BUILD IT WITH
PLYWOOD:
88 FURNITURE PROJECTS

BUILD IT WITH
PLYWOOD:
88 FURNITURE PROJECTS

BY DON GEARY

TAB TAB BOOKS Inc.

BLUE RIDGE SUMMIT, PA. 17214

FIRST EDITION

FIRST PRINTING

Copyright © 1983 by TAB BOOKS Inc.

Printed in the United States of America

Library of Congress Cataloging in Publication Data

Geary, Don.
Build it with plywood.
Includes index.
1. Furniture making.   2. Plywood.   I. Title.
TT194.043   1983   684.1′04   82-19354
ISBN 0-8306-0330-1
ISBN 0-8306-0230-5 (pbk.)

Cover photographs courtesy of
American Plywood Association.

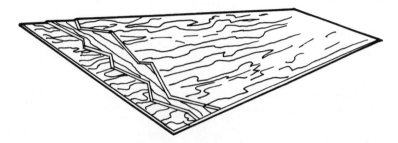

Contents

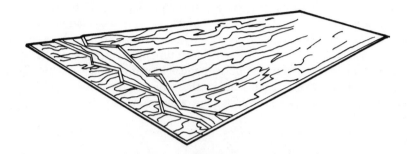

Introduction

WHETHER OR NOT YOU REALIZE IT, WE ARE VIRtually surrounded by plywood. Most of the homes in America are sheeted on sidewalls and roof decks with plywood, as are subfloors inside the home. Then there are millions of pieces of furniture that have plywood as a major building component. I find it curious that many do-it-yourselfers have little knowledge about this amazing and versatile building material. Many woodworkers use only solid woods such as oak, maple, or pine when working on a furniture project. This book will provide you with instructions for how to use plywood for furniture projects.

The first chapter in this book covers the development of plywood, which began in the early part of this century. Chapter 1 contains solid information about how plywood came into being, a brief description of the many different types of plywood, and some suggestions that you will find helpful when choosing plywood for your furniture projects.

In the second chapter the tools that are useful for working with plywood are discussed. Because of

the nature of this building material, it is actually easier to work with than solid woods. Generally, the tools that are required for working with plywood are few and simple. There are, however, a few specialized tools that can help you to achieve professional-looking results, and I discuss these as well.

Because so much of the success in building plywood furniture projects depends on working with pieces that have been cut as straight as possible, the entire third chapter is devoted to a discussion of how to cut plywood. I doubt that there is little disagreement that the best way to cut plywood is on a stationary power saw—such as a good table saw. But I also realize that many do-it-yourselfers do not own such a tool. Chances are good, however, that you will own some other type of saw such as a hand saw, a hand-held circular saw or a sabre saw. In Chapter 3, I fully explain how to achieve perfectly straight cuts using all types of saws. In the end, you should be able to cut plywood like a pro no matter what type of saw you have at your disposal.

A major part of any plywood project involves applying some type of finish to the piece. All of the popular finishes (from the varnish group) for plywood furniture are covered in Chapter 4. Solid information about how to choose a finish as well as how to properly apply it are covered in detail. In addition, this chapter also explains how to apply plastic laminate material as a finish covering to a plywood furniture project. This is a good choice, by the way, because plywood projects lend themselves well to this type of finish.

Chapter 5 is more or less the nuts and bolts chapter; here there are descriptions of the materials that are used for assembling plywood furniture projects. Included is information about adhesives, nails, screws, and specialty fasteners such as toggle bolts. There are also sections on conventional and custom-made cabinet and drawer hardware.

The remaining six chapters contain 88 plywood furniture projects. Many of the projects are provided courtesy of the American Plywood Association and the Hardwood Plywood Furniture Manufacturers Association. I would like to express my thanks for their help. Many of the other plywood furniture projects are designs that I have developed and built in my home workshop. To be sure, some of the projects are quite simple, but others require woodworking skills.

Chapter 1

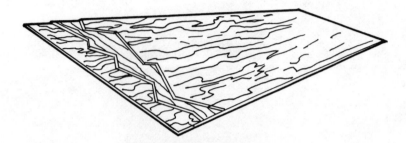

Materials

WITHOUT REALIZING IT, WE ALL COME IN CONtact with many types of plywood everyday. Just think for a minute about all of the things in our lives that are made from plywood and you will begin to see my point. For example, the home you live in—unless it is more than 50 years old—probably has plywood sheeting for the roof deck (Figs. 1-1 and 1-2), plywood sheeting for all subfloors, and, in many cases, plywood exterior siding. Additionally, plywood panels are commonly used for interior wall coverings.

Some of the many other uses of plywood include most types of kitchen cabinets and counters. Just about every home in America today has a kitchen constructed largely of plywood. Just take a close look at your counter and cabinets. Bathroom vanities are commonly constructed from plywood as well.

Plywood is truly an amazing building material that is used across the entire spectrum of construction. Almost anything that can be built with wood can probably be made from plywood. The real advantages of plywood are that it does not warp, it is much stronger than standard wood or lumber, and it is much less expensive than solid lumber.

Plywood is a relatively new building material. The first appearance of plywood was at the 1905 Lewis and Clark International Exposition held in Portland, Oregon. At this exposition, the Portland Manufacturing Company revealed a special three-ply panel for display to the general public. When manufacturers saw this Douglas fir plywood panel, they realized that it could be used for many purposes. The Portland Manufacturing Company received a large number of orders for this new plywood material.

The main users of plywood, in the beginning, were manufacturers of doors, cabinets, and trunks. As a result of this widespread acceptance of plywood, several other lumber mills in the Northwest began manufacturing plywood. By the 1920s, plywood was being widely used across the United States.

Around this time another major market for plywood developed. Automobile manufacturers discovered that plywood was an excellent material

Fig. 1-1. Plywood has thousands of applications (courtesy American Plywood Association).

Fig. 1-2. Most American homes are sheathed with plywood (courtesy American Plywood Association).

for automobile running boards. In the short period, automobile makers were competing with door manufacturers as the largest users of plywood. By 1925 there were 11 plywood plants in the Northwest. These early mills (Fig. 1-3) were producing almost 160 million square feet of plywood per year, an astounding output for the time. As a side note, the modern plywood plants of today can turn out more than that in just a few days.

The Great Depression during the 1930s severely cut plywood production, but markets nevertheless began to develop with the help of a new trade association representing the plywood manufacturers. This association was first named The Douglas Fir Plywood Association; it was formed in Tacoma, Washington in 1933. In 1964, the name was changed to The American Plywood Association (APA) but the goals remained the same: to develop new plywood markets through research,

development, and product promotion.

The association uses a staff of field representatives, plus national advertising and publicity, to reach many different markets. Its promotional efforts are based on an extensive research and development program that continually tests plywood under hundreds of different applications. The Association's Division for Product Approval conducts an inspection and testing program for all of the members in the association. The association's APA trademark is stamped on the back of every sheet of plywood and has become a standard of quality and dependability throughout the building industry in the United States and many foreign countries.

Still another major step in developing major markets for plywood was the discovery of a waterproof glue (Fig. 1-4) for gluing the plys of a panel. This development was first introduced in 1934 and, as you might expect, this opened hundreds of new

Fig. 1-3. Plywood was used for automobile running boards (courtesy American Plywood Association).

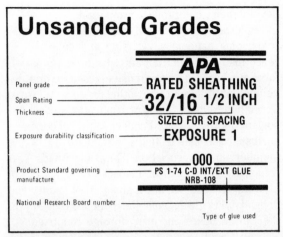

Unsanded Grades

APA
RATED SHEATHING
Panel grade ——————————————
Span Rating ——————————— **32/16 1/2 INCH**
Thickness —————————————
SIZED FOR SPACING
Exposure durability classification ———— **EXPOSURE 1**

000
Product Standard governing ———— PS 1-74 C-D INT/EXT GLUE
manufacture NRB-108

National Research Board number ————————

Type of glue used

Fig. 1-4. The symbol of The American Plywood Association is a sure sign of dependable quality (courtesy American Plywood Association).

markets to the plywood industry. These included residential and commercial construction and the marine industry (Fig. 1-5).

By 1940, plywood was being used for residential subfloors, paneling, roof decks, garages and outbuildings. Plywood was also being used for dozens of other applications such as built-in cabinets in both the kitchen and bath. Around this time, industry production exceeded 1 billion square feet per year. There were 25 plants producing plywood in the United States and 20 of these were located in the state of Washington. During the mid-1940s, a large portion of all plywood being produced was being used for war-time products. These included PT boats, assault ships, airplanes, barracks, other military buildings, and even footlockers.

After the GI's returned home from the World

Fig. 1-5. Plywood was used for a number of war-related materials during WW II (courtesy American Plywood Association).

Fig. 1-6. Plywood mill (courtesy American Plywood Association).

War II, there was an incredible demand for plywood for use in house construction. The mills in the Northwest could barely keep pace with the demand. Oregon had 13 plants (producing about 34 percent of all plywood) and California had two plants producing just over 1 percent of all softwood plywood. In a span of less than 10 years plywood production shifted dramatically. By 1954, Oregon had 47 plants that were producing more than 53 percent of all plywood in the country. The number of plants in California jumped to 19 and the state of Washington had 36 plywood plants or mills.

In an effort to cut the costs of plywood as well as increase production of plywood, special mills were developed around this time. These new mills produced only veneer instead of complete plywood sheets. Their production was then sent to plywood mills for manufacturing into the final product.

These new veneer mills enabled the plywood plants to locate closer to the marketplace and transportation lines. By 1960, the total production of plywood in the United States was more than 7 billion square feet. That production figure has doubled again and plywood production continues to grow as more uses for plywood are discovered each year.

The plywood industry of today has come an incredible distance since the 1905 Lewis & Clark Exposition. The original intention of the first industry association was to create a demand for plywood products. This has been done quite effectively. To this day, new products, manufacturing techniques, and product applications are developed with such great frequency that it is almost impossible to keep up with developments—even for those who are involved in the industry. All of these developments are aimed at producing a better plywood product, quicker and at a cost that is as low as possible.

5

During the early years of plywood production, the industry was turning out only a few thousand feet of plywood a year from a small number of plywood mills in the Northwest. Now almost 10 billion square feet of superior-grade plywood is being manufactured in several parts of the country. Industry spokesmen all agree that the plywood manufacturers of the United States will have little problem in meeting demand. Based on the short history of the plywood industry, it is easy to understand their optimism. See Fig. 1-6.

HOW PLYWOOD IS MADE

The life of a plywood panel begins in a forest, but not just any stand of lumber. In the early days of the plywood industry, suitable standing timber could be easily found in the Pacific Northwest. Millions of acres of virgin timber were available to lumbermen and it was common for loggers to simply just start cutting down forests for the nearby mills (Fig. 1-7).

In a rather short period, all of the easily obtain-able big timber was gone and, at the same time, the demand for suitable trees for plywood veneer was dramatically increasing. To help meet the demand smaller, less desirable timber had to be used. It was around this time that the lumber industry began to realize that, if they were to keep the industry alive, they had better do something to ensure that there would be usable timber available in the future.

This is about the time that *forestry management* or *tree farming* came into existence. Tree farming is nothing more than the scientific management of forests, in a manner similar to other types of farming. In this case, the "crop" takes quite a bit longer from seed to harvest (Figs. 1-8 and 1-9).

There are a number of advantages to managed forests. Through such techniques as selective thinning, fertilization, insect and disease control, genetic selection, and breeding of superior trees—plus harvest methods suited to the site and species—managed forests can easily produce at least 30 percent more lumber than an unmanaged forest or stand of timber.

Fig. 1-7. Logging has always been tough work (courtesy American Plywood Association).

Fig. 1-8. Millions of new trees are planted each year by the forestry industry (courtesy American Plywood Association).

Managed forests also provide vast areas (Fig. 1-10) that can be used for hiking, fishing, hunting, and a variety of other outdoor recreational pursuits. Because it takes at least 20 years for a managed forest to develop, it is common practice for lumber companies to allow these areas to be used for recreational purposes during the process. This ensures that there will always be forests in our future. Additionally, many managed forests offer public picnic and camping sites.

Of course, there is a lot more to forestry management than simply cutting down a forest, planting trees, and then coming back in 20 years to cut and plant once again. When a stand of timber matures, it is harvested (Figs. 1-11 and 1-12) and shortly after new seedlings are planted. Special tree nurseries produce over 1 billion seedlings a year, thus ensuring a steady supply of stock. Every year more than half a million acres of lumbered forest are replanted.

After a new crop of trees has been planted, lumbermen return to the area periodically to thin the stand of poorly growing trees. This gives the remaining trees the space that allows them to grow straighter, better and, faster. The small trees and timber that are culled during these thinning out programs are used for lumber or chips for the pulp mills. In this way, wood that would normally be wasted or useless—if the forest were allowed to grow on its own—is used.

In addition to thinning, remaining timber is fertilized to further encourage superior growth. Because quality lumber products can only come from stands of quality lumber, managed forests are also checked regularly for signs of disease or insect damage. If any such signs appear, they are delt with as quickly as possible. The result is prime timber for the lumber mills (Fig. 1-13).

After timber has been cut or *harvested* from the tree farm, it is transported to the lumber mills. Depending on where the stand of timber is located, it might make its way to the mill on the back of a special lumber truck or be floated down a wide and deep river (Fig. 1-14). The image of the lumberjack—with hob-nailed boots and log pike in hand while riding a mass of logs down a river—is still an accurate representation of a lumbering technique in a few parts of the Pacific Northwest and Alaska. Once the logs arrive at the mill, they are generally sorted according to size, length, and approximate

Fig. 1-9. Harvested trees (courtesy American Plywood Association).

Fig. 1-10. Planted forests have many uses (courtesy American Plywood Association).

Fig. 1-11. Timber for lumber and lumber products (courtesy American Plywood Association).

Fig. 1-12. Thinning operations remove poor-quality trees and give the better timber room to grow (courtesy American Plywood Association).

Fig. 1-13. Lumber for the mills (courtesy American Plywood Association).

grade quality. Then they are stacked accordingly until needed.

Before logs can be made into plywood, they must undergo a number of processing steps. The first step is removing all of the bark from the log. This can be done in a number of ways depending upon the sophistication of the mill equipment. The main methods currently being used to remove bark from logs (Fig. 1-15) include running the logs through a series of knurled wheels, using an extremely high pressure stream of water, or by running the logs through a special series of peeler knives.

Bark that is removed from logs at the mill is considered a byproduct with some value. Some mills package the bark and sell it as garden mulch (Fig. 1-16). Other mills use this bark as fuel for producing power for the mill. In any event, almost no part of a log is wasted; even the sawdust resulting from cutting is sold or formed into chipboard.

Once the logs have been relieved of their bark, they are referred to in the industry as *peelers*. The next step is to bring the logs into the mill and cut them into lengths of from 8 feet 4 inches to 8 feet 6 inches. These lengths allow the logs to be veneered slightly longer than the standard 4-×8-foot sizes.

Fig. 1-14. In some parts of the country floating logs to the mill is the best way (courtesy American Plywood Association).

Fig. 1-15. Logs are peeled of their bark in giant machines (courtesy American Plywood Association).

Fig. 1-16. Bark is used for decorative garden mulch.

Later, of course, the veneers will be trimmed to the standard size. The cut lengths are called *peeler blocks* and they are just over 8 feet in length. See Fig. 1-17.

Rather early in the development of manufacturing methods for plywood, it was discovered that a peeler block would be easier to cut into veneers if it was heated before the veneering process began. This is standard practice today. The heating method used for a particular peeler block depends on the species of log. One of the more popular heating methods involves soaking peeler blocks in a hot-water bath for several hours, then exposing them to steam for several more hours.

VENEERS

As the peeler blocks are removed from the heat treatment, they are moved into the actual veneering mill on conveyor belts or by some other means. Next they are placed into a large lathe, centered, and secured. The peeler block is then

Fig. 1-17. Peeled logs are cut into peeler blocks (courtesy American Plywood Association).

rotated—at varying speeds, depending on the species of log—while at the same time a special cutting blade comes in contact with the surface of the log. This is where the veneers are cut from the log. See Fig. 1-18.

The actual cutting of veneer goes very quickly (Fig. 1-19). With modern technology, it is entirely possible to cut over 500 linear feet of veneer from a log per minute. This depends on the type of log being cut. Generally, softwoods such as pine and fir can be cut 1/10 to ¼ of an inch thick. Hardwood such as oak or walnut can be cut as thin as 0.005 of an inch. As you can well imagine, modern veneer cutting machines can quickly reduce a large diameter peeler block to something resembling a fence post in a matter of minutes.

Only so much of a log can be cut into veneer. When the core of the log is about 4 inches in diame-

ter, the long veneer-cutting blade can no longer effectively cut. At this point, the remainder of the log is removed from the lathe and either sold as a fence post (Fig. 1-20) or other lumber item, or passed on to a chipper and ground into pulp.

As the freshly cut veneer comes off the log, it must be cut into usable lengths and widths. This is most commonly done in a machine called a *green chipper*. This machine cuts the veneer into widths of approximately 54 inches and easily manageable lengths. The green chipper machine also will slice out sections of veneer that are useless (areas with unrepairable defects, for example). See Fig. 1-21.

Next, the freshly cut and trimmed veneer must be sorted and stacked according to grade (Fig. 1-22). The stacks of veneer must then be dried before they can be worked with any further.

The drying of veneer can be accomplished in

Fig. 1-18. Peeler blocks are chucked into a giant lathe (courtesy American Plywood Association).

Fig. 1-19. Cutting plywood veneer (courtesy American Plywood Association).

two basic ways: *air drying,* and *kiln drying.* Air drying is easily the most inefficient way to accomplish the required 5 percent moisture content in veneer. In this method, the sheets of veneer are stacked out of doors during clear and dry weather until the proper moisture content in the wood is achieved. As you can well imagine, this method leaves a lot to chance and also requires an enormous amount of physical handling. As inefficient as the air drying method is, it was at one time the only means of drying veneer available to mills making plywood.

Basically, there are two methods currently being used to kiln dry veneer. The first simply places stacks of veneer in a specially designed and humidically controlled room where the veneer is allowed to dry out. The second method of kiln dry-

ing, mechanical kiln drying, uses a conveyor system to carry sheets of veneer through an extremely dry chamber (Fig. 1-23). Although there are differences in speed between these two kiln drying methods, they both offer a large amount of control over the drying process and therefore a better dried veneer can be achieved.

After the sheets of veneer have been dried to a maximum moisture content of 5 percent, they are inspected once again before actually being glued into sheets of plywood. This stage is quite important because most of the veneer strips require some type of repair or patch before they can be used for the face or back of a sheet of plywood. Very often knot holes and other defects are present on a sheet of veneer and it is common practice to simply cut

Fig. 1-20. After veneer has been cut, a fence post remains.

these areas out of the panel and install a special patch that has a slightly larger size than the cutout area. Other repairs such as filling small holes and splicing strips of veneer are also performed at this time. See Figs. 1-24 and 1-25.

The repaired sheets of veneer then move along to the layup process where they are separated according to how they will be assembled: face and back, core stock, and cross-bands (inner plys). Then various parts of each panel of plywood are passed through a gluing machine that applies a coating to a core panel of veneer. Other plys are added and more glue is applied until the plywood panel is assembled, but still rather rough looking. From here, the assembled and glued plys are fed a hot press where they are exposed to both pressure (up to 200 pounds per square inch) and heat (as high as 300 degrees Fahrenheit) and the final bonding of the glue takes place (Fig. 1-26).

As the sheets emerge from the hot press, they must be trimmed to standard lengths and run through various other processes to ensure that each panel is within certain thickness tolerances. Other tasks such as sanding the face or back, cutting patterns on the face of the panel (as for exterior siding), finishing edges so they will interlock with other panels (tongue and groove fashion) and, if required, a finish coating can be accomplished at this time.

Quality control is a very important function at any plywood mill. Even after the panels have been glued, hot pressed and trimmed to size, the panels are further inspected for defects. Very often the face or back of a plywood panel will require some additional "touch-up" or patching. In most cases, defective areas will simply be cut out with a router like machine and a special patch applied in the area. Even indentations or depressions can be repaired by filling the void with polyurethane foam and then heating to cure the problem. All of these repair tasks are done to ensure that the final product fits into a predetermined size, thickness, and grade category.

Although modern machines are used for the actual patching, all inspection and repair work is done manually. Experienced workers can make just

Fig. 1-21. Green chipper (courtesy American Plywood Association).

Fig. 1-22. Plys are sorted according to grades after cutting (courtesy American Plywood Association).

about any type of repair in less than 1 minute per panel.

After all repairs are made, the panels are sorted according to grade. The panels are stamped with the grade designation and stacked into standard-size bundles. The bundles are then strapped and warehoused (Fig. 1-27) until they can be shipped to building supply wholesalers, or other wood merchants.

The preceding description of the manufacturing of plywood is an oversimplification of the process. There are different ways of cutting the veneer from the peeler blocks and even different ways of gluing the plys. But the information given in these pages will certainly give you a very good idea of how plywood is made. In addition, technological advances and improvements in various aspects of the manufacturing process take place often in this industry. Quality is thus insured when you see the APA symbol (Fig. 1-28) on a sheet of plywood.

PLYWOOD GRADES

Generally, all plywood manufactured today can be lumped into two very broad categories: *exterior grade plywood* and *interior grade plywood*. There are also quite a number of grade designations within these two groups.

All plywood that is designated as "exterior" is made with a special waterproof glue. Such a panel

Fig. 1-23. Plys are kiln dried (courtesy American Plywood Association).

Fig. 1-24. Veneer plys are patched (courtesy American Plywood Association).

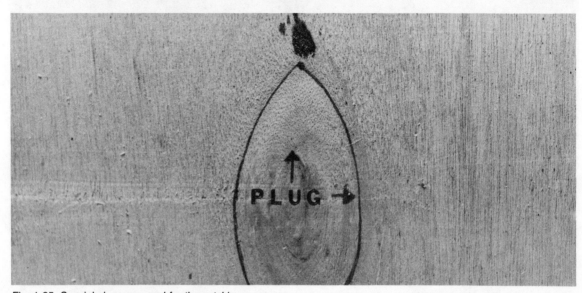

Fig. 1-25. Special plugs are used for the patching.

20

Fig. 1-26. Plys are glued and placed in a hot press to make plywood (courtesy American Plywood Association).

Fig. 1-27. Plywood is stacked for shipment (courtesy American Plywood Association).

APA

Grade of veneer on panel back

Grade of veneer on panel face ——— A-C GROUP 2
Species Group Number ————————
Designates the type of plywood ——— EXTERIOR

Mill number ———————————————— 000
Product Standard governing ————— PS 1-74
manufacture

(Also available in Groups 1, 3, and 4)

Fig. 1-28. The symbol of the American Plywood Association.

can be exposed to the weather (Fig. 1-29) for an indefinite period without any ply delamination. There are many grades within the exterior classification and all are made with a waterproof glue.

Interior grade plywood is made with a glue that could be affected by moisture. All "interior" grade plywood is made with a highly moisture resistant (but not waterproof) glue. In practice, most interior-type plywood and all exterior-type plywood are manufactured with special exterior glue.

It is possible to purchase interior-grade plywood manufactured with a special exterior glue.

Fig. 1-29. One of the most common uses of plywood is in house construction (courtesy American Plywood Association).

This type of plywood can be used for building kitchen cabinets or counters and bathroom vanities where both appearance and high resistance to water are prerequisites.

Another basic difference between exterior and interior grades of plywood is that the interior grades are generally considered to be "appearance" grades. They will be used inside the home (Fig. 1-30) and will be seen more than the exterior grades. This might sound a little confusing because there are also appearance grades that are used on the exterior of the home (exterior siding, for example).

There is also the designation *engineered* grade for both interior- and exterior-grade plywood. Basically, what engineered grade means is that the ultimate use of the plywood will be in some type of concealed installation. Examples of this include subfloor sheeting and roof-deck sheeting (Fig. 1-31). As you can well imagine, there is quite a bit of difference between a panel of plywood that will be used for subflooring and a panel that will be used on an interior wall where the face of the panel will be visible.

Generally, engineered grades of plywood will have a number of patches or plugs on both the face and back of the panel, and the panel will not have a smooth, sanded finish. This is not to suggest that engineered-grade plywood is inferior in any way to appearance-grade plywood, but only that when engineered plywood is installed it will not be visible.

The American Plywood Association's trademarks appear only on products that have been manufactured by APA member mills. These marks signify that the manufacturer is committed to APA's rigorous program of quality supervision and testing and that panel quality is subject to verification through APA audit. This is designed to assure that the manufacture of plywood is in conformance with APA performance standards for United States Product Standard PS 1:74/ANSI A199.1 for Construction and Industrial Plywood. See Fig. 1-32. The following is a line-by-line description of the label.

Line One. This will indicate the grade of the veneer, a registered trademark, a designation of the plywood's use (such as "Underlayment"), or possi-

Fig. 1-30. Many types of furniture are made from plywood.

23

Fig. 1-31. Plywood sheathing provides a good base for finish materials in house construction (courtesy American Plywood Association).

bly letters indicating the veneer grade of the face and back of the plywood panel.

Line Two. This line will indicate spacing or the span index for this particular sheet of plywood. The maximum recommended spacing for rafters is the first number on this line often followed by another number (separated by a "/"). The second number is the recommended maximum spacing for joists. The important thing to keep in mind is that rafter spacing always comes first and then spacing for joists (24/16, for example, means rafters 24 inches apart or joists spaced 16 inches on center). In addition, if the edges of the panel have been specialled milled, this will be indicated after the span index. An example for exterior siding with tongue-and-groove edges might be 24/16 T&G.

Line Three. This line tells you the thickness of the sheet of plywood on most structural types of plywood (25/32 inch, for example).

Line Four. Type of plywood (interior or exterior).

Line Five. Product standard. This special designation only appears on engineered plywoods and it refers to the industry standards that govern the

Fig. 1-32. Engineered-grade plywood is widely used for construction.

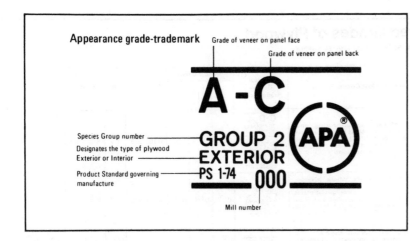

Fig. 1-33. Appearance-grade plywood is used for furniture.

sheet's manufacture. This designation may appear in Arabic numerals and letters or may be indicated by the word "Group" followed by a Roman numeral.

Line Six. Mill number. This is the APA number of the mill that made this sheet of plywood.

Line Seven. The type of glue used in making this panel of plywood (either interior glue or exterior glue).

Line Eight. National Research Bureau report, if one has been made on this grade of plywood. Because this is a special designation, it only appears on specially ordered grades of plywood.

Because the preceding descriptions are for those grades of plywood designated as engineered grades, you will need more information if you are looking at appearance grades of plywood. There are a number of classes in this group. See Fig. 1-33. The following is a line-by-line description of the label.

Line One. On this line you will find what class or type of wood veneer is used on the face and back of the plywood panel. This is always indicated by a series of letters.

N: Smooth surface, natural finish veneer; select, free of open defects. There may not be more than six surface repairs on a 4- ×8-foot sheet (standard size) of plywood. These repairs must be inconspicuous, such as oval rather than round plugs, and these repairs must match the surface in both grain and hue.

A: A veneer face (or back if it is the second letter) that is smooth, paintable, and with no more than 18 repairs on a standard-size sheet.

B: A veneer surface that is solid, but may have plugs and tight knots up to 1 inch in diameter. In addition, small surface splits are permitted.

C: Surface splits are permitted, but limited to ⅛ of an inch wide. Knotholes or other flaws are allowed on this grade providing they are no more than ¼ of an inch square. Wood paste filler repairs are permitted and so are minor breaks in the overall grain of the panel.

C (when used as the second letter in this marking): Tight knobs are permitted up to 1½ inches and so are knotholes up to 1 inch across the

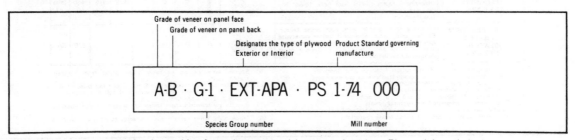

Fig. 1-34. Appearance-grade plywood is often edge stamped (courtesy American Plywood Association).

Guide to Engineered Grades of Plywood

SPECIFIC GRADES AND THICKNESSES MAY BE IN LOCALLY LIMITED SUPPLY. SEE YOUR DEALER BEFORE SPECIFYING.

Type	Grade Designation	Description and Most Common Uses	Typical Grade-trademarks (1)	Veneer Grade: Face	Veneer Grade: Inner Plies	Veneer Grade: Back	Most Common Thicknesses (inch)				
Interior Type	C-D INT-APA	For wall and roof sheathing, subflooring, industrial uses such as pallets. Most commonly available with exterior glue (CDX). Specify exterior glue where construction delays are anticipated and for treated-wood foundations. (7)	C-D 32/16 APA INTERIOR PS 1-74 000 C-D 24/0 APA INTERIOR PS 1-74 000 EXTERIOR GLUE	C	D	D	5/16	3/8	1/2	5/8	3/4
Interior Type	STRUCTURAL I C-D INT-APA and STRUCTURAL II C-D INT-APA	Unsanded structural grades where plywood strength properties are of maximum importance: structural diaphragms, box beams, gusset plates, stressed-skin panels, containers, pallet bins. Made only with exterior glue. See (6) for species group requirements. Structural I more commonly available. (7)	STRUCTURAL I C-D 24/0 APA INTERIOR PS 1-74 000 EXTERIOR GLUE	C(3)	D(3)	D(3)	5/16	3/8	1/2	5/8	3/4
Interior Type	STURD-I-FLOOR INT-APA	For combination subfloor-underlayment. Provides smooth surface for application of resilient floor covering. Possesses high concentrated- and impact-load resistance during construction and occupancy. Manufactured with exterior glue only. Touch-sanded. Available square edge or tongue-and-groove. (7)	STURD-I-FLOOR 24oc T&G 23 32 INCH INTERIOR APA 000 EXTERIOR GLUE NRB-108	Plugged C	(4)	D				19/32 5/8	23/32 3/4
Interior Type	STURD-I-FLOOR 48 O.C. (2-4-1) INT-APA	For combination subfloor-underlayment on 32- and 48-inch spans. Provides smooth surface for application of resilient floor coverings. Possesses high concentrated- and impact-load resistance during construction and occupancy. Manufactured with exterior glue only. Unsanded or touch-sanded. Available square edge or tongue-and-groove. (7)	STURD-I-FLOOR 48oc 2-4-1 T&G 1 1/8 INCH INTERIOR APA 000 EXTERIOR GLUE NRB-108	Plugged C	C(5) & D	D			1-1/8		
Interior Type	UNDERLAYMENT INT-APA	For application over structural subfloor. Provides smooth surface for application of resilient floor coverings. Touch-sanded. Also available with exterior glue. (2)(6)	UNDERLAYMENT GROUP 1 APA INTERIOR PS 1-74 000	Plugged C	C(5) & D	D		3/8	1/2	19/32 5/8	23/32 3/4
Interior Type	C-D PLUGGED INT-APA	For built-ins, wall and ceiling tile backing, cable reels, walkways, separator boards. Not a substitute for Underlayment or Sturd-I-Floor as it lacks their indentation resistance. Touch-sanded. Also made with exterior glue. (2) (6)	C-D PLUGGED GROUP 2 APA INTERIOR PS 1-74 000	Plugged C	D	D		3/8	1/2	19/32 5/8	23/32 3/4
Exterior Type	C-C EXT-APA	Unsanded grade with waterproof bond for subflooring and roof decking, siding on service and farm buildings, crating, pallets, pallet bins, cable reels, treated-wood foundations. (7)	C-C 42/20 APA EXTERIOR PS 1-74 000	C	C	C	5/16	3/8	1/2	5/8	3/4
Exterior Type	STRUCTURAL I C-C EXT-APA and STRUCTURAL II C-C EXT-APA	For engineered applications in construction and industry where full Exterior type panels are required. Unsanded. See (6) for species group requirements. (7)	STRUCTURAL I C-C 32/16 APA EXTERIOR PS 1-74 000	C	C	C	5/16	3/8	1/2	5/8	3/4
Exterior Type	STURD-I-FLOOR EXT-APA	For combination subfloor-underlayment under resilient floor coverings where severe moisture conditions may be present, as in balcony decks. Possesses high concentrated-and impact-load resistance during construction and occupancy. Touch-sanded. Available square edge or tongue-and-groove. (7)	STURD-I-FLOOR 20oc 5/8 INCH EXTERIOR APA 000 NRB-108	Plugged C	C(5)	C				19/32 5/8	23/32 3/4
Exterior Type	UNDERLAYMENT C-C PLUGGED EXT-APA	For application over structural subfloor. Provides smooth surface for application of resilient floor coverings where severe moisture conditions may be present. Touch-sanded. (2)(6)	UNDERLAYMENT C-C PLUGGED GROUP 2 APA EXTERIOR PS 1-74 000	Plugged C	C(5)	C		3/8	1/2	19/32 5/8	23/32 3/4
Exterior Type	C-C PLUGGED EXT-APA	For use as tile backing where severe moisture conditions exist. For refrigerated or controlled atmosphere rooms, pallet fruit bins, tanks, box car and truck floors and linings, open soffits. Touch-sanded. (2)(6)	C-C PLUGGED GROUP 2 APA EXTERIOR PS 1-74 000	Plugged C	C	C		3/8	1/2	19/32 5/8	23/32 3/4
Exterior Type	B-B PLYFORM CLASS I & CLASS II EXT-APA	Concrete form grades with high reuse factor. Sanded both sides. Mill-oiled unless otherwise specified. Special restrictions on species. Available in HDO and Structural I. Class I most commonly available. (8)	B-B PLYFORM CLASS I APA EXTERIOR PS 1-74 000	B	C	B				5/8	3/4

(1) The species groups, Identification Indexes and Span Indexes shown in the typical grade-trademarks are examples only. See "Group," "Identification Index" and "Span Index" for explanations and availability.
(2) Can be manufactured in Group 1, 2, 3, 4, or 5.
(3) Special improved grade for structural panels.
(4) Special veneer construction to resist indentation from concentrated loads, or other solid wood-base materials.
(5) Special construction to resist indentation from concentrated loads.
(6) Can also be manufactured in Structural I (all plies limited to Group 1 species) and Structural II (all plies limited to Group 1, 2, or 3 species).
(7) Specify by Identification Index for sheathing and Span Index for Sturd-I-Floor panels.
(8) Made only from certain wood species to conform to APA specifications.

Fig. 1-35. Charts of plywood grades and types (courtesy American Plywood Association).

Guide to Appearance Grades of Plywood [1]

	Grade Designation [2]	Description and Most Common Uses	Typical [3] Grade-Trademarks	Face	Inner Plies	Back	Most Common Thicknesses (inch)				
Interior Type	N-N, N-A N-B INT-APA	Cabinet quality. For natural finish furniture, cabinet doors, built-ins, etc. Special order items.		N	C	N,A, or B					3/4
	N-D-INT-APA	For natural finish paneling. Special order item.		N	D	D	1/4				
	A-A INT-APA	For applications with both sides on view, built-ins, cabinets, furniture, partitions. Smooth face; suitable for painting.		A	D	A	1/4	3/8	1/2	5/8	3/4
	A-B INT-APA	Use where appearance of one side is less important but where two solid surfaces are necessary.		A	D	B	1/4	3/8	1/2	5/8	3/4
	A-D INT-APA	Use where appearance of only one side is important. Paneling, built-ins, shelving, partitions, flow racks.	A-D GROUP 1 INTERIOR (APA) 000	A	D	D	1/4	3/8	1/2	5/8	3/4
	B-B INT-APA	Utility panel with two solid sides. Permits circular plugs.		B	D	B	1/4	3/8	1/2	5/8	3/4
	B-D INT-APA	Utility panel with one solid side. Good for backing, sides of built-ins, industry shelving, slip sheets, separator boards, bins.	B-D GROUP 2 INTERIOR (APA) 000	B	D	D	1/4	3/8	1/2	5/8	3/4
	DECORATIVE PANELS—APA	Rough-sawn, brushed, grooved, or striated faces. For paneling, interior accent walls, built-ins, counter facing, displays, exhibits.	DECORATIVE BD G1 INT APA PS1 74	C or btr.	D	D	5/16	3/8	1/2	5/8	
	PLYRON INT-APA	Hardboard face on both sides. For counter tops, shelving, cabinet doors, flooring. Faces tempered, untempered, smooth, or screened.			C & D				1/2	5/8	3/4
Exterior Type	A-A EXT-APA	Use where appearance of both sides is important. Fences, built-ins, signs, boats, cabinets, commercial refrigerators, shipping containers, tote boxes, tanks, ducts. (4)		A	C	A	1/4	3/8	1/2	5/8	3/4
	A-B EXT-APA	Use where the appearance of one side is less important. (4)		A	C	B	1/4	3/8	1/2	5/8	3/4
	A-C EXT-APA	Use where the appearance of only one side is important. Soffits, fences, structural uses, boxcar and truck lining, farm buildings. Tanks, trays, commercial refrigerators. (4)	A-C GROUP 1 EXTERIOR (APA) 000	A	C	C	1/4	3/8	1/2	5/8	3/4
	B-B EXT-APA	Utility panel with solid faces. (4)		B	C	B	1/4	3/8	1/2	5/8	3/4
	B-C EXT-APA	Utility panel for farm service and work buildings, boxcar and truck lining, containers, tanks, agricultural equipment. Also as base for exterior coatings for walls, roofs. (4)	B-C GROUP 2 EXTERIOR (APA) 000	B	C	C	1/4	3/8	1/2	5/8	3/4
	HDO EXT-APA	High Density Overlay plywood. Has a hard, semi-opaque resin-fiber overlay both faces. Abrasion resistant. For concrete forms, cabinets, counter tops, signs, tanks. (4)	HDO HDN RF-HI-OM 14" APA 0	A or B	C or C plgd	A or B		3/8	1/2	5/8	3/4
	MDO EXT-APA	Medium Density Overlay with smooth, opaque, resin-fiber overlay one or both panel faces. Highly recommended for siding and other out door applications, built-ins, signs, displays. Ideal base for paint. (4)(6)		B	C	B or C		3/8	1/2	5/8	3/4
	303 SIDING EXT-APA	Proprietary plywood products for exterior siding, fencing, etc. Special surface treatment such as V-groove, channel groove, striated, brushed, rough-sawn and texture-embossed MDO. Stud spacing (Span Index) and face grade classification indicated on grade stamp.	303 SIDING 6 S GROUP 1 24 oc SPAN EXTERIOR PS 1N 000 (APA)	(5)	C	C		3/8	1/2	5/8	
	T 1-11 EXT-APA	Special 303 panel having grooves 1/4" deep, 3/8" wide, spaced 4" or 8" o.c. Other spacing optional. Edges shiplapped. Available unsanded, textured and MDO.	303 SIDING 6 S W GROUP 1 24 oc SPAN EXTERIOR PS 1N 000 (APA)	C or btr.	C	C			19/32	5/8	
	PLYRON EXT-APA	Hardboard faces both sides, tempered, smooth or screened.	PLYRON EXT APA		C				1/2	5/8	3/4
	MARINE EXT-APA	Ideal for boat hulls. Made only with Douglas fir or western larch. Special solid jointed core construction. Subject to special limitations on core gaps and number of face repairs. Also available with HDO or MDO faces.	MARINE A A EXT APA	A or B	B	A or B	1/4	3/8	1/2	5/8	3/4

(1) Sanded both sides except where decorative or other surfaces specified.
(2) Can be manufactured in Group 1, 2, 3, 4 or 5.
(3) The species groups, Identification Indexes and Span Indexes shown in the typical grade-trademarks are examples only.

(4) Can also be manufactured in Structural I (all plies limited to Group 1 species) and Structural II (all plies limited to Group 1, 2, or 3 species).
(5) C or better for 5 plies. C Plugged or better for 3 plies.
(6) Also available as a 303 Siding.

grain of the panel. Paste fillers and plugs are allowed. There may also be off-color areas or defects on the panel surface that were caused by sanding, but do not impair the overall strength of the panel.

D: Knotholes and knots up to 1¼ inches in width across the grain are permitted. A limited number of splits are also allowed in this type.

Line Two. Standard group under which the sheet was manufactured. If a span index is listed (not all appearance grades have a span index), it will be on line three.

Line Four. Product standard number under which this panel was made.

Line Five. Mill number. The APA designated mill number.

In addition to the APA stamp on each sheet of plywood, there might also be a special edge grade mark. These marks are generally reserved for appearance-grade interior plywood. They will not be found on engineered-grade or construction-grade (framing or sheeting) plywood panels. Where the edge grade stamp is present, it will simply condense the information that normally would be present on the face or back of the sheet.

Because appearance grades of plywood are most commonly installed so that their face or back is visible, the conventional stamp would be unsightly. Therefore it is placed on the edge of the panel. See Fig. 1-34.

Figure 1-35 lists most of the grades of plywood that the do-it-yourselfer is likely to use. Each grade is described and included are the APA grade stamps.

CHOOSING THE RIGHT PLYWOOD

There are quite a number of choices facing the do-it-yourselfer while planning a plywood furniture project. To begin with, you must have not only a well thoughtout work plan but, you must also be able to envision the finished project. You must know, for example, if the piece of furniture will be painted, coated with a varnish or if the piece will be covered with veneer or plastic laminate. In other words, how the project will be finished will have a direct bearing on your choice of plywood.

One of the first things you must determine is if the project will come in contact with water (a kitchen counter for example). If you answer in the affirmative, then your choice of plywood must be a grade that has a waterproof glue (Fig. 1-36). Plywood with waterproof glue should be your choice if the furniture will be placed in the kitchen, the bathroom, or outside the home. If the piece of furniture will not be used in any of these applications, then you can probably use plywood with an interior rated glue.

The wise do-it-yourselfer can realize a considerable savings simply by choosing a plywood that is of a lesser grade than the best obtainable (choosing a B-C or C-C grade, for example, rather than an A-A or A-B grade). It is easy to see that a grade of

Fig. 1-36. Most bathroom vanities are made using plywood.

Fig. 1-37. Plywood provides a good base for plastic laminate.

plywood with an A designation (A-A or A-B for examples) is about the best grade of plywood that you can obtain. If the furniture project will be painted or covered with a veneer or plastic laminate, there is really no point in purchasing the best grade of plywood.

Because the surface will be covered (Fig. 1-37), there is no reason to use the best or better grades when the lesser grades will do the job as well. It is entirely possible to build a piece of furniture for a third to half the cost by using a lesser grade of plywood.

Where a furniture project will be finished with a clear coating (possibly stained first) you will be more satisfied with the results if a good grade of plywood is chosen. This means using an A-A or A-B grade of plywood. The choice is really simple. If only one side of the plywood will be visible on the finished project, then A-B or in some cases A-C plywood can be used. If both sides of the plywood will be visible on the finished project, then the only real choice is A-A.

SPECIES

Many people are surprised to learn that the face veneer (and possibly the back veneer) of plywood can be any one of over 70 different woods. Most common are the softwoods normally associated with plywood such as Douglas fir.

There are five main groups of wood species that are presently being used for the face and back veneers of plywood. Figure 1-38 shows that a panel of plywood can actually have a face veneer that is quite hard (those in group one, for example) or a face that is quite soft (those in group five). When you realize that the face and back of any given piece of plywood can be made from any one of the species listed in any of the five groups, you begin to understand the importance of knowing a little about plywood species grades.

A little explanation is in order for the group species chart. The species are divided on the basis of stiffness and bending strength. The stiffest species are in Group 1 and the most limber group is Group 5. The group number that appears in the trademark on some APA trademarked panels (primarily the sanded grades) is based on the species of both the face and back veneers. Where face and back veneers are not from the same species group, the higher group number is used except for sanded and decorative panels which are less than ⅜ of an inch thick. These are identified by face species because they are chosen primarily for appearance and used in applications where structural integrity is not a factor of any importance.

Some species are used widely in plywood manufacture and others are used rarely. If you decide that you want a particular species, such as

Yellow Birch, you might have to special order the plywood from your local lumber yard. Some species are not generally available in some areas.

HARDWOOD PLYWOOD

Plywood is made from hardwoods such as oak, walnut, and maple. The more exotic woods such as teak, rosewood and, African mahogany are also available for the do-it-yourself furniture maker. Hardwood plywood is used on a larger commercial scale. Easily 90 percent of the hardwood plywood manufactured in the United States goes into commercial furniture making. Plywood that has a face veneer of hardwood is quite a bit less expensive than actual hardwood. Therefore, it is possible to make furniture from hardwood plywood (Fig. 1-39) at a fraction of the cost of hardwood furniture. Hardwood plywood is also widely used in mobile homes (as a wall covering), aircraft, elevators, and many other industrial, commercial, and residential uses.

Hardwood plywood is manufactured with quality appearance as a primary goal. If you purchase hardwood faced plywood (at a cost per sheet of several dollars more than softwood plywood) you will want to apply a clear coating, such as varnish, so that the grain and naturalness of the wood will show through. It is a safe assumption that all hardwood plywood is manufactured in such a way as to permit this type of finishing (Fig. 1-40).

Currently there are approximately 150 species of hardwoods that are used as face veneers on hardwood plywood. In addition, there are many ways of cutting the face veneers before they are attached to the panel. These include plain sliced, quartered, and rotary-cut veneers. The cutting of hardwood veneers is illustrated in Fig. 1-41.

The agency that sets standards for hardwood plywood in the United States is the Hardwood Plywood Manufacturer's Association (HPMA). Most of the hardwood plywood produced in this country is made under a standard called the NBS Voluntary Product Standard PS 51—71. "The standard is intended to provide producers, distributors,

Group 1	Group 2		Group 3	Group 4	Group 5 [a]
Apitong [b][c]	Cedar, Port Orford	Maple, Black	Alder, Red	Aspen	Basswood
Beech, American	Cypress	Mengkulang [b]	Birch, Paper	Bigtooth	Poplar, Balsam
Birch	Douglas Fir 2 [d]	Meranti, Red [b][e]	Cedar, Alaska	Quaking	
Sweet	Fir	Mersawa [b]	Fir, Subalpine	Cativo	
Yellow	Balsam	Pine	Hemlock, Eastern	Cedar	
Douglas Fir 1 [d]	California Red	Pond	Maple, Bigleaf	Incense	
Kapur [b]	Grand	Red	Pine	Western Red	
Keruing [b][c]	Noble	Virginia	Jack	Cottonwood	
Larch, Western	Pacific Silver	Western White	Lodgepole	Eastern	
Maple, Sugar	White	Spruce	Ponderosa	Black (Western	
Pine	Hemlock, Western	Black	Spruce	Poplar)	
Caribbean	Lauan	Red	Redwood	Pine	
Ocote	Almon	Sitka	Spruce	Eastern White	
Pine, Southern	Bagtikan	Sweetgum	Englemann	Sugar	
Loblolly	Mayapis	Tamarack	White		
Longleaf	Red Lauan	Yellow-poplar			
Shortleaf	Tangile				
Slash	White Lauan				
Tanoak					

(a) Design stresses for Group 5 not assigned.

(b) Each of these names represents a trade group of woods consisting of a number of closely related species.

(c) Species from the genus Dipterocarpus are marketed collectively: Apitong if originating in the Philippines; Keruing if originating in Malaysia or Indonesia.

(d) Douglas fir from trees grown in the states of Washington, Oregon, California, Idaho, Montana, Wyoming, and the Canadian Provinces of Alberta and British Columbia shall be classed as Douglas fir No. 1. Douglas fir from trees grown in the states of Nevada, Utah, Colorado, Arizona and New Mexico shall be classed as Douglas fir No. 2.

(e) Red Meranti shall be limited to species having a specific gravity of 0.41 or more based on green volume and oven dry weight.

Fig. 1-38. Face veneer on softwood plywood can be from any of these groups (courtesy American Plywood Association).

Fig. 1-39. Hardwood plywood is used for modern furniture (courtesy Hardwood Plywood Manufacturers Association).

Fig. 1-40. Hardwood plywood is attractive and functional when used for furniture and wall coverings (courtesy Hardwood Plywood Manufacturers Association).

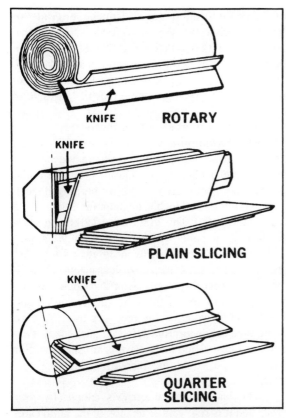

Fig. 1-41. Hardwood plywood face veneers can be cut in three different ways (courtesy Hardwood Plywood Manufacturers Association).

Fig. 1-42. The symbol of the Hardwood Plywood Manufacturers Association is a sure sign of dependable quality.

architects, contractors, builders and users with a basis for common understanding of this product." What this means for the do-it-yourselfer is that you can be certain that the hardwood plywood that you do purchase has been manufactured under various quality parameters and, that it will perform according to the stated specifications.

It is important to keep in mind that this industry standard is voluntary. It is possible that you might come in contact with hardwood plywood that has not been manufactured within these guidelines. If you want to be sure that the hardwood plywood you are about to purchase has been produced according to PS-51—71 standards, look for the HPMA trademark (Fig. 1-42) either on the back of the hardwood plywood panel or stamped on the edge. This trademark is a sure sign of quality in hardwood

faced plywood, just as the APA stamp is for softwood plywood.

Hardwood plywood is classified according to the face veneer on the panel. There are approximately 50 hardwood species currently being used for hardwood plywood face veneers. Figure 1-43 lists these. They are broken into three broad categories: A, B, and C. These three catagories are determined by the specific gravity of the face veneers in that category. The specific gravity of these veneers, in turn, determines the maximum thickness of the veneer.

Hardwood Grades

Just as there are different grades for softwood plywood, there are also different grades for hardwood plywood. There are 7 categories of hardwood-faced (veneered) plywood. As an aid in helping you to choose the right hardwood plywood grade for your furniture projects, I will briefly discuss each of these grades.

Premium grade hardwood plywood is the finest available. When two or more pieces of veneer are used on the face of the panel (which must be full size; 4×8 feet), the edges of the sheets of veneer

Categories of commonly used species based on specific gravity ranges[a]		
Category A species (0.56 or more specific gravity)	Category B species (0.43 through 0.55 specific gravity)	Category C species (0.42 or less specific gravity
Ash, Commercial White	Ash, Black	Alder, Red
Beech, American	Avodire	Aspen
Birch, Yellow, Sweet	Bay	Basswood, American
Bubinga	Cedar, Eastern Red[b]	Box Elder
Elm, Rock	Cherry, Black	Cativo
Madrone, Pacific	Chestnut, American	Cedar, Western Red[b]
Maple, Black (hard)	Cypress[b]	Ceiba
Maple, Sugar (hard)	Elm, American (white, red, or gray)	Cottonwood, Black
Oak, Commercial Red	Fir, Douglas[b]	Cottonwood, Eastern
Oak, Commercial White	Gum, Black	Pine, White and Ponderosa[b]
Oak, Oregon	Gum, Sweet	Poplar, Yellow
Paldao	Hackberry	Redwood[b]
Pecan, Commercial	Lauan, (Philippine Mahogany)	Willow, Black
Rosewood	Limba	
Sapele	Magnolia	
Teak	Mahogany, African	
	Mahogany, Honduras	
	Maple, Red (soft)	
	Maple, Silver (soft)	
	Prima Vera	
	Sycamore	
	Tupelo, Water	
	Walnut, American	

[a] Based on ovendry weight and volume at 12 percent moisture content.
[b] Softwood.

Fig. 1-43. Hardwood plywood veneers fall into one of three categories (courtesy Hardwood Plywood Manufacturers Association).

must be either book matched or slip matched. Such joints in veneer are tight and practically invisible. As you might expect, the veneers used for this grade are as close to perfect as possible (Fig. 1-44).

Good grade is second in quality only to the premium grade. When more than one piece of veneer is used on the face of the panel, the edges must be tight and the veneers themselves must be fairly close in color and grain patterns.

The third hardwood plywood grade is called *sound grade*. For this grade, the edges of the veneers—where more than one sheet of veneer is used—must be tight, but need not necessarily be matched as to color or grain pattern. There are also a number of allowable defects in this grade.

The next grade is called *utility grade* and it is

often considered a general-purpose grade of hardwood plywood. Various defects, such as worm holes and splits not exceeding 3/16 of an inch, are permitted in this grade. This is often a good choice of hardwood plywood for projects where the face of the panel is not readily visible (such as the side of bookcases).

The lowest grade of hardwood plywood is called the *backing grade*. As the name suggests, this grade is most often used for the inside back of cabinets and bookcases. This grade is similar to the utility grade, but more defects are permitted (such as knotholes up to 3 inches in diameter, splits in the face veneer, etc.). This grade is a good choice when the face of the panel will not be generally visible.

The next grade of hardwood plywood is called *specialty grade* and it is more or less a general grade category for hardwood plywood that does not conviently fit into any of the other grade categories. Hardwood plywood in this category tends to have some unusual decorative features such as striking color or unusual and distinctive grain patterns. For example, you would find Bird's Eye Maple in this grade category.

The last grade category is called *character grade* and it is really an extension of the sixth category, specialty grade. In this grade, you will find the most unusual of all hardwood plywood. I am referring to the face veneers of plywood in this group, not the inner or back plies. If the veneer has a special quality, such as interesting grain irregularities, small splits, unusual knots, and unusual natural stains, you will probably find it in the specialty grade of hardwood plywood.

Hardwood Panel Construction

Generally, hardwood-faced plywood is made in the same manner as softwood-faced plywood. An uneven number of veneers (3-ply, 5-ply or, 7-ply) are assembled and glued using heat and pressure. As with softwood plywood, the inner plies must occur in pairs of the same thickness and must be positioned so that the grain patterns are at right angles to one another. See Fig. 1-45.

The previously described method is called *veneer coring* and it is probably the most common

Fig. 1-44. Hardwood face veneers can be matched for an interesting pattern (courtesy Hardwood Plywood Manufacturers Association).

method of constructing plywood in use today (for both softwood and hardwood plywood). In addition to the veneer coring method, there are three other construction methods used for making hardwood faced plywood. These are *multiply veneer core, lumber core* and, *hardboard core.* A brief discussion of each of these construction methods follows.

The multiply veneer core construction method involves the use of seven layers of veneer, including the face and back veneers. This type of core construction results in an extremely strong plywood panel that will have little flexibility. Most other plywood is made up of no more than five layers of veneer, including the face and back veneers. Currently, there are no guidelines as to the thickness of any of the veneer plies except the face veneer thickness, which must be a thickness expressed in specific gravity for the particular species

of wood being used. The core plies must be positioned so that all grain patterns are at right angles to preceding plies (Fig. 1-46).

The lumber core construction method for hardwood faced plywood produces a very rigid finished plywood panel. This method involves the use of a number of strips of lumber that are identical in species, thickness and, width. The strips are

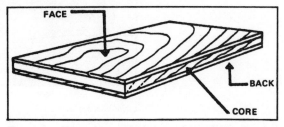

Fig. 1-45. Three-ply veneer core plywood construction (courtesy Hardwood Plywood Manufacturers Association).

35

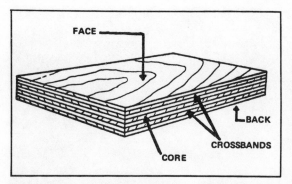

Fig. 1-46. Multiply veneer core plywood construction (courtesy Hardwood Plywood Manufacturers Association).

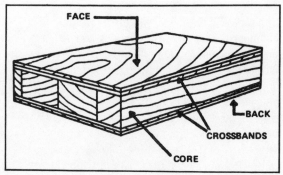

Fig. 1-47. Five-ply lumber core plywood construction (courtesy Hardwood Plywood Manufacturers Association).

edge glued to form the core of the plywood panel.

There are various requirements for the width of the strips. For example, there are three categories of lumber core hardwood faced plywood: A, B, & C. The maximum thickness for strips in category A is 2½ inches, for B-3 inches and, for category C-4 inches wide. To complicate matters even more there are four grades of lumber designations for the lumber used for the core strips. Clear

grade strips are the best obtainable. At the other end of the spectrum are lumber cores that are designated at Clear Edge Grade, and as the name suggests, only the edge strips are required to be clear and free from defects (with widths of at least 1½ inches). This core grade is a good choice if only the edge of hardwood faced plywood will receive some type of finishing or joining with other panels.

Another type of hardwood faced plywood core

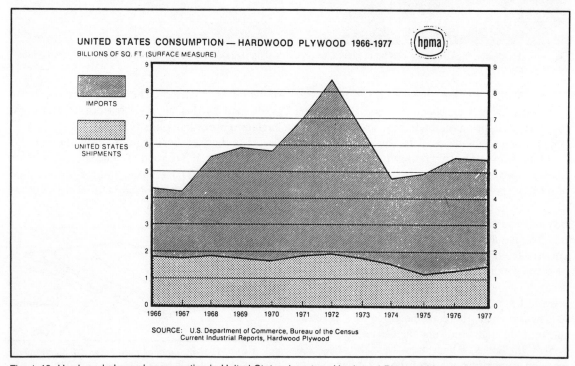

Fig. 1-48. Hardwood plywood consumption in United States (courtesy Hardwood Plywood Manufacturers Association).

is called *hardwood core.* In this category, you will find plywood with a core of either particle board or chipboard. The core panel must be manufactured under various strict guidelines. Because only the face of the hardwood plywood is visible, this type of cored plywood is a very good choice for the do-it-yourselfer who is bent on saving a few dollars per panel. Hardboard cored, hardwood-faced plywood is generally available in a very broad range of face veneers (Fig. 1-47). Because of the lower price, it is quite popular in commercial and hobbiest applications (Fig. 1-48).

PARTICLE BOARD

Although the focus of this book is on plywood, I feel that there should also be some mention of that group of sheet panel material referred to as particle board, chipboard, hardboard or fiberboard. All of these sheet materials are different panel materials. If you are looking for an alternative to conventional plywood for a furniture project, first evaluate the choices.

Particle board and chipboard are hard-surfaced panels that have been made from wood flakes, chips, and sawmill by-products such as sawdust. These solid materials are mixed with a liquid adhesive or bonding agent, and then pressed into panels and cured with heat. The result is a panel that looks like a sheet of sawdust (which it is). In addition, the panel will be rigid and hard. This makes it ideal for use as a substrate material for plastic-laminate-covered cabinets and vanities in the kitchen and bathroom. See Fig. 1-36.

Hardboard is made in almost the same manner as particle board except that the raw materials used for making the panel are processed to render them into a very fine dust before mixing with the bonding agent. The finished product will be fairly flexible (differing from particle board which is quite rigid). Generally, hardboard panels are easier to work with

Fig. 1-49. Particle board is often used for internal shelving.

conventional hand tools than particle board. This is a good alternate choice and especially where the finished project need not have a lot of internal integrity of its own.

Fiberboard is another category of recycled sawmill by-products. If you have worked with Masonite you are familiar with fiberboard. This material is rather soft and it can be easily worked with hand tools. The most common form of fiberboard is finished on only the face of the panel. The back remains unfinished and it usually shows a rather rough texture caused by mesh marks or abrasion in the press during compression of the panel. Fiberboard, because it lacks strength, is a poor choice for most furniture projects. But because of its very low cost, it is an excellent choice for parts of furniture that do not have strength as a prerequisite. Some examples of where fiberboard can be used to good advantage include the back of bookcases and cabinets and possibly the underside of some furniture projects, such as the bottom of a planter.

Generally, particle board or hardboard can be substituted for conventional plywood when the furniture plans call for covering the surface of the project with a material such as plastic laminate or wood veneer. There are also certain cases where the project builder is more concerned with a utilitarian application rather than esthetics. One example of this might be internal shelving (Fig. 1-49) in a cabinet or wall storage system. If particle board is chosen for such shelving, it can be painted a dark color or stained a dark tone and serve the purpose of providing internal shelving at a low cost. One possible drawback in using particle board materials is that they tend to be hard on conventional handtools.

Chapter 2

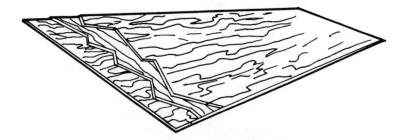

Tools and Workspace

BEFORE YOU BEGIN TO BUILD PLYWOOD FUR-niture projects in your spare time, you should first consider the need for creating a suitable workspace. This is a very important point that many do-it-yourselfer's overlook and the result, more often than not, is a project that does not turn out according to plan. There are a number of hand tools and power tools that can help you achieve professional results, but you must also have the space for working on your projects.

Probably the most apparent feature of working with plywood is that the standard-size sheets are large (4 ×8 feet is equal to 32 square feet of material in one board). Therefore, one of the most important requirements of a suitable plywood workshop is space enough for working with full-size sheets of plywood. One of the most aggravating aspects of working with full sheets of plywood is trying to maneuver a panel around so that it can be cut on a table saw or with a hand-held electrical saw. If the only space you have available for a woodworking shop is 10 × 10 feet, one solution is to do all of your

cutting of full-size panels out of doors (Fig. 2-1). Although this arrangement has limitations, it is nevertheless one way to cope with the small workshop problem.

An alternative is to have your local lumberyard do some of the cutting for you when you purchase plywood. This is certainly a very good way if you do not have a table saw. If you live in an apartment, where workspace is almost nonexistent, this might be your only choice for obtaining plywood for your projects. Because at least part of the success of any plywood furniture project depends on assembling precision-cut pieces of plywood, you can improve your chances for good results by starting out with precut plywood (Fig. 2-2).

In addition to having adequate work space, the ideal home woodworking shop should also have ample storage space. You will need room to store uncut materials and trimmings from previous projects. Because plywood does not take up much space when stacked on edge, consider using one wall in your workshop for storing uncut plywood panels

Fig. 2-1. If your workshop is small, you might have to cut full sheets of plywood out of doors.

(Fig. 2-3). Less than full-size sheets of plywood can be stored in a similar manner. Place larger pieces in the back and the smaller pieces in front.

The home workshop must also have storage space for tools. Some type of cabinet storage system is ideal for this because the tools will not only be out of harms way, but they will also be protected from sawdust and other airborne particles that could cause them to malfunction. In the ideal workshop, stored tools are out of the way at all times, but easily accessible when needed (Fig. 2-4). If you have children in your home, the need for safe storage will become very apparent as they start to explore.

While a workbench will not prove especially handy for most plywood furniture projects (large projects are best accomplished from the floor up), it

will probably come in handy for smaller projects. A large worktable, located in the center of your workshop, will be most effective if it is at least 4 × 4 feet. It will also be easier to work on if it is only about 2 feet in height. This way you can work on many different types of plywood furniture projects while standing with the work at a comfortable height. Specifications for building a suitable plywood furniture project worktable are given in Fig. 2-5.

In the process of planning a woodworking shop, there are two areas that you should give extra attention to: lighting and adequate electrical service. These are two areas that are generally deficient in most home workshops. The need for adequate lighting cannot be overstressed. If your shop is not well lighted, you open the door to accidents. The chances of a serious accident increase dramatically when electrical power tools are in use. Another very good reason for supplying plenty of light in the workshop is so that you can clearly see what you are doing. If you can not see well in the workshop, it will be almost impossible to create any kind of project worthy of your pride.

I have found that 4-foot-long fluorescent light fixtures—either two- or four-bulb types—are ideal for lighting the home workshop. Not only do these lighting fixtures provide a flood of good light, they do not become very hot to work around. They are also less expensive to run than incandescent lighting.

For specialty lighting, consider having one or two clamp-type lights (Fig. 2-6) around the workshop. You generally can pick up one of these at a photo shop. These lights are handy because you can clamp them close to the project and direct a beam of light directly where you want it. Other good choices for auxiliary lighting include a gooseneck lamp with a clamp base and a draftsmans' lamp. The latter is usually available in either fluorescent or incandescent.

Electrical service is always a problem in the home workshop. It almost always seems that there are never enough electrical outlets available for efficient work. One good way to eliminate this problem is to install a special plug-in strip on the front edge of your workbench or worktable. These units

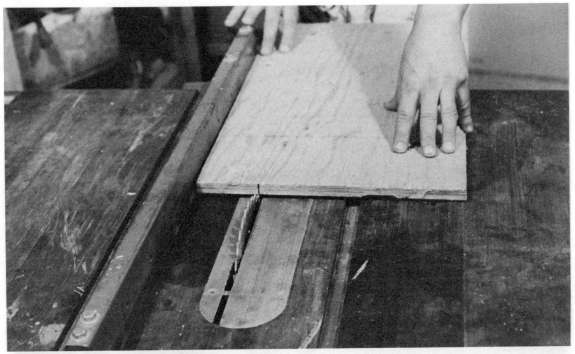

Fig. 2-2. Most lumber yards will cut plywood for a small fee.

Fig. 2-3. Stack your plywood neatly and according to size.

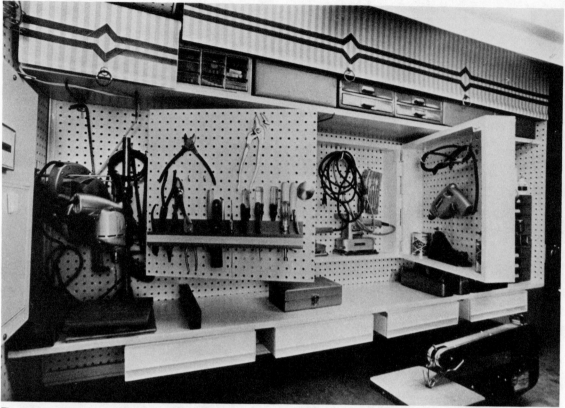

Fig. 2-4. An efficient workshop has plenty of work and storage space.

allow you to plug in a number of power tools at the same time (Fig. 2-7).

Stationary power tools such as table saws, radial-arm saws, band saws, grinders, lathes, and drill presses should all have electrical outlets close to the unit. If you have any of these machines in your workshop, you know how much easier the piece of equipment is to use if you can simply turn it on to use rather than have to first search around for an outlet.

Don't think, even for a moment, that you can work in a woodworking shop that has only one electrical outlet. Many handymen attempt to work this way and try to eliminate the problem they encounter by stringing extension cords around the shop. While extension cords are handy for special projects, they should never be relied on as a basic source of electrical power. Not only do you increase the chances of serious injury—by tripping over

loose wires on the floor—but you also run the risk of electrical shock.

The best way to provide adequate electrical service for your workshop is to install conventional

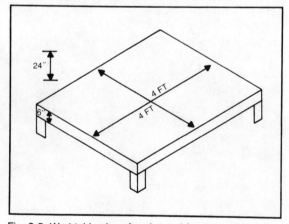

Fig. 2-5. Worktable plans for plywood furniture workshop.

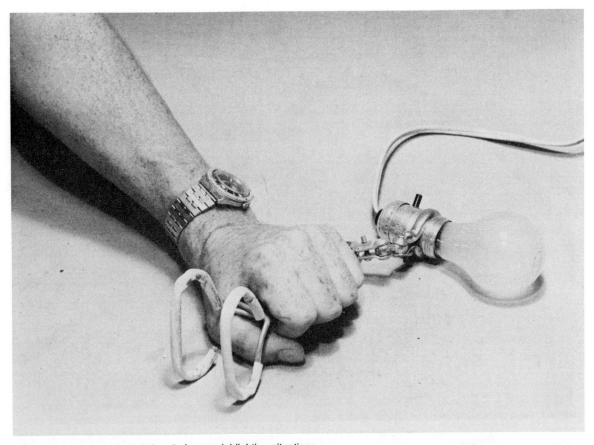

Fig. 2-6. A clamp on lamp is handy for special lighting situations.

electrical outlets around the shop. If you have the qualifications for installing electrical service—from the main circuit box in the house—by all means do the work yourself. But if you are unqualified, and you must be honest with yourself, call in a professional electrician to do the work. Remember that one of the major causes of fires in the home is faulty electrical wiring.

There are a number of other factors that you should take into consideration when you are planning your home woodworking shop. Because most of these (such as heating. ventilation, easy access, etc.) can involve a considerable amount of expense and labor to achieve, you must give them careful consideration. Most do-it-yourselfers make do with a part of a basement or garage. You should, however, try to incorporate some of the features mentioned in this chapter to make the workshop as efficient as possible.

HAND TOOLS

The basic tools required for working plywood are few and simple. If you have done much woodworking in the past, you probably have most of the tools you will require. There are also some specialized tools that are required for special projects such as covering a surface with plastic laminate.

Before you can begin working on any woodworking project, you will need some type of work plan. Most do-it-yourselfers (and professionals as well) find a detailed diagram to be most helpful. In addition to a sound work plan, you must also be able to accurately measure and lay out cut lines on the

Fig. 2-7. Provide adequate electrical service in your shop.

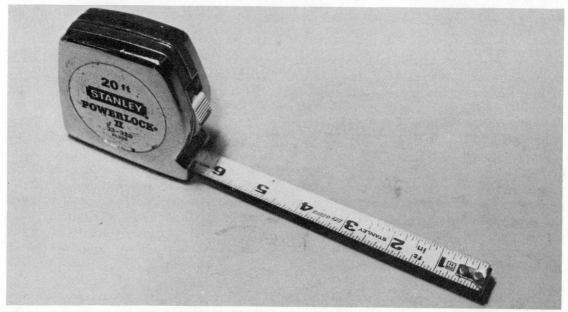

Fig. 2-8. A steel tape is handy for measuring large projects.

plywood. For measuring, the obvious and the best tool is a good ruler (Fig. 2-8). I have several around my workshop and find that I use most of them.

For long measurements, I find that an 8-foot-long steel tape is indispensable. While a steel tape of this kind is intended for general construction—such as framing and general carpentry—it is also very handy for marking off long cuts on a plywood panel. For shorter cuts, many do-it-yourselfers prefer a folding ruler (Fig. 2-9). Time was, in the not too distant past, that folding rulers were one of the real signs of a professional carpenter. Now you seldom see one on a construction site. Nevertheless, a 6- to 8-foot extension ruler is very handy around the plywood workshop. Possibly one reason many handymen shy away from folding rulers is that they are not as fast as a steel tape and they tend to break easily if handled roughly.

If you find that you do not need to work at high speed, then an old-fashioned folding ruler might be right for your measuring needs. You can easily extend the life of such a ruler by lubricating (Fig. 2-10) all of the joints in the ruler. A drop of oil on each of these metal joints will make the ruler open and close much easier. In addition, when you open a folding ruler you should hold one end of the ruler—while holding the bulk of the ruler in your other hand—and pull the ruler open smoothly (Fig. 2-11). Quick, jerking motions tend to put stress on the ruler joints. The result can be two rulers rather than one.

For small measuring tasks, foot long rulers or yard sticks are very handy. I keep a small ruler close to the table saw and it is very handy for setting up the saw for various cuts. A yard stick (Fig. 2-12) is most useful if it is strong and straight. One of the better choices is a steel yardstick. These are generally available at hardware stores and lumber yards. A good one should easily last a lifetime. In addition, a steel yardstick can do double duty as a

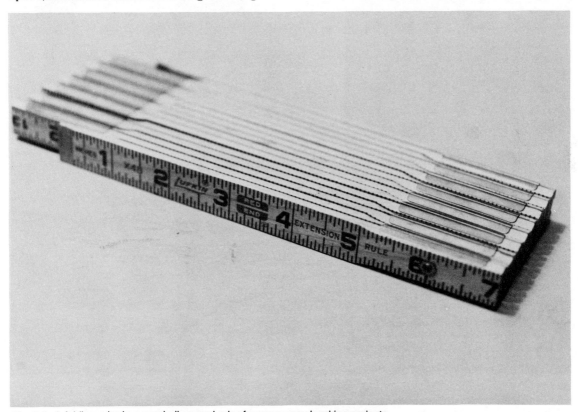

Fig. 2-9. A folding ruler is a good all-around ruler for many woodworking projects.

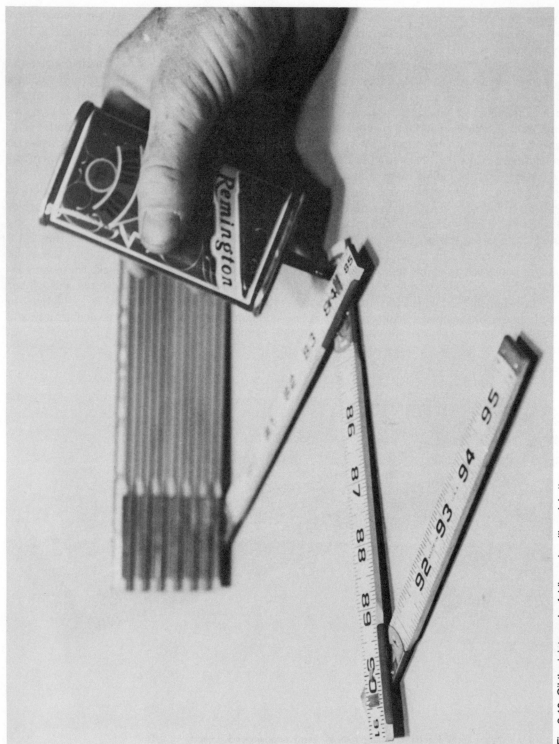

Fig. 2-10. Oil the joints and a folding rule will work better.

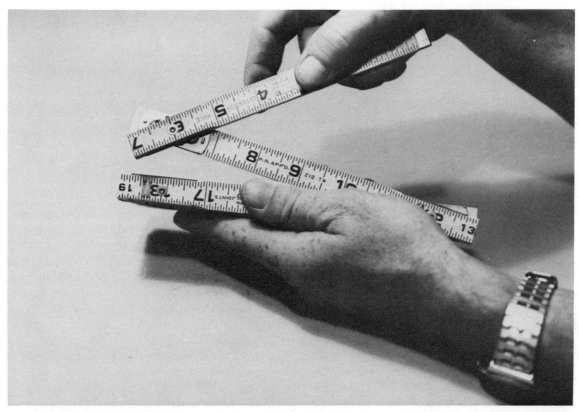

Fig. 2-11. Pull a folding ruler open.

straightedge and it is very handy for marking cuts on a sheet of plywood.

You might not have considered using a chalk line (Fig. 2-13) in your woodworking shop but, a chalk line is very useful for marking long cuts on a panel of plywood. More importantly, a chalk line will give you a very accurate mark faster than using a long straightedge.

Fig. 2-12. A yardstick is helpful around the shop.

Fig. 2-13. A chalk line is handy for marking full-size sheets of plywood.

An example of how to use a chalk line to mark a long cut may prove helpful. Let's assume that you need to cut a full panel of plywood in half (lengthwise) so that you end up with two equal pieces measuring 2 feet wide by 8 feet long. Begin by marking one end of the panel 2 feet in from the edge; place a pencil mark at this point. Next, mark the other end of the panel—also 2 feet in from the edge. Then strike a chalk line between these two points and you will have a clear cut mark running down the center of the plywood panel. This method of marking a long cut is so simple, fast, and accurate that you will use it whenever you need to mark a long cut on plywood. This same method of marking long cuts also works very well for other materials such as wall paneling, gypsum panels, and other long or wide sheet materials.

The home woodworking shop should have an assortment of marking tools. The most common and useful examples include a combination square, a try square, a framing square, a sliding T-bevel, and a pair of dividers or a simple compass.

A combination square is a very handy and quite common tool that is used for various types of squaring off marking. A typical combination square (Fig. 2-14) will have a 12-inch-long steel ruler,

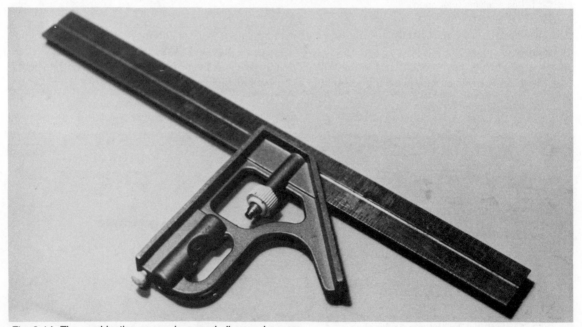

Fig. 2-14. The combination square is a good all-around square.

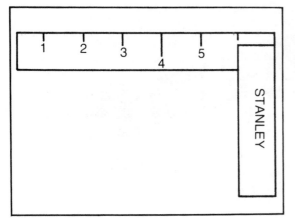

Fig. 2-15. Try square.

along which slides a special head that can help you to mark off either a 45- or 90-degree angle. Because the head slides along the ruler, this square can be adjusted for different widths of lumber. Most models also have a pin-like scribing tool that slips into the head. This way you always have a squaring off tool and a marking tool at your fingertips.

The try square is most commonly available in a fixed 90-degree angle. Because of its small size, it is very handy around the woodworking shop. Some of the more common uses of a try square include marking lumber at a 90-degree angle, setting up a table saw or hand-held saw so that the blade is at a perfect 90-degree angle to the saw table, and other tasks where a 90-degree angle is essential. Generally, inexpensive models can be knocked out of alignment easily, but the more expensive versions, as result of precision machining, remain true.

Another squaring-type tool is called a framing square or rafter square. If you have ever measured and cut roof rafters, you have probably worked with one of these. A framing square is very handy for laying out cut lines on plywood. Additionally, one can be used for checking the squareness of any piece of lumber. The 2-foot size (Fig. 2-16) is probably the most common and readily available. This is a good size for the home workshop as well.

A sliding T-bevel (Fig. 2-17) is a marking tool that is indispensable for copying almost any angle. Because the blade and head can be turned to conform to any angle, the sliding T-bevel is the tool to

Fig. 2-16. Rafter or framing square.

Fig. 2-17. The sliding T-bevel is handy for making angle cuts.

use if you want to duplicate an angle. It is simple to use, and in a matter of seconds, you can determine any angle and transfer it to a surface.

A handy marking tool for the home woodworking shop is a pair of dividers or a simple compass. With such a tool, you will be able to mark out curved cuts on plywood. Dividers are used for marking circles (or half circles) up to about 8 inches in diameter.

For larger circles, most woodworkers prefer to use a string, a nail, and a pencil. To do this, you must first determine the center of the circle and drive a small nail into the plywood at this point. Then tie one end of a string to the nail (with a slip knot) and the other end to the shaft of a pencil. It is important to tie the end of the string to the pencil at the proper distance from the nail. A little experimenting will be required to obtain the desired diameter circle. To mark a circle, the pencil is held straight up and down while at the same time keeping the string taut. Then the pencil is moved around the nail until the circle is complete. With a little practice, you can turn out perfect circles every time (Fig. 2-18).

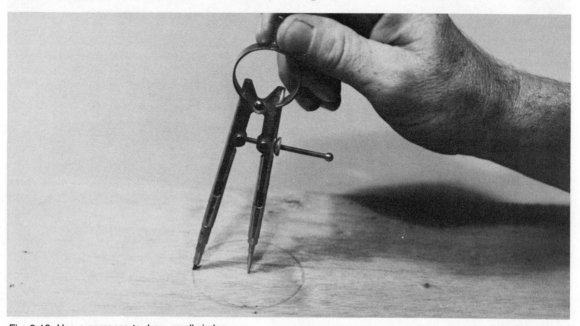

Fig. 2-18. Use a compass to draw small circles.

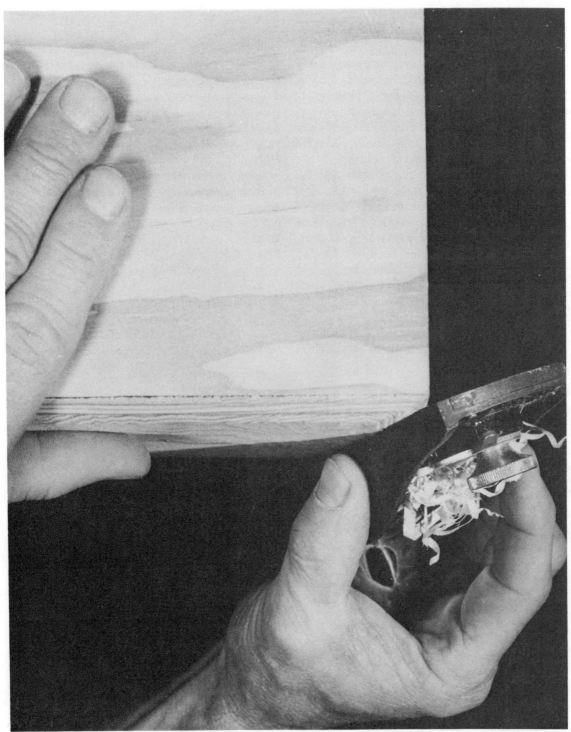

Fig. 2-19. A small plane is useful for light trimming on plywood furniture (courtesy American Plywood Association).

SHAPING AND SANDING TOOLS

There are a number of very special tools that are used in the forming and finishing of plywood furniture. In this group are planes, rasps, and other specialized tools that are used for various forming tasks such as shaping the edges of plywood. In addition, sanding tools are used to smooth out surfaces of a plywood furniture project. These include abrasive papers (commonly called sandpaper) and a sanding block. The first group of tools is generally used to remove large amounts of wood material rather quickly. The latter tools are used for final smoothing and general surface preparation prior to and during finishing with a coating (either clear coatings such as varnish or solid colors of paint).

The well-equipped home woodworking shop should have an assortment of planes for working with plywood. The most useful types are a small hand plane, a block plane, a larger bench plane, and possibly one or two Surform tools.

A small hand plane (Fig. 2-19) is very useful for little edge trimming projects where only a bit of plywood needs to be removed. For trimming the edges and ends of plywood, a block plane is more than handy—it is essential. A good block plane will be about 6 inches long and fit comfortably in the hand. The blade of a block plane is set at a low angle. It is just the tool for planing end or edge grain in general woodwork. Because every edge and end of a piece of plywood has edge grains, a block plane is very useful for smoothing these edges quickly and efficiently. For long edge planing, a block plane can be used, but the work will go quicker and be easier to accomplish if a larger bench plane is used. There are two general sizes of bench planes. The smooth plane measures from 8 to 10 inches in length and the large jack plane is approximately 15 inches long. Either one of these bench planes will make short work out of smoothing long edges on a sheet of plywood. The longer jack plane is probably the best for the longer smoothing tasks.

Stanley Tool Company's Surform tool (Fig. 2-20)—available in a number of different sizes and shapes—is one of the handiest forming tools to

Fig. 2-20. The Stanley Surform Tool is handy for trimming and shaping operations.

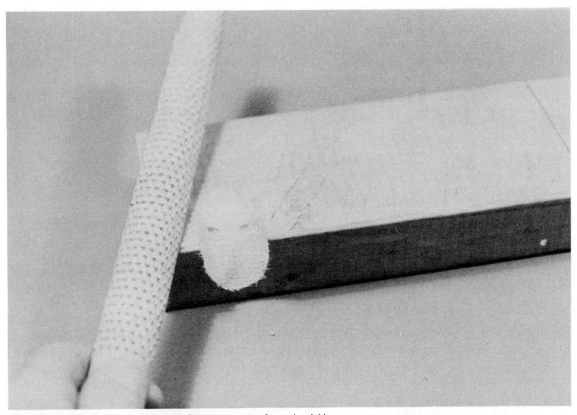

Fig. 2-21. The wood rasp can remove large amounts of wood quickly.

come down the pike in many years. The replacement blade in the Surform tool is made from a thin piece of sheet steel, and it has hundreds of tiny holes in the surface. Each of these holes has a high and a low end. When the blade is inserted in the conventional manner, it will quickly remove material on the push stroke. By varying hand pressure, the user can remove a little or a lot of material from most types of surfaces—wood, plastic, filler-type materials, etc. Unlike a true plane, the Surform tool can be used to shape irregular surfaces. While this tool is not really capable of producing a finished surface, it can come fairly close. Usually the only additional work necessary is sanding.

You will also need a selection of wood rasps (Fig. 2-21) and files for your home woodworking shop. Wood rasps are capable of removing significant amounts of wood quickly. They are very handy for forming irregular shapes. The Stanley Surform

is actually a modern-day wood rasp, that does about the same type of work, but not as quickly.

One of the more useful wood rasps is called a four-in-hand rasp. This tool is made with four different types of rasping surfaces. It is quite versatile in the woodworking shop. The four surfaces—ranging in texture from very coarse to very fine—can be used for shaping many types of angles and is especially useful for rounding or forming special decorative edges on plywood. This tool should take care of most types of forming or shaping tasks in the home woodworking shop.

Files are used for removing small amounts of wood and generally smoothing the surface after it has been worked on with a wood rasp. Files are also used for finishing off the edges of plastic laminate after they have been cut with a router equipped with a special plastic laminate trimming bit.

A good selection of files for the home work-

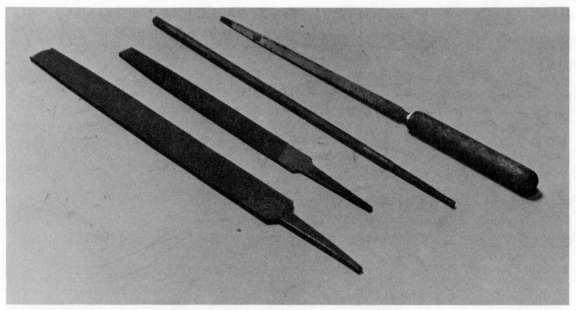

Fig. 2-22. An assortment of files will find use around your workshop.

shop should include the following: large, flat-mill bastard; cabinet; and one or two round files similar to those used for sharpening the teeth on a chain saw. Whenever you are using a file or rasp, the tool should have a handle. You can purchase one of these when you buy your file or make one from a section of old broom handle. See Fig. 2-22.

Whenever you work with a file to smooth the edges of plywood—or any wood or metal for that matter—the file grooves will tend to become clogged with the material. In a short time, the file will be much less efficient at doing its job simply because the cutting edges are filled. For this reason, you should have a file card in your workshop. A file card is simply a brush-like cleaning tool (Fig. 2-23) that is used for unclogging a file or rasp. One

Fig. 2-23. Use a file card to clean out file grooves.

side of a file card will have steel bristles and the other side will have fiber bristles.

When you feel that the file is not removing material as efficiently as it should, simply brush it with the file card to clean out the cutting edges. Then the file will work as good as new.

Even though most people refer to abrasives as "sandpaper," there is not sand on them. There are four basic types of abrasives used in the woodworking industry: *flint, garnet, aluminum oxide* and, *silicon carbide*. The first two abrasive materials occur naturally in nature. The second two are man-made materials. Each of these abrasives have various characteristics suitable for specific sanding projects.

Flint paper is probably the most familiar of all the abrasives sold in this country. It is easy to identify because it has an off-white face color that is very much like the color of sand. Even though flint paper is widely available, it is generally considered by professionals as the poorest choice. It is not very hard. Therefore it will not cut as well as most other abrasives. About the only strong point flint paper has is low price, and this is really a false economy.

Garnet is harder than flint and, therefore, a better choice for finish or light sanding. Garnet abrasives are easy to recognize because its color is a reddish-brown earth tone. Garnet is popular among serious woodworkers, It is available in sheets, belts, and disks.

Aluminum oxide is the third hardest abrasive. This man-made material is an excellent choice for sanding most hardwoods such as oak and walnut. Aluminum oxide is a by-product of aluminum ore (bauxite) to which small amounts of other adhesive materials are added to create a rich brown-colored abrasive that is fast cutting, and therefore, a good choice for most sanding projects.

The hardest and sharpest of all abrasives is silicon carbide. This is truly a remarkable man-made abrasive that is suitable for almost any sanding project under the sun—from softwoods to metal. Carbide is used for sharpening stones and there are a wide range of cutting edges such as carbide-tipped saw blades and router bits. Silicon carbide is easy to identify because it is almost black in appearance. As you might have suspected, silicon carbide abrasives are costly to produce and abrasive papers are expensive. Nevertheless, many woodworking enthusiasts prefer silicon carbide abrasives over all others.

Abrasives for woodworking projects are available in a wide range of papers, belts, disks and pads. For sanding by hand, most abrasives are available in 9- × -12 sheets (that can be cut to fit sanding blocks) or in pre-cut strips that generally fit most conventional hand sanding tools. It is probably a safe assumption that if you have a sanding block, a hand-held sander (belt, orbital or disk), or a stationary sanding machine, you should have little problem in finding an abrasive paper, a belt or a disk to fit your tool.

It is important to use the right abrasive for the project at hand. It is equally important to work your way up to the smaller grit sizes as you get closer to the final finish (applying a coating of wax, varnish, or paint). Figure 2-24 gives you an indication of the proper grit sizes of abrasive papers to use for various sanding projects.

CUTTING TOOLS

While the majority of home woodworkers today use electrically powered saws for most cutting tasks, there are still some cuts that are best made with a handsaw (Fig. 2-25). Unfortunately, the art of using a handsaw (from a crosscut saw to a hacksaw) is falling by the wayside largely because of the convenience and speed of modern electrical saws.

The carpenters' handsaw has been in use for centuries. Modern versions will cut plywood admirably, but there is obviously more effort required for this type of work than if the same task is accomplished with a power saw. Basically, there are two different types of handsaws for woodworking: *crosscut* and *ripsaw*. The main differences between these types of saws is that the crosscut saw is designed (Fig. 2-26) to be used while cutting across the grain of wood while a ripsaw is designed for cutting with the grain of wood.

When cutting plywood—with multi-directional layers of veneer—you will encounter both types of grain. The first inclination is to use the ripsaw for

	Grit Number	Grade	General Uses
Very Fine	400 360 320 280 240 220	10/0 - 9/0 8/0 7/0 6/0	Polishing, finishing after stain, varnish & paint. Last paper to be used.
Fine	180 150 120	5/0 4/0 3/0	Finish sanding prior to staining or sealing.
Medium	100 80 60	2/0 1/0 1/2	Final removal of rough surface texture.
Coarse	50 40 36	1 1 1/2 2	For sanding after rough sanding has been done.
Very Coarse	30 24 20 16	2 1/2 3 3 1/2 4	For sanding very rough textured surfaces.

Fig. 2-24. Grit size table.

cutting plywood, but the result will be a wide cut that lacks smooth edges. Because a ripsaw cuts with the grain as a result of wide tooth spacing, it is really a poor choice for cutting plywood. It tends to rip the plywood rather than provide a smooth cut. The best choice of saw for cutting plywood is a crosscut saw.

All saws are described according to the number of teeth (properly called *points*) per inch of saw blade. Generally, the greater number of teeth per inch, the finer or smoother the finished cut will be. Most authorities seem to agree that the coarsest crosscut saw that can be used to neatly cut plywood is a 10-point-per-inch saw. A much smoother cut can be achieved by using a crosscut saw with 12 points per inch. The basic rule is that the more teeth per inch on the saw blade the finer the cut.

A keyhole saw (Fig. 2-27) is quite handy for making irregular-shaped cuts and hole-type cuts in

Fig. 2-25. Handsaw use requires control and practice.

plywood. This saw has a long, tapering blade that is ideal for making hole cutouts after a small starter hole has been made in the plywood. A keyhole saw enables you to make a cutout anywhere on a panel of plywood without having to cut in from the edge of the panel. A keyhole saw is very handy for many other general carpentry tasks. If you are planning to buy a keyhole saw, look for one that has a selection of interchangable blades (usually fine, coarse, and metal-cutting) because this type is extremely versatile.

A coping saw (Fig. 2-28) is another handy, special-purpose saw to have around the woodworking shop. While a typical plywood furniture project will not require a coping saw, the more detailed projects will. Because the blade of a coping saw is thin and narrow, it is indispensable for making intricate cuts. All coping saws can use a variety of blades that increase the saws capabilities. Blades range from very coarse to extremely fine, and they are probably the least expensive saw blades that you can buy today.

While the traditional use for a hacksaw (Fig. 2-29) is for cutting metals, it is also handy for cutting small pieces of plastic laminate and making small, straight cuts on plywood. Because the points on hacksaw blades tend to be many (over 12 per inch), the quality of the cut you can obtain with a

hacksaw is often quite good. The hacksaw will not receive that much use in the plywood furniture shop, but there are a few instances where this tool will prove its worth. A wide assortment of blades will make the hacksaw even more versatile.

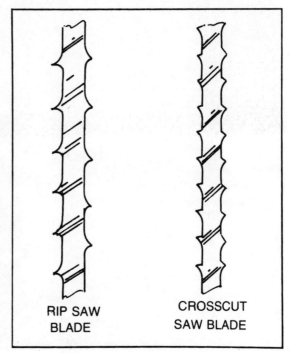

RIP SAW
BLADE

CROSSCUT
SAW BLADE

Fig. 2-26. Diagram of rip and cross-cut saw teeth.

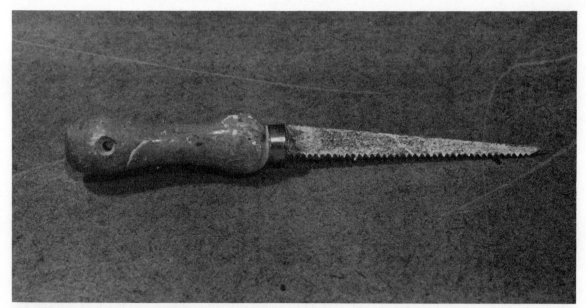

Fig. 2-27. Keyhole saw.

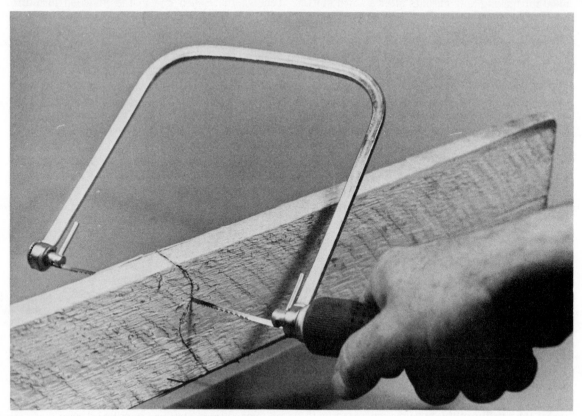

Fig. 2-28. The coping saw is useful for irregular cutting tasks.

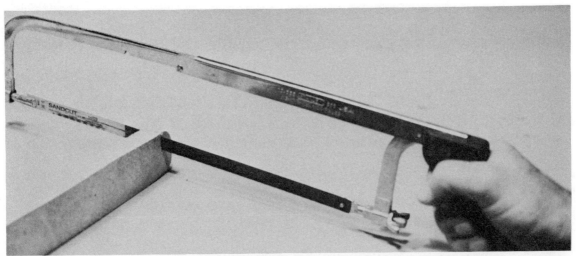

Fig. 2-29. A hacksaw is useful for small cutting operations such as cutting thin strips of plastic laminate.

HAMMERS

Certainly every do-it-yourselfer has one or more hammers in the tool box or in the workshop. It is interesting to note that the concept of a hammer has remained pretty much the same for centuries, but there have, of course, been improvements in metallurgy, design and handle material. If you purchase a hammer today, chances are very good that the tool will outlast you. Modern hammers are made to last; A one-piece design hammer will never suffer from a loose head or broken handle (Fig. 2-30).

Generally, there are three basic hammer designs that will be found around the average home workshop. These include a framing or ripping hammer, the claw hammer and, specialized cabinetmakers' hammer. Of the three, the framing hammer is probably the least useful when building plywood furniture projects. The main reason is that a framing hammer is just too heavy for the often delicate nails and nailing of plywood furniture. A framing hammer will weigh at least 20 ounces. As the name suggests, it is the type of hammer used for general construction. It is also an excellent hammer for fastening plywood to roof rafters or floor joists; usually only a few blows will drive 10d nails home.

The claw hammer (Fig. 2-31) is probably the most common hammer in existence today. The familiar curved claw, opposite the striking face,

Fig. 2-30. A 20-ounce framing hammer is considered too heavy for plywood furniture building.

59

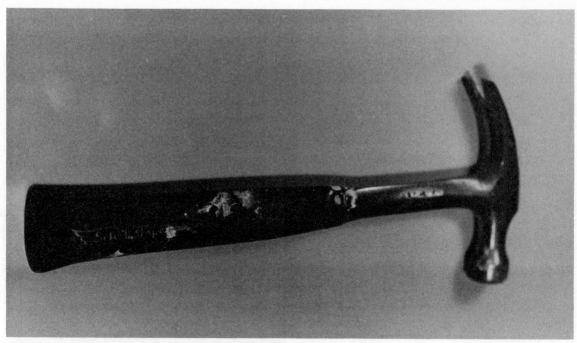

Fig. 2-31. This claw hammer design has not changed much in hundreds of years.

gives this hammer its name. The 16-ounce weight is the most popular and it will handle most types of general carpentry for constructing plywood furniture projects. Some experts suggest that a lighter weight—13- or even 10-ounce head—is more efficient at driving small finishing nails and brads. If you are planning to build many plywood furniture projects, you should consider buying a lightweight claw hammer.

The cabinetmakers' hammer (Fig. 2-32) is a rather specialized hammer that is just the ticket for building cabinets. The standard weight of this

Fig. 2-32. Some experts feel that the cabinetmakers hammer is the best choice for furniture building.

hammer is 10 ounces. This is ideal for driving wire brads and light finishing nails. Instead of a nail pulling claw, the cabinetmakers' hammer has a wedge-shaped peen opposite the striking surface of the hammer.

Most of the cabinetmakers' hammer designs are two-piece: head and handle. More often than not, this will be a metal head and a wooden handle. The head design is useful for driving light nails or brads into tight places. The conventional striking surface is used to drive the nail almost home. Then the peen end is used to finish off the driving. Because most plywood furniture projects—as well as more advanced woodworking projects—require only light nails, the traditional cabinetmaker's hammer is an ideal tool for this type of work.

While constructing plywood furniture projects, you might find occasion to use a soft-faced mallet. Various tasks, such as fitting parts of a project together, are best accomplished with a special hammer. There are several types of mallets currently available. These include rubber mallets,

wooden mallets, and plastic-head hammers. These soft-headed hammers make good additions to your basic tool chest. In a pinch, however, a block of wood covered with a soft material (such as a strip of carpeting) can be struck with a lightweight hammer (Fig. 2-33) to achieve a tight fit without fear of marring, denting or otherwise damaging the surface of the plywood furniture project.

CHISELS

Wood chisels are handy for many plywood furniture projects such as cabinets and built-ins. Wood chisels have traditionally been used for removing sections of solid wood material and carving.

There are several styles, shapes, sizes and grades of wood chisels available to the woodworker. Probably the most useful style for the plywood woodworker are referred to as *butt chisels* (Fig. 2-34). This style is moderately priced and can easily handle most general construction tasks. Quality is very important when purchasing a wood chisel (as well as most other types of woodworking

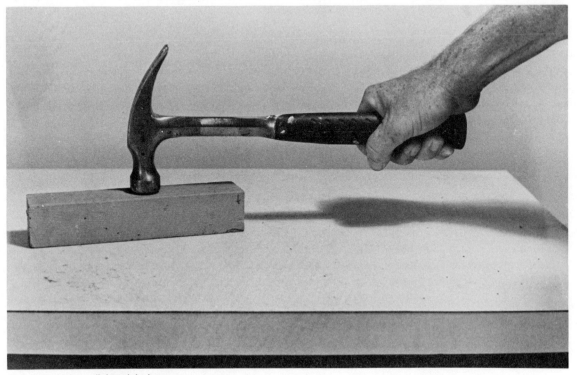

Fig. 2-33. Using a lightweight hammer.

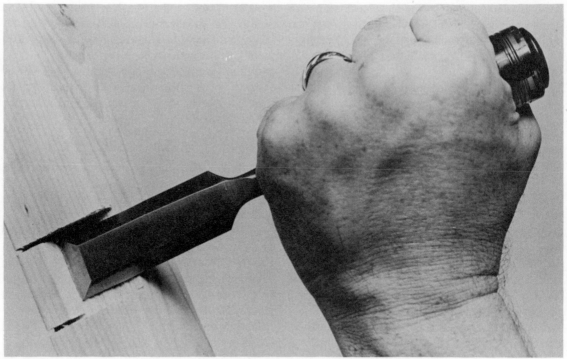

Fig. 2-34. A sharp chisel works best (courtesy The Stanley Company).

tools). A quality woodworking butt chisel will have a durable handle (wooden or molded hard plastic) and the business end will be made from a good-grade tool steel.

It is important to keep in mind when buying wood chisels that good steel can be sharpened, will hold and edge, and will not nick or chip easily. Poor-quality wood chisels (price is one guideline) will not hold an edge, tend to suffer tip chips, cannot be sharpened easily, and usually have handles that become loose after they are struck with a mallet a few times.

The best way to buy chisels is one at a time. Start with the ¾-inch-wide blade (Fig. 2-35) because it is probably the most useful. This size blade can handle most chiseling projects with ease (except removing miniscule amounts of wood). Many woodworkers prefer to buy all of their chisels at one time, but I don't see the point of having a set of five chisels—which may cost as much as $70—when the purchase of one or two quality woodworking chisels—at a cost of about $8 to $10 each—will take care of all of your chiseling needs.

A sharp woodworking chisel is a joy to work with and it is the only type of chisel that you should use for removing a section of wood. The best way to touch up your woodworking chisel is with a sharpening stone (Fig. 2-36). Use hard Arkansas for light touch-ups or coarse aluminum oxide for restoring badly worn or chipped edges.

The importance of a sharp edge on a wood chisel—or any cutting tool for that matter—cannot be overstressed. I once worked with a finish carpenter for a number of years, and one of my tasks was to keep all of the tools sharp. A wood chisel was considered sharp enough when the tip could be used to cut the hair on the back of your hand. That's how sharp a woodworking chisel should be before you use it.

SCREWDRIVERS

A number of plywood furniture projects in this book

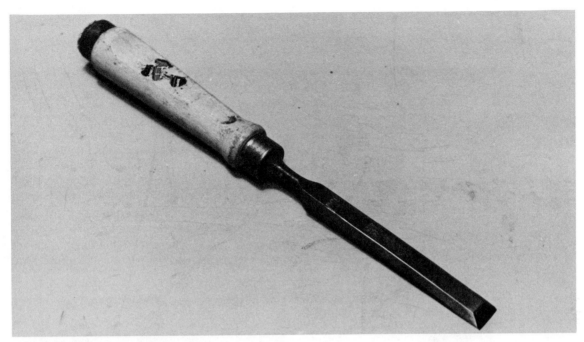

Fig. 2-35. Buy good chisels one at a time.

call for joining the pieces of the project with glue and screws for strength. There are also a number of other tasks—such as attaching hardware—that can only be accomplished with a screwdriver. The well-equipped home woodworking shop will have a selection of screwdrivers.

Even though screwdrivers are very common, there is no such thing as an all-purpose screwdriver. A quick glance in a catalog that offers fine woodworking tools will reveal screwdrivers described as cabinet, London, Scotch, spindle-bladed, ratchet or mechanical (of which there are several versions), gentlemans', gunmakers', model makers', military and, even undertakers'. These are further divided into square tip, Phillips, crosspoint, Allen head, and a few other tip designs.

With such a vast assortment of styles and tip configurations available, it is easy to become confused when buying a screwdriver. More often than not, when the need for a tool arises, the first thing that comes to hand is the screwdriver. Just as often the blade of the nearest screwdriver does not fit the screw slot well and the result is that the screw is difficult to turn or the blade slips out of the screw slot and mars the work surface.

The easiest way to avoid problems is to choose the right driver for the task at hand. The tip of the screwdriver must fit snugly in the screw slot (Fig. 2-37). The tip must not be too wide or too short, and the bottom edge of the blade should be flat and square.

A good selection of screwdrivers for the woodworking shop should include one of each of the following screwdrivers: 3-inch, 4-inch, 5-inch, 6-inch, 8-inch, and 10-inch standard bladed screwdrivers, a small, medium, and large Phillips screwdrivers, and one ratchet-type screwdriver with an assortment of tips (both standard and Phillips head). With such a selection, the do-it-yourselfer will surely be well armed to attack any task that requires turning a screw.

POWER TOOLS

There is just no getting around the fact that this is the age of power tools for the woodworker. As great as the appeal is of working solely with your hands

Fig. 2-36. Keep your chisel sharp with frequent touchups.

these power tools far outnumbered the basic tools, you might find enough reason to revert to simple hand tools.

Although many power tools are reasonably priced—when you consider their capabilities—there are some power tools that are rather specialized and not necessarily a good investment.

A power tool can be considered portable if it can be hand held during use. Part of the reason that there is such a large selection of hand-held power tools is industry response to consumer demands. According to an industry spokesman, "the average do-it-yourselfer wants power tools that are light-weight, portable, efficient, and he wants them at a reasonable price. The same requirements are required by professional carpenters and contractors,

and simple tools, almost any woodworking task can be accomplished in a fraction of the time if the proper power tool is used instead of a simple hand tool.

Responding to consumer demands, the power-tool industry has developed a vast array of electrically powered tools. Currently, it is possible to find over 50 models of hand-held circular saws, ranging in price from $20 to over $200. Add to this the choices in sabre saws, table saws, radial-arm saws, band saws and jigsaws and you have a vast assortment of saws.

There are also hand drills, routers, jointer-planners, sanders, and other special-purpose power tools. The variety of power tools is enough to confuse even experienced woodworkers and carpenters. And when you realize that the accessories for

Fig. 2-37. The screwdriver tip should fit snugly into the screw slot.

who also want durability in portable power tools. Our industry has responded to these needs by developing hand held power tools that will accomplish almost any task that a stationary power tool will do, and these tools will do the job faster and at a much lower initial cost."

All of the plywood furniture projects described in this book can be constructed using portable power tools. Many can also be built using only simple muscle-powered tools, but the task will take longer to accomplish.

HAND-HELD SAWS

By far, the largest group of portable power tools are hand-held saws; circular saws are the most common. Another very popular hand-held saw is the sabre saw. According to industry sources, the 7¼-inch blade size is the biggest seller. In this group it is possible to find models ranging in price from about $20 to $200. There is quite a difference between the low-priced and high-priced models. The main differences in price are a result of the horsepower rating of the electric motor used to power the saw as well as general features and attachments for the saw. Some of the added features of the higher-priced saws include adjustments for depth of cut, tilt adjustments, and ripping guide attachments. Generally, the higher the horsepower of the saw the higher the selling price of that unit.

For most types of general carpentry, a circular saw with a rating of around 1½ horsepower is sufficient and the unit will be light enough to use without undue arm fatigue. For cutting plywood (all thicknesses), the 1½-horsepower circular saw is ideal. Some do-it-yourselfers prefer a lighter unit that has ¾ horsepower or 1 horsepower. There are also a few professional carpenters that I know who prefer ½-horsepower, 5-inch bladed, hand-held circular saws for working with plywood paneling.

It is probably a safe assumption that the 1½-horsepower saw will be quite suitable for all your plywood work and light carpentry. If the saw will be used for cutting framing lumber (2-×-4, 2-×-6, 2-×-8 inch dimensional lumber), then you would want more horsepower as well as a tougher overall saw. These bigger saws are commonly called *contractor saws* and they have a horsepower rating of at least 2 horsepower.

Contractor's saws (Fig. 2-38) are more heavily constructed so that they stand up well to the kind of abuse that is prevalent on a construction project. The hand-held circular saw that we have today—as well as the many versions of the basic saw—was designed after World War II for speeding up general house construction.

While a hand-held circular saw is primarily designed for general carpentry, it can also be used for making accurate cuts on plywood if some type of guidance system is used to help the saw blade cut along a given cut line (Fig. 2-39). One way of doing this is to use a ripping guide; this is an accessory attachment on many saws. The only limitation of a ripping guide is that it cannot be used for guiding the saw for very wide cuts; about 12 inches is maximum. For guiding a hand-held circular saw through wider cuts—which are quite common when working with plywood—it is more practical to use some type of straightedge for the base of the saw.

A professional tip worth mentioning concerns the use of a strip of metal, a straight length of 2 × 4 lumber, or even a 4-foot level as an edge guide for a hand-held circular saw. Let's assume that you require a 4-×-4 foot piece of plywood that will cut from a full sheet of plywood (4-×-8 feet). Begin by measuring up 4 feet from one end of the panel (place a mark there, and do the same on the other side of the panel). Now you will have a full sheet of plywood with a 4-foot high and 4-foot wide section marked off. Next, take a 4-foot (or longer) straightedge and place it at a distance from the marks so that when the edge of the saw base is resting on the straightedge. The saw blade will cut a straight line across the panel at the 4-foot mark. Now you must clamp (or otherwise temporarily fasten) the straightedge to the panel. Then start up the saw and, while keeping the edge of the saw pressed against the straightedge, cut the panel along the 2-foot mark. This method of saw guidance—if set up properly—will enable you to obtain perfectly straight cuts on a panel of plywood. See Fig. 2-40.

The only area where you might run into dif-

Black & Decker
7397 7-1/4" VERTICALLY ADJUSTING SAWCAT® CIRCULAR SAW TRADE

2.25 HP (max. motor output). Builders, professional carpenters have their most demanding needs met by this saw. 10 ft. low temperature vinyl cord. Double insulated, needs no grounding. Easily maneuverable vertical adjustment. Maintains same balance and hand position at any depth of cut. Oversize retracting lever keeps hands away from saw. Ball bearings. Wraparound shoe for added support. 20 amp. long life heavy-duty switch. Shunted brush system guards against brush failure due to short term overloading. Accepts optional U1915 rip fence. Upper blade guard covers more of blade; safer. Equipped with 73-107 Premium Quality Supersharp Combination Blade. Depth of cut: 90° 2-7/16", 45° 2", 5500 RPM, 11.5 amps, 120V AC/DC, net wt 12-1/4 lbs, ship wt 14 lbs.

Fig. 2-38. The modern circular saw has helped to build America (courtesy Black & Decker).

ficulties while using this method is in determining just where to place the straightedge. When using a straightedge as a saw guide, you must place it "X" distance from the cut line. The "X" distance is defined as the distance from the edge of the saw blade to the outside of the saw plane (as in Fig. 2-41). For example, if the distance from the saw blade to the outside of the saw plane is 2¾ of an inch, the straightedge must be placed 2¾ of an inch below the cut line.

Another point that will help you produce straight cuts is to hold the straightedge in place with C-clamps or spring clamps. If the plywood will be covered with a plastic laminate, you could even nail the straightedge in place with lightweight nails.

In any event, the straightedge must be held securely in place as it is being used (Fig. 2-42).

Whenever you are using a hand-held circular saw for a cutting project, it is important to use the proper type of blade for the cutting task at hand. At least part of the success of the cutting task will be determined by the saw blade you use for the cutting. You might be surprised to learn that there is no such saw blade as an "all-purpose" blade. Instead there are several special-purpose saw blades. Generally, a special plywood blade or an 18- to 20-tooth, carbide-tipped blade is best for cutting all types of plywood. The following list can be used as a guide for choosing the right type of circular-saw blade for any cutting task.

Fig. 2-39. A special rip guide attachment is useful for narrow cuts.

Fig. 2-40. Use a straightedge for long cuts on plywood.

Fig. 2-41. Measure from the edge of your saw blade to the outside of the saw table.

Fig. 2-42. Clamp the straightedge to the work.

Combination Blade. Chisel tooth configuration means this blade is the fastest cutting blade available. Designed for general purpose cutting—ripping and crosscuts—on solid woods as well as plywood, where finish on the cut edge is not the most desired effect.

Framing/Rip Blade. An all-purpose blade for smooth, fast cutting in any direction. Rips, crosscuts, miters, etc. One of the most popular of all saw blades for general-purpose cutting. Best when used for cutting with the grain on all types of woods.

Hollow Ground Planer. Specially hollow ground for satin-smooth finish cuts in all solid woods. Professional-quality blade for use in making cabinets and furniture.

Carbide Tipped (8 Teeth per Blade). Specially designed for cutting tough-to-cut materials such as plastic laminate. Also used for cutting framing lumber.

Carbide Tipped (18 or 20 Teeth per Blade). Chisel tooth combination blade for fast general purpose cutting in all types of woods and plywood. Tips are tungsten carbide material that outlasts regular steel blades 10 to 1. Long life and smooth edges on cuts. More teeth per blade produce "glass-like" edges on all woods.

Cross-Cut. Specifically designed for smooth, fast cutting across the grain of hard and softwoods. Not a good choice for smooth cuts on plywood.

Rip. Specially designed for cutting with the grain on all types of woods. Can be used for cutting plywood when the finish of a cut is unimportant.

Plywood Blade. A specially designed blade for cutting all types of plywoods. The many-toothed blade—about 80 teeth—will produce a smooth cut. Should be used for cutting plywood where the finish of cut is important.

SABRE SAWS

A sabre saw is a very handy portable power tool that can be used for a variety of different cuts. Its real value, however, is in making curved cuts on plywood and almost any other material. The blade is the reciprocating type (up and down cutting motion) that cuts on the upstroke. Prices for sabre saws range from under $20 to over $75. Sabre saws are

quite popular because they are relatively safe to use and a perfectly servicable model.

A wide variety of sabre-saw blades are available, but only a few are really suitable for making cuts on plywood. Generally, you should only use a sabre-saw blade that is specifically labeled "plywood" and not a general purpose blade. A special plywood blade will have a large number of fine teeth that will enable you to make a smooth cut in plywood. General-purpose blades, on the other hand, tend to give a very ragged cut when used to cut plywood and, for this reason should not be used. See Figs. 2-43 and 2-44.

When using a sabre saw to cut plywood, it is necessary to cut the panel from the back side, rather than to cut on the face. The face in this case is that side of the panel which will be exposed when the project is assembled. Because the blade cuts on the up stroke, the veneer, which is closest to the saw plane, might splinter slightly. By cutting from the back of the plywood panel, you will not mar the face of the panel. Of course, cutting from the back rather than from the front of a plywood panel requires that you be doubly certain of your measurements. Cutting from the back is particularly important when you are cutting thin plywood such as wall paneling and plastic laminate materials.

ELECTRIC DRILLS AND BITS

Hand-held electric drills (Fig. 2-45) you can buy today are vastly different from the electric drill of just 10 years ago. Gone forever are the shiny metal drill housings and the excess weight of older drills. The modern electric drills are constructed with an ABS plastic case that will not break or conduct electricity (thereby eliminating the possibility of electrical shock). The plastic case is much lighter to use and less expensive to make. The result is a powerful electric drill that has greater capabilities than older drills and yet can be purchased for under $20 dollars. Special features such as variable speed, reversing action, greater horsepower and large chuck size (standard size for noncommercial drills is ¼ inch) will all contribute to make the price higher.

My recommendation for the all-around best

Black & Decker®
7580 *VALUE-PLUS*™
VARIABLE SPEED JIG SAW

1/3 HP (max. motor output). Slide control switch on handle lets you choose the speed to suit the job and material. Calibrated tilting shoe for making bevel, compound mitre cuts. A good choice for all-purpose use. Easier pocket cutting. Better control. Double insulated. Sleeve bearings. Detachable 6 ft. cord. Two prong convenience. Includes U2151 Combination Rip Fence and Circle Guide plus wood cutting blade. Capacity: hardwood 1", softwood 2", infinite settings 0 to 3200 SPM; 3 amps; 6 ft. cord: 120V AC; net wt 3-1/4 lbs. Ship wt 3-1/2 lbs.

TM: A trademark of The Black & Decker Mfg. [

Fig. 2-43. A jigsaw (courtesy Black & Decker).

drill for the do-it-yourselfer is one with a ⅜-inch chuck, variable speed, and reversing action. With such a drill, you will be able to tackle almost any boring or drilling operation you will come in contact with around the home. Current price for an electric drill with these features is approximately $40, but you can expect your investment to last for a long time—even with a lot of use.

A portable drill stand attachment can be bolted to a workbench and your hand-held electric drill can be fastened in place (Fig. 2-46). There are certain limitations to a portable electric drill stand but, it will handle most drilling projects with a fair amount

of accuracy. The real advantage of a portable drill press is that they don't cost very much.

The more common and useful drill bits for plywood furniture projects include twist drill bits, spade bits, auger bits, countersink bits, and hole or circle-cutter bits.

Twist Drill Bits

The most common type of drill bits are twist drill bits (Fig. 2-47). If you own an electric drill, chances are that you have at least a few of these. Twist drill bits were first developed for drilling holes in metal. It was learned that they were also quite capable of

Fig. 2-44. Choose the right sabre saw blade for cutting plywood.

Black & Decker

7190 3/8" VARIABLE SPEED
REVERSING DRILL with Infinite Speed Lock

VSR

VALUE-PLUS™
Added features for versatility.

1/3 HP (max. motor output). Use as a drill or screwdriver. Reversing switch for backing out screws, removing jammed drill bits. The further you pull back the trigger the faster the speed. Trigger can be locked at correct speed for each job. Double insulated. Gearing and 3/8" chuck for bigger, tougher jobs. Precision ball-thrust bearing system. Exclusive recessed center locking button guards against accidental "lock-on." Detachable 6 ft. cord can be locked away for safety. Capacity: steel 3/8", hardwood 3/4"; 0 to 1200 RPM; 120V AC; 3 amps; 6 ft. cord; net wt. 2-3/4 lbs., ship wt. 3 lbs.

Fig. 2-45. Electric Drills are quite popular (courtesy Black & Decker).

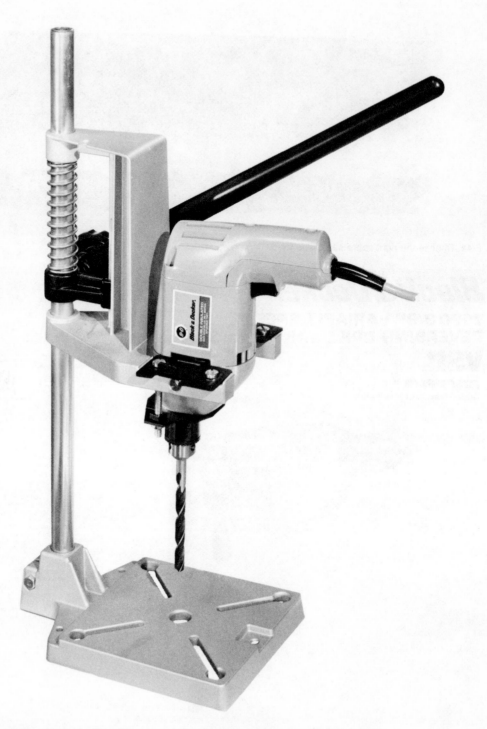

Fig. 2-46. A portable drill stand will enable you to make straight holes (courtesy Black & Decker).

Fig. 2-47. An assortment of twist drill bits is very useful.

drilling admirable holes in wood, glass, plastic, and similar materials. These drill bits have chisel-like cutting edges and a pair of spiral channels that twist up the shank of the bit. These help to carry away cut material from the resulting hole.

The most available sizes of twist drill bits are from 1/16 of an inch to ½ of an inch. While it is possible to buy twist drill bits made from exotic metals—very hard alloys—most of the drill bits that are generally available to the consumer are made from high-speed steel (Fig. 2-48). This steel will hold a sharp cutting edge for a long time when drilling in materials other than metal. Although expensive initially, the best way to buy twist drill bits is in a set containing all of the sizes from 1/16 to ½ inch.

Spade Drill Bits

Spade drill bits (Fig. 2-49) are a little less common

Fig. 2-48. A high-speed steel twist drill.

Fig. 2-49. Spade drill bit.

screw holes in wood. Not only does this bit drill a hole for the screw, but it also drills a larger hole near the surface that enables you to countersink the screw head. Before countersink drill bits came into existence, two holes had to be drilled if the screw was to be countersunk. One hole was needed for the screw shank and another (close to the top of the hole) was needed for the screw head. If you are working on a plywood furniture project that requires countersunk screws, the countersink drill bit will not only save you a lot of time, but do the job better as well. A complete set of countersink drill bits—containing all of the major screw sizes—can be purchased for just a few dollars.

Rim-Cutting Drill Bits

Rim-cutting drill bits enable you to drill the smoothest and truest holes of all. The bit has a thin steel rim with cutters that quickly bore through wood and similar materials. Inside the rim tip are special chisel-like cutters that are very efficient at peeling away material after it has been first cut with the rim. Rim-cutting drill bits are ideal for boring holes in plywood, but they must, generally be used at a lower rpm than most other types of drill bits. If you want to bore perfect holes in plywood—up to about 3 inches in diameter—this is the right drill bit to choose. See Fig. 2-50.

than twist drill bits. Their real value is for boring holes that are larger than a half inch in diameter and up to about 1½ inches in diameter. Spade drill bits are simply a shaft of high-speed tool steel with a flattened end. This is beveled so that it scrapes material as it bores the hole. Spade bits are intended for use on wood and other wood-like (soft) materials. Spade bits tend to splinter the bottom side of a hole unless care is exercised. This is especially important when boring holes in plywood where you are cutting through several layers of veneer. Even with these limitations, spade bits are valuable for drilling fair-sized holes in wood.

Countersink Drill Bits

A rather specialized drill bit, the countersink drill bit (Fig. 2-50) is extremely handy when drilling

Fig. 2-50. Countersink drill bit.

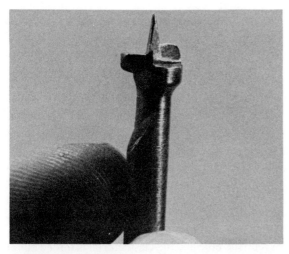

Fig. 2-51. Rim-cut drill bit.

Hole-Cutting Drill Attachments

If you need to drill a large hole in plywood or similar material, a hole-cutting attachment might be just the tool you need. Of course, you can use a rim cutting bit (Fig. 2-51) for large holes, but a simple hole-cutting attachment (Fig. 2-52) for your electric drill will be much less expensive. Basically, a hole-cutting attachment is a simple device that looks like a cookie cutter with a drill bit in the center. This device is chucked into an electric drill and the drill bit center is placed on the drill hole mark. As the drill turns, the pilot drill bit bores into the center of your mark; then the actual cutter begins to bore the large hole.

Hole-cutting attachments are available for cutting holes up to about 4 inches in diameter. While a

Fig. 2-52. Use a hole cutter for large size holes in plywood.

Fig. 2-53. Auger bits are designed to be used in a brace.

certain amount of care must be exercised when using these attachments—especially when making a hole in plywood or paneling—they will do the job of making a hole quite well. It is possible to purchase a set of hole-making attachments—from 1-inch to 4-inch diameters—for under $10. That is about the price for one rim cutting bit.

Auger Bits

Auger bits (Fig. 2-53) are designed to be used with a brace—the old muscle powered drill. An auger bit is simply a steel spiral that has a cutting end, a tip to guide the hole, and a cutting edge or edges that do the actual cutting of the hole. The cutting edges scrape the hole and the cut material is forced out of the hole via the spirals on the bit shank. Auger bits should only be used in a brace because they are designed to be used at only very low rpms. These

Black & Decker
7604
3/4 HP ROUTER
VALUE-PLUS™

Excellent value in 3/4 HP Router. Double insulated. Large positive control handles. Keeps chips clear from working area. 1/4" collet-type chuck. Ball bearings. Flat top supports router for easy bit changing. Vertical depth adjustments calibrated in 1/64". Non-marring base. Shunted brush system guards against brush failure due to short-term overloading. Specs: 30,000 RPM, 120V AC, 5 amps, 3/4 HP (max. motor output), 6 ft. cord. 3-7/16 lbs. net wt., 5 lbs. ship wt.

Fig. 2-54. The hand-held router is useful for many tasks around the woodworking shop (courtesy Black & Decker).

drill bits cut amazingly fast and were about the only way a precise hole could be bored in wood until electric drills came on the scene.

ROUTERS

Many woodworkers have discovered that a portable router (Fig. 2-54) will enable them to put various finish edges on woodworking projects (in addition to other tasks) much quicker and at less cost than by any other means. In addition, a router equipped with a special plastic laminate trimming bit is the best way to finish off the edges of plastic laminate.

Basically, a router consists of an extremely high-speed motor (approximately 25,000 rpm), a chuck for holding any one of a vast selection of router bits, and an adjustable base that enables you to cut, trim, or add a decorative edge. There are several versions of routers currently available from three or four manufacturers, but basically all routers are the same.

The two sizes of routers are one handed units and two-handed units. The one-handed router is really designed for trimming plastic laminate material, and it will accomplish this task very well. The two-handed router can rightly be considered a general-purpose router. It will easily handle any router related project you will ever come in contact with. Of course, some versions of routers are designed for the woodworking hobbyist, while other models are for commercial use and are therefore offered with more precise adjusting capabilities and larger horsepower motors. Nevertheless all routers are basically the same in design and operation. See Fig. 2-55.

The real business end of any router is, of course, the router bit and there is a very broad selection. Figure 2-56 describes the most popular of these but, there are others as well. As with twist drill bits, the best way to buy router bits is in a set. While the initial cost is high, easily over $50, you will greatly expand the capabilities of your router with a selection of router bits. Most experts agree that carbide-tipped router bits cut better and last at least 10 times as long as high-speed steel router

Fig. 2-55. Adjustments to the router are simple.

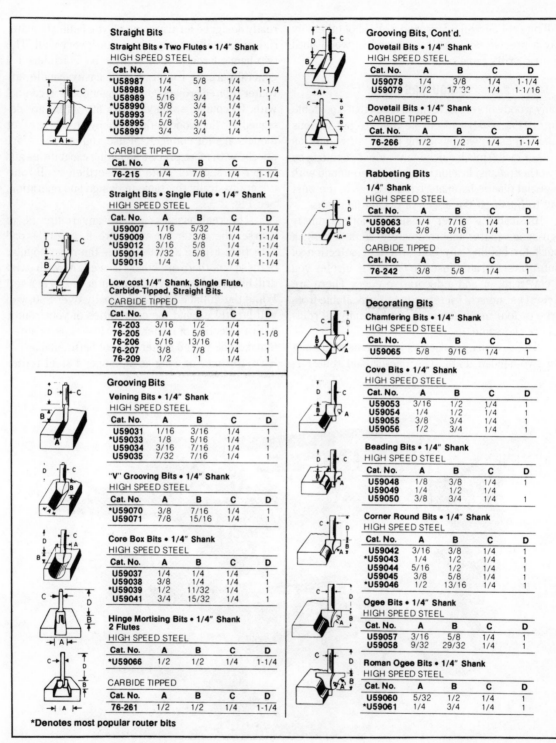

Straight Bits

Straight Bits • Two Flutes • 1/4" Shank
HIGH SPEED STEEL

Cat. No.	A	B	C	D
*U58987	1/4	5/8	1/4	1
U58988	1/4	1	1/4	1-1/4
U58989	5/16	3/4	1/4	1
*U58990	3/8	3/4	1/4	1
*U58993	1/2	3/4	1/4	1
U58995	5/8	3/4	1/4	1
*U58997	3/4	3/4	1/4	1

CARBIDE TIPPED

Cat. No.	A	B	C	D
76-215	1/4	7/8	1/4	1-1/4

Straight Bits • Single Flute • 1/4" Shank
HIGH SPEED STEEL

Cat. No.	A	B	C	D
U59007	1/16	5/32	1/4	1-1/4
*U59009	1/8	3/8	1/4	1-1/4
*U59012	3/16	5/8	1/4	1-1/4
U59014	7/32	5/8	1/4	1-1/4
U59015	1/4	1	1/4	1-1/4

Low cost 1/4" Shank, Single Flute, Carbide-Tipped, Straight Bits.
CARBIDE TIPPED

Cat. No.	A	B	C	D
76-203	3/16	1/2	1/4	1
76-205	1/4	5/8	1/4	1-1/8
76-206	5/16	13/16	1/4	1
76-207	3/8	7/8	1/4	1
76-209	1/2	1	1/4	1

Grooving Bits

Veining Bits • 1/4" Shank
HIGH SPEED STEEL

Cat. No.	A	B	C	D
U59031	1/16	3/16	1/4	1
*U59033	1/8	5/16	1/4	1
U59034	3/16	7/16	1/4	1
U59035	7/32	7/16	1/4	1

"V" Grooving Bits • 1/4" Shank
HIGH SPEED STEEL

Cat. No.	A	B	C	D
*U59070	3/8	7/16	1/4	1
U59071	7/8	15/16	1/4	1

Core Box Bits • 1/4" Shank
HIGH SPEED STEEL

Cat. No.	A	B	C	D
U59037	1/4	1/4	1/4	1
U59038	3/8	1/4	1/4	1
*U59039	1/2	11/32	1/4	1
U59041	3/4	15/32	1/4	1

Hinge Mortising Bits • 1/4" Shank 2 Flutes
HIGH SPEED STEEL

Cat. No.	A	B	C	D
*U59066	1/2	1/2	1/4	1-1/4

CARBIDE TIPPED

Cat. No.	A	B	C	D
76-261	1/2	1/2	1/4	1-1/4

Grooving Bits, Cont'd.

Dovetail Bits • 1/4" Shank
HIGH SPEED STEEL

Cat. No.	A	B	C	D
U59078	1/4	3/8	1/4	1-1/4
U59079	1/2	17/32	1/4	1-1/16

Dovetail Bits • 1/4" Shank
CARBIDE TIPPED

Cat. No.	A	B	C	D
76-266	1/2	1/2	1/4	1-1/4

Rabbeting Bits

1/4" Shank
HIGH SPEED STEEL

Cat. No.	A	B	C	D
*U59063	1/4	7/16	1/4	1
*U59064	3/8	9/16	1/4	1

CARBIDE TIPPED

Cat. No.	A	B	C	D
76-242	3/8	5/8	1/4	1

Decorating Bits

Chamfering Bits • 1/4" Shank
HIGH SPEED STEEL

Cat. No.	A	B	C	D
U59065	5/8	9/16	1/4	1

Cove Bits • 1/4" Shank
HIGH SPEED STEEL

Cat. No.	A	B	C	D
U59053	3/16	1/2	1/4	1
U59054	1/4	1/2	1/4	1
U59055	3/8	1/4	1/4	1
U59056	1/2	3/4	1/4	1

Beading Bits • 1/4" Shank
HIGH SPEED STEEL

Cat. No.	A	B	C	D
U59048	1/8	3/8	1/4	1
U59049	1/4	1/2	1/4	
U59050	3/8	3/4	1/4	1

Corner Round Bits • 1/4" Shank
HIGH SPEED STEEL

Cat. No.	A	B	C	D
U59042	3/16	3/8	1/4	1
*U59043	1/4	1/2	1/4	1
U59044	5/16	1/2	1/4	1
U59045	3/8	5/8	1/4	1
*U59046	1/2	13/16	1/4	1

Ogee Bits • 1/4" Shank
HIGH SPEED STEEL

Cat. No.	A	B	C	D
U59057	3/16	5/8	1/4	1
U59058	9/32	29/32	1/4	1

Roman Ogee Bits • 1/4" Shank
HIGH SPEED STEEL

Cat. No.	A	B	C	D
U59060	5/32	1/2	1/4	1
*U59061	1/4	3/4	1/4	1

*Denotes most popular router bits

Fig. 2-56. Router bit chart (courtesy Black & Decker).

Panel Pilot Bits

HIGH SPEED STEEL

Cat. No.	A	B	C	D
U59072	1/4	3/4	1/4	1-5/16
U59073	3/8	7/8	3/8	1-1/8

CARBIDE TIPPED

Cat. No.	A	B	C	D
76-245	1/4	3/4	1/4	1-1/4

Trimming Bits

Low cost Carbide-Tipped, Combination Straight and 22° Bevel Bit.

Cat. No.	A	B	C	D
76-250	3/16	7/16	1/4	1

Laminate Trimming Bits

22° Bevel Trimming Bit • Carbide Tipped 2 Flutes

Cat. No.	A	B	C	D
76-254	7/16	1/4	1/4	5/8

Straight & 22° Bevel • Carbide Tipped 1 Flute

Cat. No.	A	B	C	D
76-253	3/16	17/32	1/4	13/32

7° Bevel • Solid Carbide

Cat. No.	A	B	C	D
76-255	3/16	3/8	1/4	1

Flush Trim • Solid Carbide

Cat. No.	A	B	C	D
76-256	1/4	3/8	1/4	1

Trimming Cutters

Low cost 1/2", 2 Flute, Carbide-Tipped, Veneer Flush Cutter with Screw, Washer & Ball Bearing.

Cat. No.	A	B	C	D
76-251	1/2	1/2	1/4	1-1/4

Low cost 1/2", 2 Flute, Carbide-Tipped, 22° Bevel Cutter with Screw, Washer and Ball-Bearing.

Cat. No.	A	B	C	D
76-252	11/16	1/2	1/4	1-1/8

Veneer Trimmer Arbor

Cat. No.	A	B	C	D
U59124	5/8	1-3/32	1/4	1

Oversize Ball Bearing Assembly for use with 22°, 45° Cutters.

Cat. No.	A	B	C
U59125	13/16	1/4	1/4

Trimming Cutters, cont d.

22° Bevel Trimming Cutter • Carbide Tipped

Cat. No.	A	B	C
U59132	57/64	3/8	1/4

45° Bevel Trimming Cutter • Carbide Tipped

Cat. No.	A	B	C
U59133	1	1/4	1/4

Flush Trimming Cutter • Carbide Tipped

Cat. No.	A	B	C
U59134	5/8	3/8	1/4

Use 3 items above on U59124 Arbor

Trimming Saw • Solid Carbide

Cat. No.	A	B	C	D
U59131	3/4	1/32	1/4	1

Low Cost Router Bit Cutters and Arbor

High quality, low cost router bit cutters used with 76-000 Arbor with pilot. Makes your router more useful because they're more affordable. Arbor fits any router with 1/4" collet.

Rabbeting Cutter

Cat. No.	A	B
76-064	3/8	11/16

Decorating Cutters

Cove Cutter

Cat. No.	A	B
76-055	3/8	11/16

Beading Cutter

Cat. No.	A	B
76-049	5/16	11/16

Corner Round Cutter

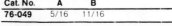

Cat. No.	A	B
76-045	3/8	11/16

Roman Ogee Cutter

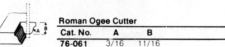

Cat. No.	A	B
76-061	3/16	11/16

Arbor With Pilot for Router Cutters

Cat. No.	C
76-000	1/4

Fig. 2-57. Spray your router bit often with a silicone spray.

bits. As you might expect, carbide-tipped router bits cost at least twice as much as steel router bits.

After a router bit has been chucked into the router, give it a quick spray (Fig. 2-57) with silicone or other modern lubricant such as WD-40 or Tri-Flon. This will help the bit to cut easier with less heat buildup. If you are working on a large project with a lot of router work, stop the router every few minutes and give the bit another quick spray of the lubricant. The theory behind this is very simple. A lubricated router bit will cut better and last longer than a dry router bit.

One accessory that you might find worth investing in if you do a lot of edge finishing is a router table (Fig. 2-58). The router table I have has an adjustable fence that allows me to run lengths of lumber or plywood past the spinning router bit. The router table is adjustable (as is the router itself) and therefore a wide range of possibilities are easily obtained.

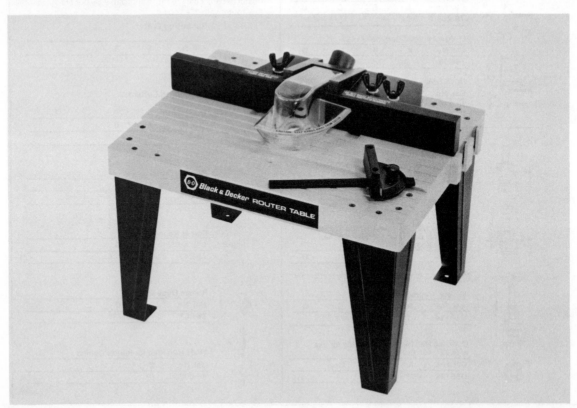

Fig. 2-58. A router table can extend the capabilities of your hand-held router (courtesy Black & Decker).

SANDERS

Generally there are two basic types of portable sanders available: *belt sanders* or *disk sanders,* and *finish sanders.* Belt and disk sanders are capable of sanding large areas very quickly. Finish sanders are used for sanding where the surface is only lightly sanded (prior to or between coats of varnish or paint).

Belt sanders (Fig. 2-59) are powerful sanding machines. They can be used for shaping or forming woodworking projects to give a project an overall softness. Belts for belt sanders sell for approximately 1 dollar each. They are generally available in three grit sizes: fine, medium, and coarse. It is probably fair to say that most sanding on plywood furniture projects should be done with the fine grit belts. The other two sizes are a bit too strong for sanding veneer faces.

An operating tip for belt sanders is that the machine must always be kept in motion to avoid creating low spots on the surface. Additionally, a belt sander will sand well without putting a lot of pressure on the machine. Some people bear down on the sander while sanding and this not only puts undue strain on the motor, but also tends to make the sanded surface uneven. When using a belt sander, it is important to remember that sanding with the grain is always the best procedure. Sanding across the grain will remove a lot of surface material, but this will also tend to roughen the surface. That means more sanding with the grain will be necessary before a finish coating (paint or clear coating) can be applied with any success.

Disk sanders (Fig. 2-60) are similar to an electric drill with a pad attachment (which holds the abrasive paper) that spins during use. In fact, there are attachments for standard electric drills that can be used for sanding. While you will find very little

Black & Decker®

7451 3" x 24" DUST COLLECTING LCG BELT SANDER

Black & Decker's **BEST** home-use tool

LCG (low center of gravity). Motor between pulleys puts weight where it counts. No tilting, gouging, rocking. Dust collector, powered by sander motor, keeps most dust under control. Up-front controls for easy belt installation and tracking. Gear driven for smooth power transmission. Long life roller bearings. Takes 3" x 24" belts. Includes 1 coarse grit sanding belt. 1200 SFPM; 13.8 sq. in. of sanding surface; 120V AC; 5.2 amps; .75 HP (max. motor output); 10 ft. cord; net wt 8-3/4 lbs, ship wt 11 lbs.

Fig. 2-59. Belt sander (courtesy Black & Decker).

Black & Decker®
7965 7" DISC SANDER
TRADE

Packed with power at the right speed for excellent performance. Well balanced, good weight distribution for less operator effort. 2-position side handle. Ball and needle bearings. Shunted brush system guards against brush failure due to short-term overloading. 10 ft. low temperature vinyl cord. Double insulated, needs no grounding. When brushes wear out, check-point brush system stops motor. Includes 7" phenolic disc, clamp washer, non-marring tool rests, 3-1/2" quick-changing backing pad, extra heavy-duty spindle lock for changing the different attachments. Specs: 4800 RPM (no-load speed), 120V AC/DC, 5/8"-11 spindle thread, 10 amps, max. backing pad diameter for sanding: 9", 10 ft. cord, net wt 9-7/8 lbs, ship wt 11-3/4 lbs.

Fig. 2-60. Disk sander (courtesy Black & Decker).

use for a disk sander around the plywood furniture workshop, they are widely used in metalworking (welding and automobile body work). Nevertheless, if you are working on a plywood furniture project that requires a lot of forming or removal of large sections, a disk sander might be the tool that you need for the task at hand. Not only are different grit size abrasives available for disk sanders, but there are also abrasive stones that will cut metal.

Generally, finish sanders (Fig. 2-61) are driven by either an orbital or an oscillating motion. They are the sanding tool to use when only light sanding is required. The basic difference between the two types is that the orbital sander can be moved in any direction over the surface and the oscillating sander should only be used while sanding in the direction of the grain of the wood. Finish sanders give the impression of a quiet, efficient

machine and they are very useful for sanding projects that fall within their limitations. Almost any abrasive grit size can be used with these sanders. To make sanding more economical, sheet abrasive paper can be purchased and then simply cut to fit the sander.

STATIONARY POWER TOOLS

When you start to become serious about your woodworking and furniture building projects, you will begin to see the limitations of portable hand power tools. When this happens you will probably start shopping for power tools that are capable of much greater accuracy. That means stationary power tools. The stationary power tools that are most useful to the plywood furniture maker are table saws. Radial-arm saws, band saws, jigsaws, and possibly a drill press. While not all of these

Black & Decker
7465 1/2 SHEET FINISHING SANDER
TRADE

Powerful. Rated for continous production service. For heavy-duty finishing sanding and fastest material removal. Large 1/2 sheet sanding surface and fast orbital action get job done fast. Three ball-bearings for long life. Shunted brush system guards against brush failure due to short-term overloading. 10 ft. low temperature vinyl cord. Flush sands on 3 sides. Specs: 4-1/2" x 11" (1/2 standard sheet) abrasive paper, 120V AC, .25 HP (max. motor output), 10,000 OPM, 3 amps, net wt 7-1/2 lbs, ship wt 8-3/4 lbs.

Fig. 2-61. Finish sander (courtesy Black & Decker).

stationary power tools are required for building plywood furniture projects, all of them are helpful for accomplishing various tasks.

Table Saw

Probably the most useful stationary power tool for plywood furniture building projects is the table saw. Because the most common cut for furniture is a long rip-type cut, the table saw is the best choice for an all-around, useful, stationary power tool. In addition to straight rip cuts, a table saw can make cuts such as miter, bevel, dado, rabbet and others that are useful for constructing plywood furniture. Any quality table saw will also have a depth of cut adjusting feature. This simply raises or lowers the blade. A ripping fence is another common feature on table saws so you can make perfectly straight precision cuts with the greatest of ease.

Table saws (Fig. 2-62) range in price from

Fig. 2-62. Table saw.

Fig. 2-63. Carbide-tipped blades last the longest.

about $200 to over a thousand dollars. When you go shopping for a table saw it is important to have a clear understanding of your requirements. Many experts seem to agree that the best all-around table saw will have a 10-inch blade, and will be of the variety known as *contractors' table saw.* Such a table saw currently sells for approximately $500. You will want to be fairly serious about woodworking before you buy one.

A saw of this type is quite an investment, but it is also quite a saw. There are very few, if any, cutting tasks that such a saw cannot tackle with ease. The wide table allows you to work with full sheets of plywood and the large-horsepower motor will speed cutting through any wood or similar material. It will cut through lumber that is up to 4 inches thick, in addition, it is completely adjustable for depth of cut as well as angle of cut.

The best all-around blade for a table saw is a carbide-tipped blade (Fig. 2-63). A table saw blade with from 40 to 70 carbide teeth will produce a finish cut that will not require any sanding. "Smooth as glass" is one common description of a cut that has been made with a carbide-tipped saw blade. Carbide tipped saw blades of this type are commonly called *cabinetmaker blades* and you can expect to pay up to about $80 for one. It will enable you to make perfect cuts in plywood (and any other wood as well). As an added bonus, you can expect a carbide-tipped blade to stay sharp and last at least 10 times as long as a standard steel-saw blade.

When all is said and done, a good table saw is probably the best choice for the home woodworker who can only afford one stationary saw. One way of getting around the high cost of a new contractors' table saw is to buy one second hand. If you shop around—check your local newspaper for used tools, or consult your telephone directory for a firm that deals in used woodworking equipment—you should be able to pick up a quality table saw for close to half the asking price of a new unit. It is important, however, to spend as much as you can possibly afford when buying a table saw. A poor-quality saw is more of a headache than an aid to successful woodworking.

Radial-Arm Saw

The second most popular stationary saw is the radial-arm saw (Fig. 2-64), and it can be used for a variety of woodworking cuts on plywood and all other types of woods. In addition, most radial-arm saws can also be used as a fixed-position router simply by chucking a router bit into the special chuck on one end of the motor. To use the router the saw motor must be turned 90 degrees and locked in that position. This is a simple matter as radial-arm saws are quite adjustable.

Part of the appeal of using a radial arm saw for a

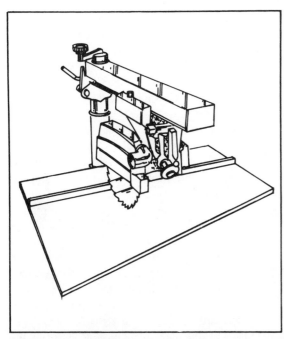

Fig. 2-64. Radial-arm saw.

cutting task is that, because the blade is above the work, you can always see what is taking place. This differs from work done on a table saw where the blade spins and cuts from below the work.

A radial-arm saw can be adjusted in a number of positions. This enables the user to make a variety of cuts. Some of the more obvious cuts include straight cuts in or through relatively narrow pieces of wood, angle cuts, and even long ripping-type cuts (although these are limited to about 2 feet in width). A quality radial-arm saw is a nice addition to the home woodworking shop. With such a large selection of attachments and blades, it is possible to expand your woodworking capabilities into the range of professional quality. As with the table saw discussed previously, a carbide-tipped blade will produce the most satisfactory cuts on or through plywood.

Band Saw

The band saw has rather limited application in the plywood furniture shop because it can only be used

Fig. 2-65. Band saw attachment for the Shopsmith Mark V.

for rather small pieces of plywood. A band saw is used for making fine, curved cuts in all wood materials; it does this type of work very well. Most models are freestanding and they are rather expensive. It is therefore tough to justify this sometimes useful tool unless, of course, you have a frequent need for a power tool with these capabilities. See Fig. 2-65.

Jigsaw

The jigsaw (Fig. 2-66) is a stationary power tool designed for making curved cuts. Unlike the band saw, the jigsaw can handle relatively large pieces of plywood. But like the band saw, it is hard to justify the expense (and shop space) unless you find that a lot of this type of cutting is necessary in the work you do. In most cases, a hand-held sabre saw can be used in place of either the band saw or the jigsaw. While there will be a certain sacrifice of accuracy, a sabre saw can handle most curved cutting quite well. In addition, a sabre saw does not cost very much (a good one can be purchased for approximately $50) and it will not take up valuable shop space.

The most useful stationary power tool for the plywood furniture shop is a table saw. An alternative to the conventional table saw is the Shopsmith Mark V system. The Shopsmith Mark V is actually five stationary power tools in one (Fig. 2-67). These include a 10-inch table saw, a 34-inch wood lathe, a horizontal boring machine, a 12-inch disk sander and, a 16½-inch vertical drill press. This same machine employs a single table, spindle, stand, and motor. In addition to being precise at everything it does, the Shopsmith Mark V requires less storage space (Fig. 2-68) than a full-size man's bicycle.

Each of these five machines is a full-blown, professional-quality tool. The table saw, for example, can be used to cut full-size sheets of plywood accurately and with little effort. The other four basic machines of the Shopsmith are equally accurate and versatile. See Figs. 2-69 through 2-74.

There are a number of accessory attachments for the Shopsmith Mark V that really expand the capabilities of this machine. These accessories include an 11-inch band saw, a 4-inch jointer, a 6-inch belt sander and, an 18-inch jigsaw.

The Shopsmith—which is advertised and sold

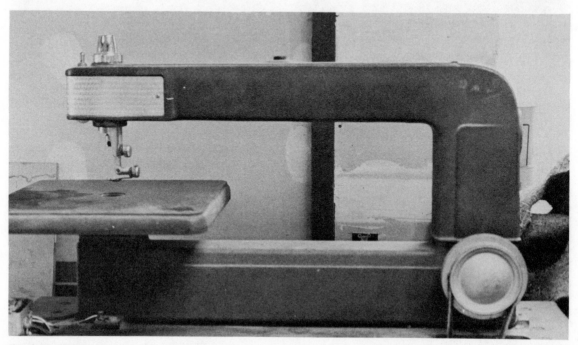

Fig. 2-66. Jigsaw.

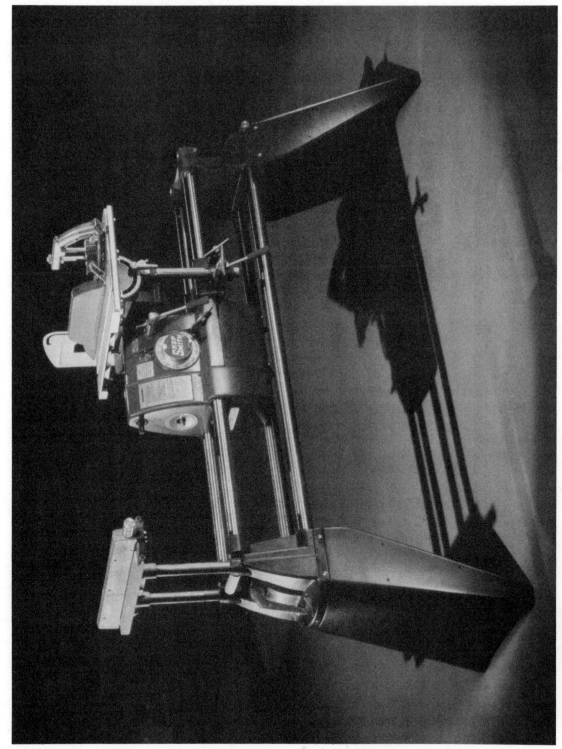

Fig. 2-67. Shopsmith Mark V.

Fig. 2-68. Shopsmith Mark V takes very little space to store.

Fig. 2-69. Shopsmith Mark V is a quality table saw.

Fig. 2-70. Shopsmith Mark V is a wood lathe.

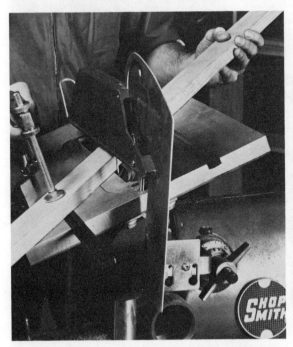

Fig. 2-71. Shopsmith Mark V can be used for cutting compound miters.

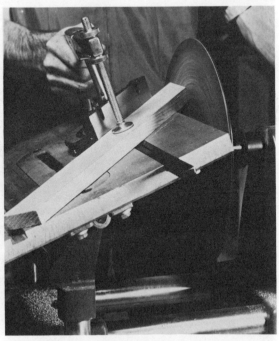

Fig. 2-72. Shopsmith Mark V is also a disc sander.

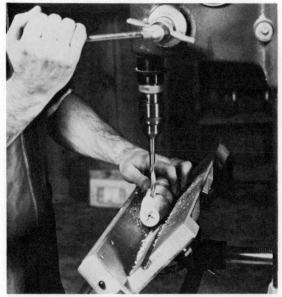

Fig. 2-73. Shopsmith Mark V can be used as a drill press.

nationally—offers a very good alternative to conventional stationary power tools, and at a very reasonable price. Each unit comes with an extensive operational manual that will show you how to use the Shopsmith equipment and all of its accessories.

WOODWORKING SHOP SAFETY

All of the power tools described in this book are powerful units capable of performing various woodworking tasks quickly and accurately. They are also potentially dangerous. For this reason there are a number of rules that should always be followed to make woodworking a safe hobby. Follow them at all times.

☐ Always wear eye protection (Fig. 2-75).

☐ When operating power tools, wear ear plugs.

☐ Support all work to prevent saw bind or buck.

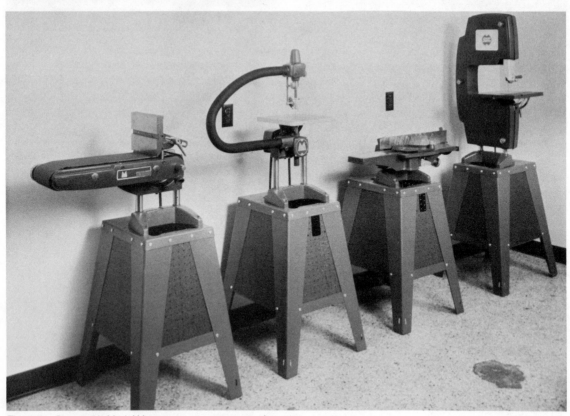

Fig. 2-74. Shopsmith Mark V has many accessory attachments.

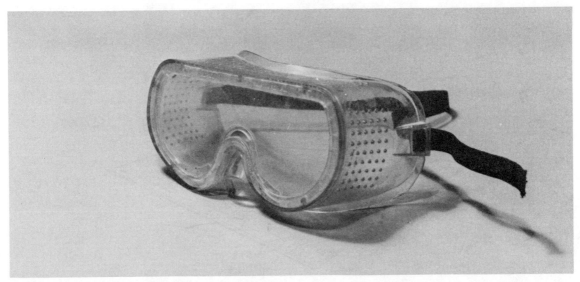

Fig. 2-75. Eye protection is a necessity in the workshop.

☐ Never force a tool through the work, guide it for best results and long tool life.

☐ Unplug your tools before changing blades or bits.

☐ Make certain your tools are off before plugging them in.

☐ Keep both hands on a tool while using it.

☐ Always keep your mind on the work; avoid distractions.

☐ Never operate a tool in need of repair.

☐ When not actually in use, store power tools where children cannot get them.

☐ Do not use a power tool for cutting small pieces.

☐ Provide adequate ventilation and lighting in the home workshop.

☐ Wear a respirator when sanding or spray painting.

☐ Keep all tools sharp; a sharp tool works best.

Chapter 3

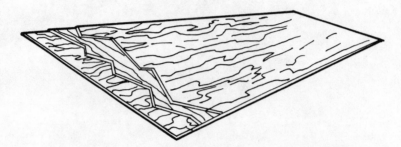

Cutting Techniques

I T IS A SAFE ASSUMPTION THAT ALL OF YOUR PLY-
wood furniture projects will require some cutting. Generally, the best way to slice up a sheet of
plywood is on a table saw (Fig. 3-1) but, many
do-it-yourselfers cut plywood with a handsaw, a
sabre saw or a hand-held circular saw. Because so
much of the success of any plywood furniture project depends on making straight, clean cuts, it will
be well worth your while to learn how to accomplish
this task effectively.

CUTTING PLYWOOD

Certainly the simplest way to cut plywood is with a
handsaw (Fig. 3-2), but this is by no means the
easiest, quickest, or most accurate method. Using a
handsaw properly is a skill that takes some time to
develop. Oddly enough, this ancient cutting tool is
not used properly by most people. The result, more
often than not, is a cut of poor quality—beveled,
curved, irregular, or with torn rather than smooth
edges.

Because many of the forthcoming operations

and tasks are common in all types of cutting—with
both electrically powered and muscle-powered
saws—it will be well worth your while to learn
them. If you are somewhat experienced at woodworking, this will be a good time to refresh your
memory.

Any cutting project begins with accurately
marking your cut on the workpiece (Fig. 3-3). There
is an age old carpenters' expression that is worth
passing along: "measure twice, cut once". This is a
worthwhile sign to put up in your woodworking
shop.

After you have determined the exact dimensions of your cut, begin by marking the workpiece
with a cut line. It is important to keep in mind that
the saw blade, as it cuts through the plywood, will
waste a bit of wood. This is due to the width of the
kerf of the saw blade. For this reason, it is best to
mark only one cut at a time, make the cut, then mark
and cut again.

When working with a handsaw it is necessary
to draw a straight cut line across the entire work-

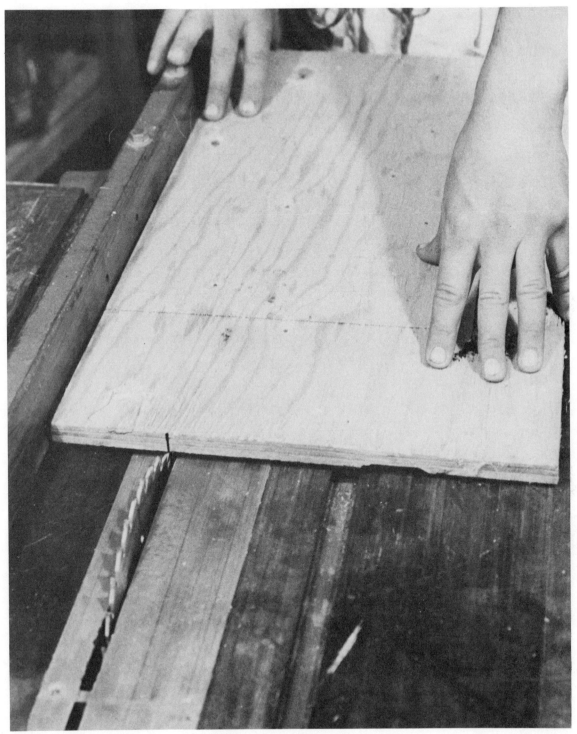

Fig. 3-1. Cutting plywood requires careful attention and good saw control.

Fig. 3-2. You can cut plywood with a handsaw but keep in mind that this task will take time.

piece. After the initial mark is made, the cut line can be drawn with the aid of a suitable-size square such as a try square (Fig. 3-4) or the larger rafter square or framing square.

The next step is to carefully start the cut (Fig. 3-5). This is the task that is most often done incorrectly. You must begin a cut by making two or three "backward" strokes with the saw. This should be done with only enough pressure to start the cut. Keep in mind that most handsaws are specifically designed to cut on the forward stroke. Your intention should not be to cut, but to create a starting slot for the saw blade. Once this slot has been created, then you can begin stroking forward with a smooth, long, and deliberate action. This type of sawing will

help you to make a straight cut and prevent the saw blade from moving from side to side.

Generally, cuts on plywood are best accomplished when the saw blade is held at about a 60-degree angle to the work surface. Cross-grained cuts on conventional lumber (other than plywood) are best made with the saw blade held at an angle of about 45 degrees.

A large part of the success of your handsaw cut will be determined by just how much pressure you exert on the blade while cutting. The secret of proper handsaw use is to apply only a small amount of pressure. In other words, you should bear down gently on the saw and only on the forward stroke. The weight of the saw combined with the natural

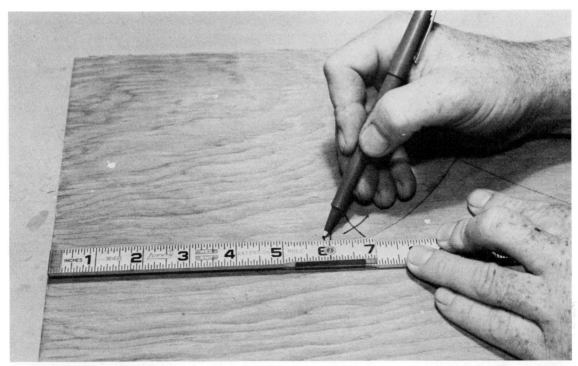

Fig. 3-3. Mark your cuts accurately.

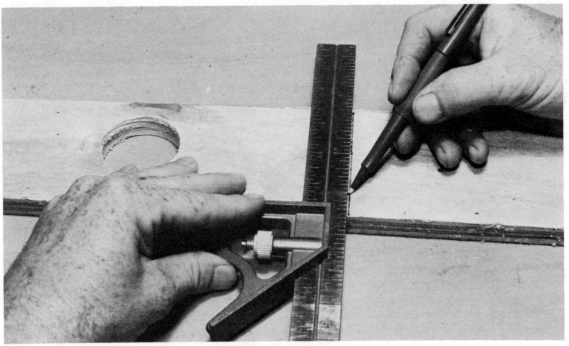

Fig. 3-4. Use an aid such as this try square to make a straight cut line.

Fig. 3-5. Keep the saw at an approximate 60-degree angle to the face of the work.

action of the stroke is all that is really required for a straight, clean cut.

Most experts agree that you should make a cut on the waste side of your cut line; as the pro's say "leave the line." You must take into consideration the kerf of the saw blade when you begin your cut or you will be off your mark. As you cut, keep the saw blade as close to the line as possible without actually touching the line. See Fig. 3-6.

As you near the end of your cut, shorten your strokes and don't apply any pressure on the saw blade. You might also find it helpful to support the waste end so that it's weight does not cause it to fall off before you have completed your cut. An extra pair of hands are handy for this or you can place a piece of scrap lumber under the cut. The scrap must be long enough to support the waste end. The cut should be finished off with light strokes.

The whole secret to using a handsaw correctly is to let the saw do the cutting for you rather than trying to hurry the cutting by applying a lot of unnecessary pressure. Do-it-yourself wood-worker's often try to muscle a handsaw through a cut and the result is usually a cut of poor quality. On the other hand, if you work in a fluid motion, you will find that a handsaw cuts quite well and without a lot of effort.

Occasionally, you will find it necessary to re-move only a small amount of plywood—a cut of under one inch in width, for example. The amount that must be removed is actually too thick to take off with a plane and too thin to cut with a saw. The best solution to this type of problem cut is to use a scrap piece of lumber as a guide for the saw blade. In effect, you will be cutting two pieces of material rather than one, but at least you can be fairly certain that the required cut will be true.

Clamp or nail a guide to a workbench, and place the piece to be cut next to this. Then begin your cut on the scrap lumber. Make long strokes that will cut both pieces. You will be amazed at how thin of a piece of plywood can be cut when using this technique (Fig. 3-7).

One reason often offered for poor-quality cuts, when using a handsaw, is that it is difficult to hold the saw in a verticle position while making the cut. There are a few aids that can be used to help you guide the blade so it is at a perfect 90-degree angle to the surface. One such aid is a conventional miter box. While this aid is primarily intended for making perfect cuts in relatively narrow pieces of lumber, it can often be used to good advantage when working with plywood. As a rule, if you must cut a piece of plywood that is less than about 5 inches in width, a *miter box* (Fig. 3-8) might be very useful to you.

One other aid for making straight cuts with a handsaw, and one that can be used for any width cut, is to rig up an *edge guide* (Fig. 3-9) for the handsaw. For this, you will need two clamps (C-clamps work well) and a length of 2-×-4-inch lumber that is slightly longer than the cut you must make.

Begin by marking your cut on the face of the plywood. Next, position the length of 2 × 4 along the cut line and clamp it in place. Now you can make your cut, keeping the side of the handsaw flush with the edge of the 2 × 4 for the entire length of the cut. The handsaw is used in the conventional manner— that is slow, long strokes—while at the same time

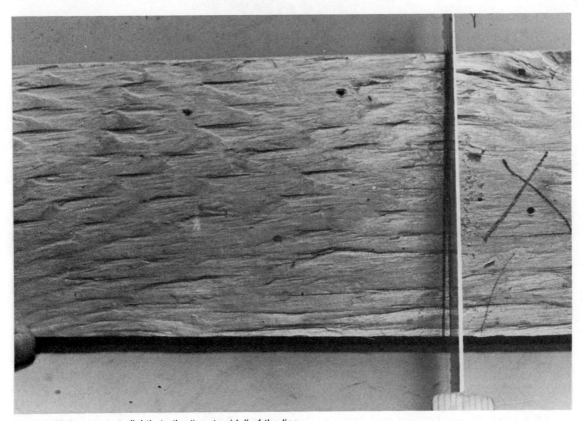

Fig. 3-6. Make your cut slightly to the "waste side" of the line.

Fig. 3-7. Clamp a piece of scrap lumber to the work and use it as an edge guide.

Fig. 3-8. A miter box is very handy for making accurate cuts on narrow pieces.

Fig. 3-9. A end of a scrap piece of 2-×-4 inch lumber is a good edge guide when making a cut with a handsaw.

keeping the side of the saw blade flush with the edge of the 2 × 4. While this method requires a little extra effort, at least in setting up, it will help you to produce almost perfect cuts with a handsaw.

HAND-HELD ELECTRICAL SAWS

In all probability, the average do-it-yourselfer will have at least one electrically powered saw around the home workshop. Sabre saws and circular saws are relatively inexpensive to purchase and can be relied upon to make accurate cuts through plywood.

The sabre saw (Fig. 3-10) can be used for both straight and curved cuts on most types of materials. Curved cuts are most often made freehand. While this same technique can be used for making straight cuts, it is generally better to use some type of guide to ensure straightness.

One of the first types of cuts that you may want

to learn how to make with a sabre saw is called the *plunge cut*. This type of cut is made when you want a hole or section cut out of a piece of plywood without having to start the cut from the edge of the panel. One way to approach this type of cut is to first drill a hole in the panel (Fig. 3-11). Then you can use a sabre saw to make the exact cut. But with a little practice, you can eliminate the drill work and simply make a plunge cut.

After carefully marking the area to be cut out of the plywood panel, begin by placing the sabre saw in the center of the area. The blade of the saw should not be touching the work. Turn on the saw and, when top RPM's are reached, slowly lower the moving blade onto the surface of the plywood. As the blade comes in contact with the work, it will begin to make the cut. As it cuts, you should lower the blade further into the cut until the sabre saw is

Fig. 3-10. Sabre saw.

Fig. 3-11. One way to make a cut out is to start with a drilled hole for the saw blade.

Fig. 3-12. Both hands are required for making a plunge cut with a sabre saw.

perpendicular to the surface. It is a simple matter of moving the saw to the cut line and making your cut along it (Fig. 3-12).

A plunge cut is a very handy technique to know when working with a sabre saw; it will enable you to quickly remove a section of plywood. There are a few things that you can and should do, however, to ensure that your cut comes out the way you want it to. Cut from the backside of the plywood panel. It is important to keep in mind that a sabre saw cuts on the upstroke. To achieve a small face cut, you must cut from the backside. Hold the saw with both hands throughout the cutting process. Often a bit of resistance will be encountered (especially when the moving blade first comes in contact with the plywood surface). If you have the saw securely held

in both hands, you should not encounter any problem. If you are holding the saw with only one hand, it will very likely jump off the work and cause damage to the project or *you*.

Straight cuts with a sabre saw require a steady hand and a good eye. One way to increase your chances of success when making a straight cut in plywood is to use some type of edge guide for the sabre saw. Edge guides for sabre saws are available both commercially and jury rigged.

Commercial edge guides for sabre saws most often consist of a device that attaches to the base of the saw while, at the same time, the far edge rides along the edge of the workpiece (and thus guides the sabre saw blade). All of the better-made sabre saws come with this attachment that is commonly

Fig. 3-13. Some sabre saw cuts can be aided by a ripping guide attachment.

Fig. 3-14. Measure from the edge of the saw blade to the edge of the saw table.

called a *ripping guide* (Fig. 3-13). These are simple to use and require only accurate measurements and adjustments to the guide. Edge guides are, however, limited in use to the length of the guide arm. This is usually only about 12 inches long. If a wider cut is required, you must rig up some type of guide for the saw base rather than simply rely on the ripping guide.

An edge guide for a sabre saw is not unlike the same type of guide discussed in the section on handsaw use. It is simply a length of lumber fastened along the cutline with clamps. The difference, of course, is the distance from the cut line which the guide must be placed (Fig. 3-14). When using a handsaw, the guide is placed very close to the cutline. When using a sabre saw, the edge guide must be placed several inches from the cut line.

To determine the distance, measure from your sabre saw blade to the edge of the saw base and place the guide at this distance from the cut line

(Fig. 3-15). Once you realize that the guide is used for guiding the base of the saw—rather than directly guiding the saw blade—it is a simple matter of positioning the device so that the saw blade cuts exactly where you want.

Just because you are using an edge guide you should not become overconfident that the cut will come out straight with little effort. In fact, you must exercise care when working in this manner. Use two hands to hold the saw. Do not force the saw through the work; guide the saw and let the saw do the cutting. You must also gently press the saw base so that it rides along the edge guide. If too much pressure is exerted, the sabre saw blade—because it is long and thin—will tend to bind. The result will be a cut of poor quality.

The hand-held circular saw (Fig. 3-16) is probably one of the most popular power saws in existence. It is also one of the most abused tools. When used properly, a hand-held circular saw will enable

Fig. 3-15. Place the edge guide 1⅞ of an inch away from cut line.

Fig. 3-16. The modern circular saw has played an important part in building American homes.

you to make straight cuts, beveled-edge cuts, and even plunge cuts with ease. While there is certainly an inherent inaccuracy—because it is hand held—it can nevertheless be used for a variety of wood-working projects with excellent results.

All saw cutting must begin by determining dimensions and marking the plywood accordingly. There are two basic types of cuts that can be made with a hand-held circular saw: *freehand cuts* and *guided cuts*.

For the guided cut, begin by marking the plywood accurately. Place a suitable straightedge at the proper distance from the cut line. This distance is, of course, equal to the space between the edge of the saw blade and the edge of the circular saw base. Clamp the edge guide to the workpiece (Fig. 3-17). Before turning on the saw, position the saw on the edge of the plywood and check that the saw blade will cut just off the cut line—leaving the line.

If it looks as if the saw blade will be off the mark, adjust the edge guide until you are satisfied that all is correct. Next, turn on the saw (with the blade not yet touching the work). After the saw develops maximum rpm, slowly move the saw into the work. The edge of the saw base should be touching and riding along the edge guide and the saw blade should be cutting just off the line on the waste side of the work. Gently push the saw through the cut while at the same time keeping an eye on where the blade is cutting.

If the guide was attached properly, the cut should be straight and true. Goggles, face shield, or some other type of eye protection will enable you to watch where the blade is cutting. As you get near the end of the cut, support the waste end of the plywood so it does not break off prematurely.

The better hand-held circular saws usually come with a ripping guide attachment (Fig. 3-18)

Fig. 3-17. An edge guide will help you to make straight and true cuts with a circular saw.

Fig. 3-18. For narrow cuts, a ripping guide is useful.

that can be used for guiding the saw on narrow cuts (up to about 8 inches). If you find that you require a straight and narrow piece of plywood and, you have such an attachment, by all means use it. If you do not have a ripping guide attachment or you are required to make a wide cut, then you will have to rig an edge guide.

The freehand cut is easily the most often-asked type of cut with a hand held circular saw. In fact, the saw was designed to be used in this fashion. You will almost never see an experienced carpenter use an edge guide for a hand-held circular saw. If you require a long, straight cut and you have not fully developed your woodworking skills, you will be better off using the edge guide method.

Before you attempt a freehand cut with the hand-held circular saw, you must first know where your saw cuts. On all hand-held circular saws, the front of the saw base will have a notch (Fig. 3-19) or other mark that tells you where the saw blade will cut. Because there is a lot of variation between saws, it is not possible to do more than make general comments here. Some saws cut on the left, others cut on the right, and still others cut in the center. If you do not know where your saw cuts in relation to this guide, make a few practice cuts.

Before you attempt a freehand cut, you must mark the workpiece so you will know where the cut is to be made. You can mark the work with a chalk line or a straightedge and pencil, but first use a ruler to place tick marks at the exact location of the cut. You must also support the plywood so that it is off the ground and relatively stable. This can be done with saw horses laid across a few pieces of dimensional lumber (scrap 2 × 4's) or some other means that you have at your disposal.

Position the saw cutting guide on the mark, but with the blade not yet touching the workpiece. After the saw is in position, turn it on and, with both hands on the saw, move the spinning blade into and along the cut line (Fig. 3-20). As with any type of cutting, the saw should be allowed to cut at its own speed. It should not be forced.

Listen to the whine of the saw motor. If it begins to slow or labor, you know that you are forcing the saw rather than letting it cut naturally.

As you proceed through the cut, it is important that you keep the guide riding along the cut line. If you go off course, chances are that the motor will start to labor because the blade is starting to bind. Cor-

Fig. 3-19. Use this notch as a "sight" when cutting with a circular saw.

Fig. 3-20. Accurate freehand cuts can be made with a circular saw.

rect this problem by backing up, and then going forward once again.

STATIONARY SAWS

The most accurate cuts on plywood are made using a stationary power saw—specifically a table saw (Fig. 3-21) or a radial-arm saw. Probably the most useful of the two types is the table saw. With such a tool, long, straight cuts as well as many other types of cuts are possible and relatively easy to achieve. I am sure that some readers will disagree with this statement, especially those who own a radial arm saw, but the fact remains that a table saw is much more versatile when working with full-size (4-×-8) sheets of plywood.

The Shopsmith Mark V (Fig. 3-22) can be used as a lathe (wood turnings), a verticle drill press (precision, of course), a full-blown (10-inch blade) table saw (depth of cut, table tilt relative to blade, powerful motor), a horizontal boring machine, and a 12-inch disc sander all put together in a semistationary configuration.

In addition, Shopsmith offers a thorough instruction program with every machine. Even a casual user can accomplish a wide range of woodworking tasks with a single machine. There are also a few accessories that can be attached to the basic Shopsmith Mark V. These include an 11-inch band saw, a 4-inch jointer, a 6-inch-wide belt sander, and an 18-inch jigsaw. Any of these accessories can be

Fig. 3-21. A modern table saw is about the best way to make accurate cuts.

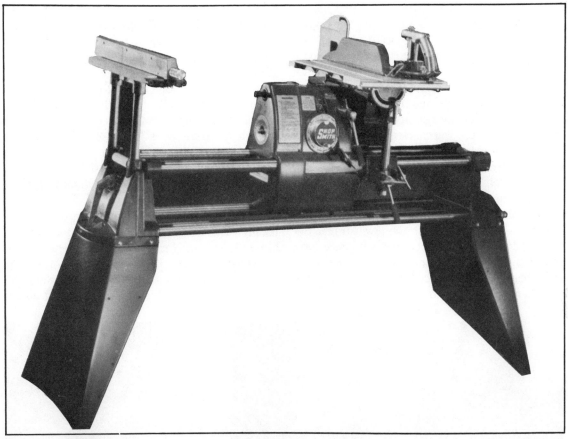

Fig. 3-22. Shopsmith Mark V is handy for a myriad of woodworking projects.

quickly setup to work on the basic Shopsmith system.

The Shopsmith Mark V and accessories offer an alternative to anyone wanting to set up a quality woodworking shop for a fraction of the cost if each of these machines were purchased separately. Their system is very easy to follow, and in almost no time you can be accomplishing advanced woodworking projects that in the past you only dreamed about.

Cutting Plywood with a Table Saw

The first step in cutting a full-size sheet of plywood on a table saw is to make certain that the panel will be well supported during the actual cutting. This can be accomplished in a number of ways, but the best way is to use a saw that has a large table and full extensions at the sides. If you own a small table

saw, you will have to rig up some type of support system for the saw or get one or more people to help you with the cutting. The old saying "many hands make light work" certainly applies here.

Adjustable roller stands—available from Sears, Roebuck and Co., for one example are probably the best bet for the do-it-yourself woodworker. Roller stands can be adjusted and positioned to help hold the sides of the panel as they pass by the cutting blade, or to catch the cut pieces as they come off the back end of the table. A helper is also of value because a full sheet of plywood is heavy and cumbersome for one person to handle.

After you have set up the area around the table saw and you are ready to work, the next step is to make certain that the saw blade is at a perfect 90-degree angle to the saw table. This task is best accomplished with a try square, making adjustments as required (Fig. 3-23). Next, the ripping fence must be adjusted so it is located the required distance from the saw blade. It is important to keep in mind that some saw blades are wider than others. A carbide-tipped blade is wider than a conventional steel blade, for example, and you will have to adjust the ripping guide accordingly if the blade is changed. Make sure you check the ripping guide at both the front and rear of the table. This is one area that lends itself to being out of alignment. See Figs. 3-23 and 3-24.

When making cuts on a table saw, the workpiece is placed face up. This is necessary because the table saw blade cuts on the downstroke. Because the blade first contacts the workpiece form below, alignment can present a little problem. One of the best ways to make certain that the blade will cut where you want it to is to extend the cut line over the edge of the piece of plywood (Fig. 3-25). Then when you place the plywood on the table—one edge along the ripping fence—you can clearly see just where the blade will cut and you can adjust the ripping fence accordingly.

One last operation that should be done before actual cutting begins is to adjust the height of the saw blade. The blade should extend only about ¼ of an inch above the work (Fig. 3-26). Adjusting the height of a table saw blade is a simple matter of cranking the blade or table up or down (depending on the type of adjustments you have on your table saw).

After all adjustments have been made, position the plywood on the saw table without it touching the blade of the saw. Next, turn on the saw and move the plywood toward the spinning blade. Make certain that one edge of the plywood rides along the ripping fence. As with all types of cutting opera-

Fig. 3-23. Check the blade angle with an aid. It should be at a perfect 90-degree angle.

Fig. 3-24. Position the rip fence carefully and accurately.

tions, it is important to let the saw do the cutting at its own speed. Do not try to force the cutting to go quicker.

Listen to the whine of the saw motor. This is the best indication of how the cutting is progressing. There should be a high-pitched whine. If the motor starts to labor, you might either be pushing too hard on the workpiece or you might not be moving in a straight line. Gently pull the work towards you and away from the spinning blade (Fig. 3-27), and the motor should once again achieve maximum rpm. Then proceed again.

As you near the end of the cut, slow down the rate at which the work advances toward the saw blade. The last ½ to ¼ inch of the workpiece should be fed into the saw blade very slowly. This action will prevent tearing or splintering of the corners as the two pieces separate.

Fig. 3-25. Mark the end of plywood.

After the cut has been completed, continue pushing the plywood past the blade until it is entirely clear of the blade—then turn the saw motor off. After the saw blade comes to a full stop, then and only then, should you remove the cut piece. Fingers are very handy for a number of woodworking projects. The best way to keep them is not to get near a spinning saw blade. Safety first in all cases.

Small cuts to plywood on a table saw can be a little tricky and slightly dangerous if approached in the wrong manner. There are a number of aids that are available for working with small pieces of lumber and plywood on a table saw. A few of these aids can even be made quite easily in the home workshops. The intention of all of these gadgets is to allow you to cut small pieces of lumber without having to place your fingers close to the saw blade.

Fig. 3-26. Saw blade height should be no more than ¼ inch above the work.

Fig. 3-27. Guide the work through the spinning blade.

Fig. 3-28. The table saw miter gauge is invaluable for angled cuts.

One such accessory is called a *miter gauge* (Fig. 3-28).

The miter gauge is a standard accessory on most table saws sold today, and it is useful for guiding a piece of stock past the saw blade. The base of the unit is a flat piece of strap steel that rides in a groove—inset on either side of the saw blade—and on top of which is a swiveling head with a flat face.

The piece to be cut is held tightly against the face of the miter gauge as it is slowly pushed forward into the spinning blade. When used properly, the miter gauge keeps the operator's fingers well away from the saw blade and thus eliminates or at least greatly minimizes accidents. For very small pieces, one trick worth mentioning is to clamp the work to the miter gauge (Fig. 3-29). Not only will this permit you to cut small pieces of lumber or plywood, but it will also eliminate kickbacks and allow you to work with a certain degree of precision.

Another feature of the miter gauge is that it can be used for making angle cuts. Because the head of any miter gauge is marked in degrees, it is a simple matter of making, say a 45-degree angle cut, on lumber or plywood.

One other aid for working on a table saw, and one that is very handy for small pieces of work, is a push stick. There are probably 20 different designs for this tool and they all have one thing in common. They allow you to push a piece of lumber or plywood past the spinning saw blade without having to place your fingers very close. Generally, a suitable push stick can be made from almost any piece of lumber. Nevertheless, many woodworkers prefer hardwood such as oak or maple. The stick should not be too wide or it will touch the blade when you attempt to push work past it. A piece of lumber

Fig. 3-29. Clamp small pieces to the miter gauge for safety's sake.

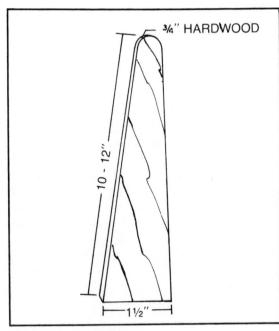

¾" HARDWOOD

10 - 12"

1½"

Fig. 3-30. Push stick diagram.

measuring ¾ × 1½ × 10-12 inches is ideal for making a push stick (Fig. 3-30).

Cutting Plywood with a Radial-Arm Saw

Woodworkers who have used a radial-arm saw (Fig. 3-31) with any frequency will often state that this stationary power tool is more versatile and safer than a table saw. When you consider the seemingly infinite adjustment possibilities for cutting, and the other operations (such as drilling, routing, planing), the radial-arm saw does indeed seem quite versatile.

Probably the greatest limitation of a radial-arm saw (when working with plywood) is that it cannot be used to cut across the entire width of a full sheet of 4-foot plywood. This is because the saw can only cut as far as the arm extends over the saw table. In most cases, this will be about 24 inches. Of course, many radial-arm saw users get around this shortcoming by making two cuts: both of 24 inches. Still another way of overcoming this limitation is to

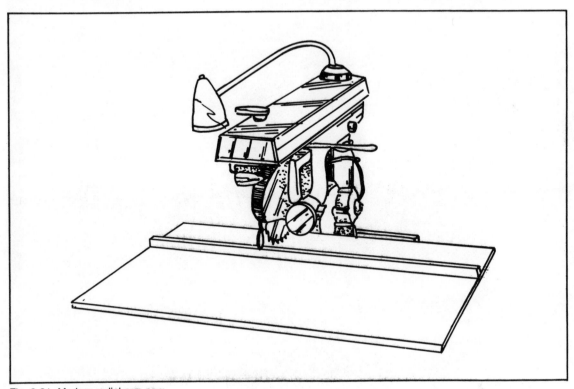

Fig. 3-31. Modern radial-arm saw.

rough cut the full sheet of plywood on a table saw or with a handsaw and then finish cutting on the radial-arm saw.

Another shortcoming of the radial-arm saw is that working with full sheet of plywood tends to be a cumbersome task. Although radial-arm saws are capable of ripping (making a lengthwise cut) a full sheet of plywood, the sheet must be supported along its entire length during the process. Because the table of the radial arm saw is only about 2 feet wide—and a full sheet of plywood measures 4 feet in width—this obviously means that a piece of plywood measuring 2 × 8 feet will extend out from the radial-arm saw table. The two ways of effectively supporting this overhang are with a set of roller stands or several pairs of hands.

Because the radial-arm saw cuts from above, it is a simple matter to make a cut exactly where you want it. Begin by placing the workpiece—with suitable cut lines inscribed on the top—on the table and positioning it so that the saw will cut on the waste side of your mark. This same task on a table saw, because it cuts from below, requires a lot of eyeing up before actual cutting can begin.

The tasks that the radial-arm saw performs well are straight cuts and miter cuts. Because a number of plywood furniture projects require such cuts, a radial-arm saw is an ideal stationary power saw for the do-it-yourself plywood furniture builder.

Chapter 4

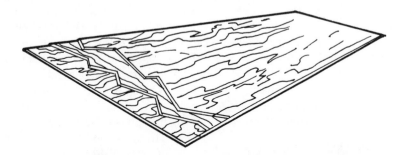

Finishing Techniques

BUILDING A PIECE OF PLYWOOD FURNITURE IS only half the task of the project. Once constructed, the next step is to finish the piece in such a way as to make it attractive and make it blend or contrast with your other furnishings. During the finishing stages, a lot must be accomplished. This includes repairing or correcting some things that have been done incorrectly during the cutting and assembly.

This chapter deals with several ways for finishing plywood furniture. If you are still in the planning stages of your plywood furniture project, you would be wise to read this entire chapter. There are a number of things that you should take into consideration before you buy your raw materials. The type of finish you plan to have on the completed project will have a bearing on the type of plywood you purchase. It is entirely possible, for example, to realize quite a savings in material costs simply by choosing an economical finish, if low-cost, functional furniture is your goal.

Generally, there are two basic ways of finishing a plywood furniture project. You can cover all or most of the surfaces with some material such as plastic laminate or a true wood veneer or you can coat the project with stain, a clear coating (such as varnish) or a solid color paint. Your choice of finish for your furniture project should be based on how much time and money you are willing to invest and the overall effect you are trying to achieve.

Very little surface preparation is required if the surfaces of the furniture will be covered with plastic laminate material. If this method is chosen, almost any plywood or particle board can be used for the project, and it is therefore possible to realize quite a savings. But you must take into consideration the cost of the plastic laminate. This cost may very well offset the savings gained on the purchase of the plywood.

If you choose to apply a stain and clear coating or paint your plywood furniture project, you must realize that a lot of time will be required to complete the project. Consider also that a better grade of plywood must be purchased in the first place and that after carefully constructing the piece you must fill and finish the edges before the entire project can be sanded very smooth. All this must be accomplished before a stain and clear coating or paint can be applied.

As you can see, there are a number of important considerations that you must be aware of when planning your plywood furniture project. It is possible to realize a savings in materials, but this is often offset by the required investment in labor. On the other hand, you can save a great deal of labor by covering the project with plastic laminate, but this will surely increase the overall cost of the project. In the end, you are the one to decide how much money and time you really want to invest in the project. For my part, I will explain how to accomplish the various ways of finishing the project.

PLASTIC LAMINATE

If the heading of this section is a little confusing to

you, just think of the typical kitchen counter that is covered with a version of this material. Most people think of the brand name Formica instead of the generic term plastic laminate. There are several companies that produce plastic laminate materials.

The beauty of plastic laminate is that it effectively forms a hard, durable covering that withstands moisture, most household stains, and moderate heat. This material has enough integrity to bridge small surface irregularities such as cracks, holes, and poor-fitting wood joints. It must, however, be attached to a surface that is flat and resistant to being flexed. In most cases, this will mean constructing the plywood furniture project from ¾ inch thick plywood or from thinner plywood that has been strengthened by internal ribs or some other type of bracing (Fig. 4-1).

Plastic laminates are sold in sheet form and in

Fig. 4-1. For a strong piece of furniture, use ¾-inch thick plywood or ½-inch thick plywood and internal bracing.

several thicknesses. The most common for residential use is called *general purpose* or *standard grade*, and it is 1/16 of an inch thick. Standard sheet inch widths are 24, 30, 36, 48, and 60. Lengths range from 60, 72, 84, 96, 120, and 144 inches. When designing plywood furniture, keep these standard sizes in mind. You might be able to use a smaller standard-size sheet and save a few dollars.

There are special-purpose grades of plastic laminate material. These include *postforming* grade (which is about 1/20 of an inch thick) that can be heated and bent or formed around a curved surface. You will see this material used on many kitchen counter tops where both the backsplash and front edge have a curved finish. There is also a grade known as *vertical grade* (measuring about 1/32 of an inch thick) that is used for vertical surfaces such as bookcases, cabinet doors, and stereo speaker cabinets. Vertical-grade plastic laminate is also commonly available in 1⅝-inch and 2-inch wide strips that are very handy for finishing off the edges of a project.

One type of plastic laminate is called *backer sheets*, and these are commonly used on the back or underside of a project to add dimensional stability. Backer sheets are inexpensive, but they do not have the overall strength of the standard grade. Nevertheless, backer sheets are very useful for interiors of cabinets, backsides of doors, and for covering shelves.

While there are a number of adhesives that can be used for attaching plastic laminate to plywood, the best choice is contact cement. As the name implies, bonding happens upon contact and therefore eliminates the need for any type of clamping. Contact cement is applied to both surfaces—the face of the plywood and the back of the plastic laminate—with a paint brush and allowed to dry before the two pieces are fitted together.

Plywood furniture that will receive a covering of laminate material should be built from ¾-inch-thick plywood so it will not flex during use. All surfaces must also be flat and free from anything such as paint, oil, or grease that will hamper the contact cement from doing its job. All areas that will receive a covering of plastic laminate must be

checked for squareness (Fig. 4-2). A framing square is helpful for this type of checking. After you are satisfied that the piece of furniture is sturdy, all joints are tight, and all edges are square, you can begin attaching the plastic laminate to the project.

For our purposes, almost all plastic laminate work begins by attaching the laminate to the edges of the project and then to the sides and top. In some cases, however, the sides or top are attached first and then the sides.

There are a number of ways to cut plastic laminate. Because all plastic laminates are hard, thin, and brittle, they have a tendency to break if handled or cut improperly. For this reason, you must always provide support for the sheet during the cutting process. When marking plastic laminate prior to cutting, make your marks at least ½ inch

Fig. 4-2. Check your project with a rafter square.

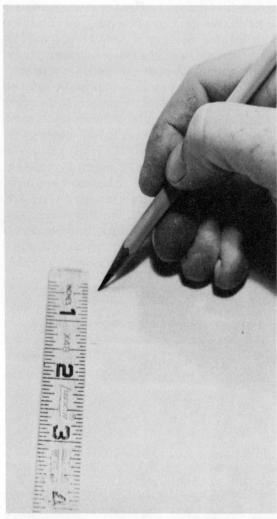

Fig. 4-3. Mark and cut laminate wider than needed. Excess is trimmed off later with router and special trimmer bit.

knife (Fig. 4-4), an awl, or an ice pick. If you use a utility knife you will find it necessary to change the blade often. To make a cut, you must score the face of the laminate along your cut line. It is necessary to make several passes and you will find a straight-edge handy as a guide.

Once the face has been scored to a depth of about half of its thickness, the next step is to bend the plastic laminate upward. This action should be all that is required for a controlled break. This method is easily the most laborious of all cutting methods. Nevertheless, it is one of the best ways for making an irregular cut on plastic laminate material.

A handsaw can also be used for making cuts in plastic laminate material. The two best choices are a crosscut saw (with 12 points per inch) or a hacksaw (Fig. 4-5) with about 32 teeth per inch. The former is useful for long, straight cuts and the latter is a good choice for cutting up small pieces such as trimming edge strips that are usually less than 3 inches in width. In either case, the saw must be held perpendicular to the surface and the laminate should be firmly supported with the face up.

The easiest and probably the best way to cut plastic laminate material is with electric power tools. These include table saws, radial-arm saws, hand-held circular saws, sabre saws, and routers.

Plastic laminate will dull conventional wood-working tools rather quickly so it is always best to use tools that have a carbide edge or tip. You should always wear some type of eye protection when cutting plastic laminate because the potential al-ways exists for bits of this material to become flying projectiles. Always set up a special work area so that the laminate is well supported. More often than not, it is better to have someone help you with the cutting because a sheet of plastic laminate can be difficult to cut single-handedly.

If you are using a table saw to cut plastic laminate, make certain that the sheet of material is well supported before attempting the cut. Adjust the height of the saw blade so that it is not more than about ¼ of an inch above the surface of the material. (Fig. 4-6). Plastic laminate is cut face up on a table saw. This way any chipping will be confined to the

wider than required (Fig. 4-3). If you need a strip that measures 2 inches wide, for example, cut the laminate at least 2½ inches wide. This excess will be trimmed off after the laminate has been attached to the plywood furniture project. If you are planning to use woodworking tools for cutting plastic lami-nate material, keep in mind that this material will dull standard saw blades very quickly. Carbide tipped cutting tools are a good choice.

One method that can be used to cut plastic laminates is to use a pointed tool such as a utility

Fig. 4-4. Plastic laminate can be scored with a sharp utility knife.

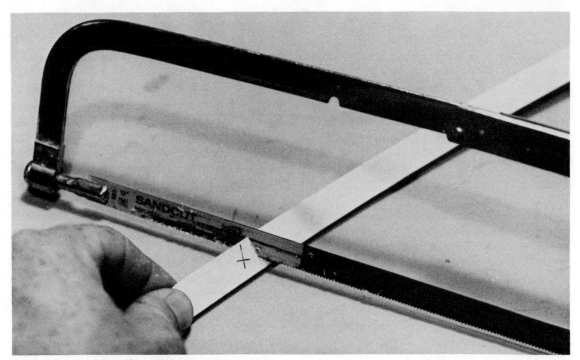

Fig. 4-5. Use a hacksaw for cutting edge strips.

Fig. 4-6. A table saw can be used to cut laminate, but make sure that the blade is not more than ¼ inch above the work.

back of the sheet rather than on the face. Guide the laminate into the spinning blade slowly for best results.

When cutting plastic laminates on a radial-arm saw, the face of the material should be down and the work must be fully supported. This means, of course, that your cut line or lines must be on the back rather than the front of the material.

A hand-held circular saw can also be used for cutting plastic laminate, but there are a few pre-requisites. The material must be securely sup-ported or it will shatter more than be cut by the saw. The face of the plastic laminate must be face up during the cutting. For long, straight cuts, some type of edge guide for the saw base is advisable for success. As for all types of cutting, a carbide-tipped crosscut blade is best for this type of cutting.

A sabre saw can also be used for cutting plastic

laminate and it is especially useful for making ir-regular cuts or contour cuts. The material must be cut with the face of the work down and fully sup-ported. Special metal-cutting blades, with approxi-mately 16 teeth per inch, are the best choice. Make sure you have several blades because they will become dull in a short time.

A hand-held portable router is probably the best choice for cutting plastic laminate material. A special carbide cutting tip is required along with some type of guidance system for the tool. For best results, the face of the material should be up and the material itself must be solidly supported or the laminate will tend to shatter and chip.

Once you have cut the plastic laminate—remember at least ½ inch wider than you re-quire—it is time to dry fit the material to the surface of the plywood furniture project. Your inten-

Fig. 4-7. Use a paint brush for applying contact cement.

tion, at this point, is simply to make certain that you have an excess of the laminate. This additional material will, of course, be trimmed off during the finishing stages. Once you are confident that the plastic laminate material will fit—and that the plywood surface is in the proper state, flat, dry, and sound—you can begin applying contact cement to the surface of the plywood and the back of the plastic laminate.

The easiest and probably the best way to apply contact cement is with a paint brush (Fig. 4-7) or, for very large surfaces, with a roller. It is important to apply this adhesive evenly on both surfaces. In most cases, two coats will be required—especially on the plywood. The adhesive must dry to the touch before either applying a second coat or fitting the pieces together.

There are several different types of contact cement. Read the container label for specific instructions about working with the contact cement you are using. Follow all instructions because some contact cements are toxic and others are highly flammable.

You must wait for the contact cement to dry to the touch (Fig. 4-8) before assembling the pieces. Depending on the amount of area, temperature, and relative humidity, this drying may take as long as 45 minutes. If you are in a bit of a rush, you can speed up drying by blowing warm air over the surfaces with a hair dryer (Fig. 4-9). Once the cement is dry, you can begin fitting it to the plywood furniture.

Generally, on tables the edges are the first to receive strips of plastic laminate and then the top is attached. On bookcases, the sides, top and bottom

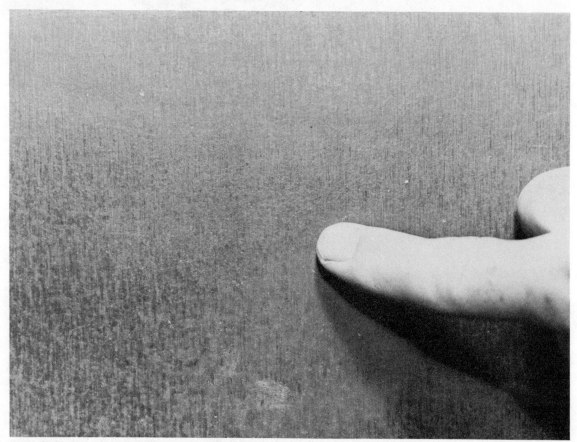

Fig. 4-8. Contact cement is ready when it is dry to the touch.

124

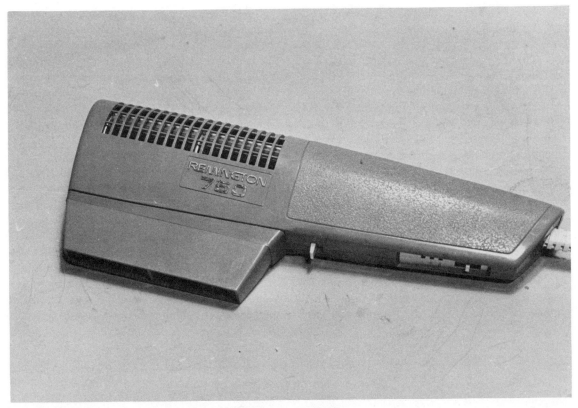

Fig. 4-9. A hair dryer can be used to speed up drying of contact cement.

of shelves are covered and then the front facing edge is covered. This procedure should be followed so that the joint—where the edge of the plastic laminate meets the other edges—is not visible. On a table, for example, you want the top laminate to overlap the edges. One reason is so that liquids cannot get between the layers of laminate material. On bookcases, where both the vertical and horizontal edges are visible, you do not want to see the joints between the layers of plastic laminate.

As you begin to attach the strips and sheets of plastic laminate material to your plywood furniture project, there is one very important point to keep in mind. Once two surfaces—which have both been coated with contact cement—come in contact bonding takes place. Once this happens, it will be difficult or impossible to reposition the plastic laminate material. This fact cannot be overstressed. Many a project has suffered as a result of poor

positioning of the laminate. Remember that the adhesive is called *contact* cement for a very good reason.

Small pieces of plastic laminate such as edges are best applied to a surface by beginning at one end, positioning the end of the strip, and then slowly and carefully bending the strip into place (Fig. 4-10). Because this edge strip on a table or bookcase edge will be trimmed with a router, your only real concern is to make certain that the edge of the piece of furniture is covered entirely with the plastic laminate. A little planning is required here. For example, if all edges of a table are to be covered with strips of plastic laminate, it is usually better—from an esthetic point of view—to apply the laminate to the short edges first and then to the long sides.

Once the plastic laminate strip has been securely fastened to the edge of the furniture being covered, it must be trimmed so that it is flush with both the top and bottom edges. In this instance, the trimming is done before the top of the piece receives its covering of plastic laminate. The best tool for trimming plastic laminate is a hand-held router that has been fitted with a special carbide-tipped, plastic laminate trimmer bit (Fig. 4-11).

There are two types of these special router bits: *flush trimmer* and *22-degree angle trimmer*. Generally, the flush trimmer can be used for all types of plastic laminate trimming. The 22-degree angle trimmer is used primarily for the edges of tabletops, counter tops and other flat, horizontal surfaces. Because these special router bits cost over $10 each, I recommend that if you could only afford one, it should be the flush trimmer. The results you can obtain with this one are more than satisfactory. In addition, if you find that you want an angled edge on a plastic laminate, you can usually obtain one by working the edge with a flat file.

Edge trimming is a fairly simple operation. Begin by chucking the special trimmer bit into the router, and then place the router flat on the surface that is to be trimmed. Turn on the router and let the motor develop maximum rpm before coming in contact with the plastic laminate. Then slowly push the router into the work until contact is made. The trimmer bit will cut through the excess plastic laminate and stop cutting as soon as the pilot bearing—on the bottom of the bit—comes in contact with the flat surface. Push the router along the edge of the work and let the bit do the trimming at its own speed. Just before you come to the end of the edge, stop the motor and, once it has stopped turning, remove it from the surface.

A router bit works best when pushed into the work rather than pushed out of the work. Therefore, the ends of the edge should be trimmed separately. Simply push the router into the edges from the outside. By trimming the edges of your project in

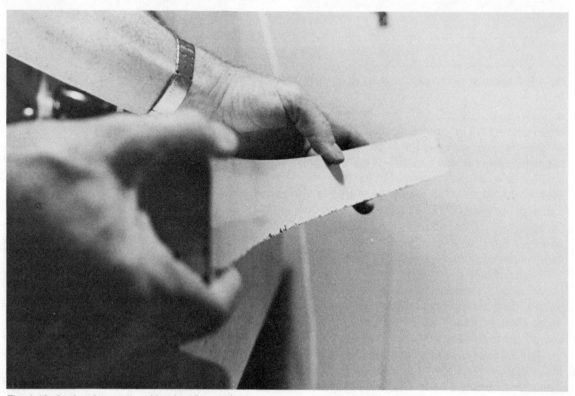

Fig. 4-10. Apply edges strips with a bending motion.

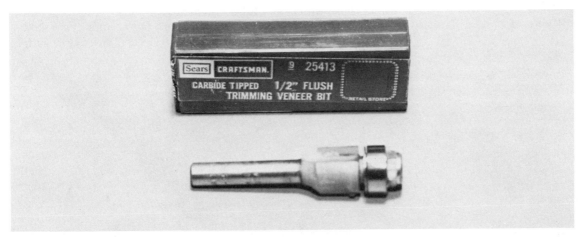

Fig. 4-11. A carbide trimmer bit.

this manner, you can be fairly certain that they will come out the way you want them to—with crisp edges. Each of the edges of a project are trimmed in this manner. Then the top or sides can be covered with plastic laminate. Then the edges of these sur-faces are trimmed with the router (Fig. 4-12) and special plastic laminate trimmer.

After the entire project has been trimmed, you must go back over the work and check for any sharp edges. Most professionals like to go over all

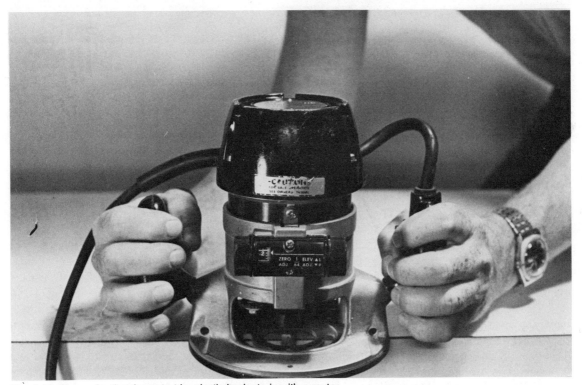

Fig. 4-12. The professional way to trim plastic laminate is with a router.

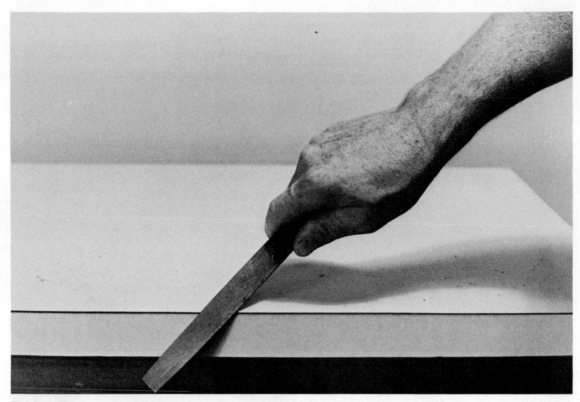

Fig. 4-13. File the edges of plastic laminate after trimming.

trimmed edges with a flat file. You may want to do this also. The effect of this touching up will give a slight roundness to each of the edges and make them smooth (Fig. 4-13).

When working with a flat file, hold the file at a 20- to 30-degree angle to the surface being touched up. Work the file downward gently from the top or outside of the project. It is important that you do not exert too much force on the file or you will cause one area to be uneven from the rest. Remember that your intention is to create a slight roundness to the trimmed edge and to remove any sharpness. This can be easily accomplished with the flat file in slow, even strokes.

The next step is to go over all joints and remove any contact cement that might have oozed out (Fig. 4-14) when the pieces were pressed together. This is easily one of the most time consuming and laborous tasks involved in a plastic laminate project. In most cases, the only thing that will remove

hardened contact cement is a special solvent applied with a cloth and lots of elbow grease. Check the can of contact cement you are using to see if the manufacturer recommends a special solvent. Do not, under any circumstances, try to remove the dried contact cement with any type of abrasive cleaner. These often have a tendency to scratch the surface of the plastic laminate.

As you clean up the edges and surfaces of the plywood furniture project, you will also have to remove the printed label that is present on some plastic laminates—Formica brand especially. These decals are printed on the surface and usually come off with bar soap and a damp rag (Fig. 4-15).

The only tools that are suitable for cutting or trimming plastic laminates are those that have carbide tips or cutting surfaces. These special blades and cutters (router bits) will start to clog up after a short period of use and especially when trimming laminate that has been fastened in place with con-

Fig. 4-14. Clean off excess contact cement.

tact cement. As this buildup of contact cement and plastic laminate bits occurs, the tip of the tool will start to get very hot and thus become a lot less effective at its task. For this reason, you should check your router bit often. If you discover a build-up, remove it with a pocketknife (Fig. 4-16) or solvent and a damp rag.

Many professionals spray plastic laminate trimming bits with a silicone preparation before starting work and periodically during the trimming.

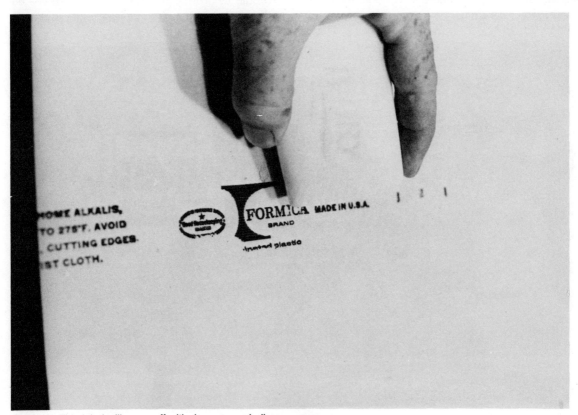

Fig. 4-15. This label will come off with dry soap and elbow grease.

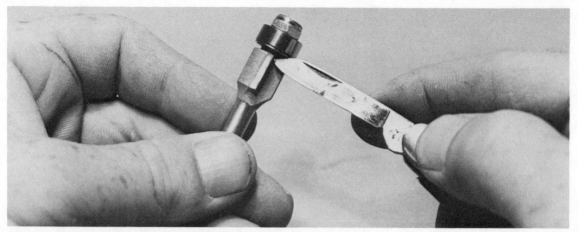

Fig. 4-16. Clean up the trimmer bit with pocketknife.

Some of the brands that are popular are WD-40 (Fig. 4-17) and Tri-Flon. These silicone sprays will prevent excess buildup and make the trimming go that much easier. Because of the lubrication, the cutter will not get very hot.

One of the tricky parts of applying plastic laminate to a large surface—a tabletop for example—is positioning the large sheet of laminate for good coverage before the two surfaces that are coated with contact cement come together. Because

Fig. 4-17. A quick spray of lubricant will help to keep your trimmer cool.

Fig. 4-18. Use wooden dowels during positioning of plastic laminate.

bonding takes place as soon as contact is made, you want to be certain that the laminate is positioned properly. There are two things that you can do to prevent contact while positioning a large sheet of plastic laminate. Both involve placing something between the two surfaces to prevent bonding.

The first method is called the *dowel method* and the technique is as follows. After the contact cement has dried to the touch, ½-inch diameter dowels (Fig. 4-18) are placed on the furniture surface. The dowels must be longer than the surface is wide so you will be able to slip them out afterward. Next, lay the plastic laminate on top of the dowels and position for full coverage. Then when you are satis-

fied with the fit, slowly pull the dowels out and let the surfaces meet. As you pull the dowels out, you must keep the plastic laminate in the proper position.

After one or two of the dowels have been removed, and you are satisfied with the alignment of the plastic laminate, you can usually pull the rest of the dowels out and be reasonably certain that the fitting will be correct. The next step is to apply pressure (Fig. 4-19) over the entire surface to ensure good overall bonding. This can be done with either a special hard rubber roller or a carpet-covered block and hammer. Next the plastic laminate is edge trimmed with a router.

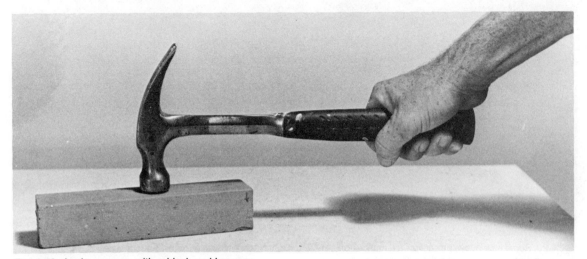

Fig. 4-19. Apply pressure with a block and hammer.

The second method that can be used to prevent immediate contact while positioning a large piece of plastic laminate involves the use of two pieces of heavy brown paper or heavy wax paper. After the plastic laminate has been cut and dry fitted, apply a coating of contact cement to both surfaces and let it dry to the touch. Next, lay two sheets of paper over the area. The pieces must be wider and longer than the area. Then position the plastic laminate.

After you are satisfied with the fit, remove one of the sheets of paper. Be very careful not to reposition the laminate. Next, ever so carefully, remove the second sheet of paper. Make sure that positioning of the laminate remains the same.

As the second sheet of paper is removed, press on the surface of the plastic laminate to help bonding occur. Once part of the laminate is secure, you can usually remove the last sheet of paper quickly without fear of repositioning the laminate. It is important to keep in mind that contact cement will not adhere to a surface unless it also has a coating of contact cement. The next steps include rolling or tapping the surface to ensure sound bonding, and then trimming the excess plastic laminate from the edges as previously described.

Because all router work results in quite a bit of airborne chips, some type of eye protection (Fig. 4-20) is required. Not only will this protect your eyes from possible damage, but you will also be able to watch the work progress with little fear of a mishap.

PAINT AND NATURAL FINISHES

After you have completed construction of your plywood furniture project, finish off the project with some type of protective coating. This is done for protection and decoration. The choices are painting

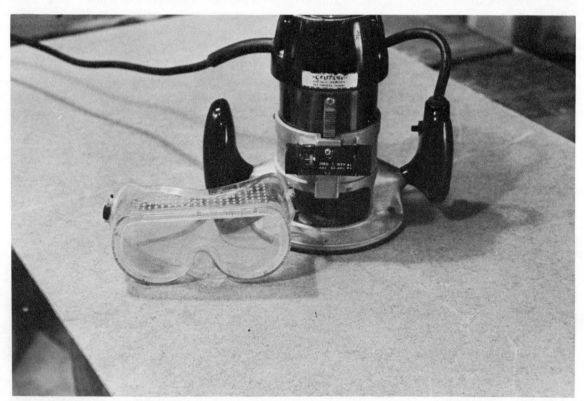

Fig. 4-20. Some type of eye protection is a must when trimming plastic laminate with a router. Your eyes will be protected and you will be able to clearly see the work as it progresses.

with a solid color, staining and applying a clear coating, or staining and applying a wax coating. Before any finish coating can be applied, however, the surface of the project must be suitably prepared. You cannot expect to obtain professional-looking (and enduring) results when finish coatings are applied to a poorly prepared surface. By most estimates, surface preparation accounts for about 90 percent of the finishing process.

In all cases where some type of finish coating will be applied over a plywood furniture project, there are a number of things that must be accomplished during the surface preparation stage. These include some type of edge treatment, sanding, and, in general, making all surfaces ready to receive the finish coating. In addition, when applying a stain and clear coating on many types of woods (the top veneers on plywood), some type of filler or sealer must be used. When coating a project with a paint, the bare wood must be primed before you apply the topcoating.

Finish materials include fillers, sealers, primers, paints, clear finishes, stains, and waxes. Fillers are used as the first step in the finishing process for surface veneers with large pores—oak, walnut, mahogany, ash, etc. The purpose of a filler material is to fill and level the pores of the wood and sometimes to add a bit of color to the finish. Color choices range from almost clear to ebony. Proper application of a filler (Fig. 4-21) is just as important as proper application of a topcoating because the filler is the base on which the topcoating is applied. Fillers are available in powder, paste, or liquid form. Fillers are not commonly used for tight- or close-grained wood veneers such as fir, pine, basswood, etc., but the application of a sealer is commonly used instead.

Sealers are also used for surface veneers that have first been filled. This is necessary to prevent the filler from migrating into the finish topcoating. Sealers are often used on tight-grained woods. Usually this is to prevent any bleeding of natural resins or dyes in the wood. The two most common wood sealers are *shellac* and *synthetic resins*.

Fig. 4-21. Filler paste is applied with a putty knife.

Fig. 4-22. Shellac sealer is painted on.

Shellac sealer is made by mixing 1 part shellac (4-pound cut) and, 7 parts alcohol. Most woodworkers seem to prefer white shellac because it is easy to apply and it dries quickly. Synthetic resin sealers (Fig. 4-22) are sold ready for use and they are a good choice for plywood furniture projects. Both types are applied in the same manner—usually with a good bristle brush—and work almost the same at preventing moisture absorption and sealing the naturalness of the surface veneer. Sealers and fillers are used for all finishing where a clear topcoating will be applied.

For plywood furniture projects that will receive a solid-color paint coating, a good primer is used. As a rule, all unpainted wood that will ultimately receive a topcoating of water- or oil-base enamel should be primed with an enamel undercoat (Fig. 4-23) to seal the wood and to provide a better subsurface.

If the unpainted piece of furniture is not primed, the enamel coat will be uneven and, generally, not what you had in mind for the piece when you started. I prefer an oil-base primer (exterior grade) for all surfaces that I paint with either an oil- or water-base topcoating.

Generally, the best choice for a solid-color paint for plywood furniture is one that can be cleaned easily. That means either semigloss or full-gloss paint. Paint with a flat appearance, particularly latex, are not generally recommended for plywood furniture because this coating is not as easy to maintain. If small children are in your home, you will find that washable furniture is a necessity. There are a lot of good choices of enamel-type paints. You should pay a visit to your local paint store to see what is available. Try to choose a color that you can live with and that will enhance the furniture you have created.

Use colors to create a mood or atmosphere. For example, paint children's furniture bright acrylic-type colors or even create some type of graphic design. Plywood furniture lends itself to bright and exciting designs. You should be able to find large decals or other aids at an art supply house.

If the natural grain of the wood is pleasing, you will want to protect and display this. More often than not, some type of stain is applied to all bare woods to bring out the characteristics of the grain or unusual patterns. Wood stains are available in a wide range or tones and in various forms. These include water stain, oil or wiping stains, nongrain raising stains, and sealer stains.

Water stains are the least expensive of all the stains and they are probably the simplest to use (Fig. 4-24). These stains are sold as powders that must be mixed with hot water before use. The stain, when applied with a brush, is absorbed by the wood fibers. This results in a stain that does not fade with time. On the negative side, water stains do swell the wood fibers and tend to raise the grain. Water stains are available in a wide range of tones and they are used commercially with great frequency.

Oil stains are sold as pigment or penetrating types. Pigment oil stains are best used on wood surfaces with an uneven color. They tend to give an overall uniformity when applied properly. Pigmented stains do not penetrate very deeply into the surface of the wood and can, therefore, be sanded to achieve a lighter tone or to remove them entirely. Of the two, most people seem to prefer the penetrating types because they are easier to apply. Both types are generally available in a variety of premixed tones.

Nongrain-raising stains are widely used in commercial woodworking and they are usually sprayed rather than brushed on. They are excellent for cabinets that will receive a finish coating of varnish or other clear topcoating. These stains, as their name suggests, do not raise the grain of the wood and result in predictable, transparent colors. Nongrain-raising stains are usually referred to as *NGR Stains.* You should see some reference to this on the packaging.

Sealer stains are another commercially popular

Fig. 4-23. All bare wood must be primed.

Fig. 4-24. Stir all stains well before and during use.

stain because they perform two functions in one application. Sealer stains are considered to be partly penetrating (the sealer) and partly a surface stain. The actual tone you select is achieved by adding drops of pigment to the base liquid. As you can imagine, this approach offers almost unlimited tone possibilities. So-called standard colors, colonial maple for example, are achieved by adding a specific number of drops of pigment. Your local paint specialty shop is the best place for more details.

There are several types of clear coatings (Fig. 4-25). All are usually referred to as *varnish*, but this is actually only one type of clear coating. Varnish forms a durable and attractive finish for plywood furniture. In addition, varnish seals the wood to form a tough, transparent film that will stand up to repeated scrubbings and a bit of abuse. Varnish is available in flat, semigloss and high gloss. The soft, golden tone of varnish is pleasing to the eye, and especially when used over many types of softwoods. One problem that many people encounter with varnish is that it forms such a brittle film that it can be damaged by scratching. Often the only way to touch up a scratched varnish surface is to recoat it entirely. A good paste wax will help to provide a little protection for varnish, but in time all varnish needs to be recoated.

Fig. 4-25. Several types of clear finishes.

Shellac and lacquer are two other clear coatings that are worth mentioning. They differ from varnish in that they can be easily repaired with a simple touchup. Shellac is easy to apply with a brush, it dries hard and fast, and it also seals the wood. Lacquer is most often applied with a sprayer. In both cases, several light coats rather than one or two heavy coats give the best results. Often a paste wax (Fig. 4-26) is applied over a multilayered shellac finish with very pleasing and soft results.

Polyurethane and epoxy varnishes are good examples of modern paint developments. These synthetic, clear coatings are very durable and have a high resistance to stains, abrasions, acids, strong cleaners, petroleum fuels, alcohol, and many chemicals. This overall toughness makes these clear coatings popular in industry and around the home. They are easy to apply with a brush, give predictable results, and have a long life. One point that some woodworkers find objectionable, however, is that both epoxy and polyurethane develop a yellowish cast with age.

Waxes are often applied to furniture to give a natural, polished look to the piece. In most cases, a few light coats of shellac should be applied to the furniture before waxing. This will provide a good substrate for the wax. The best types of wax for furniture are the paste varieties. Oddly enough, the most popular type of furniture waxes in use today are liquid types. These are probably the worst type to use. I suppose that the popularity of these waxes lies in how easy they are to use. Liquid waxes do not stand up at all to abuse and they require frequent applications. This means a wax buildup that does nothing to enhance your furniture.

Paste wax should be applied with a soft, clean cloth and rubbed with the grain. If your wax surface becomes dirty with age, it can be cleaned with a mild household detergent, followed by a rinsing with a clean, damp cloth. After the piece dries, reapply a new coating of paste wax.

One note of caution about waxes in general is that if you ever plan to refinish the piece of furniture and apply another type of topcoating—such as varnish—know in advance that wax is difficult to remove from furniture. Often some type of special wax stripper must be used to totally remove the old wax. This can be quite a project in itself.

EDGE TREATMENT

A large part of the surface preparation for plywood furniture, which will receive a natural finish of stain

Fig. 4-26. Paste wax forms a soft and pleasant finish on furniture.

137

Fig. 4-27. Edges of a project must be filled.

and clear coating of some type, must concern itself with finishing off the exposed edges of the plywood (Fig. 4-27). Not only are exposed edges aesthetically displeasing, but they also tend to be rough to the touch. Even plywood furniture that will be covered with a primer and solid-color paint must have some type of edge treatment. The most popular methods include filling, covering with some type of wood veneer, and applying some type of wooden inset on the edges.

Filling the exposed edges on a plywood furniture project is a common practice when the piece will be painted a solid color. In many cases, all edges and outside corners are first rounded with a power sander (disk or belt) or a rasplike hand tool.

After all edges have the proper contour, they are filled with some type of wood filler paste. There are a few different types of this filler material available. One brand that I use often is Zar Wood Patch (from United Gilsonite Laboratories). Another brand is Plastic Wood. These products seem to have about the same consistency. Some plywood furniture makers also use joint compound or Spackle. The point is to fill in the edges of the plywood furniture project and, after the filler has dried, sand it smooth.

When filling the edges of a plywood furniture project, there are a few points that can help you to achieve professional-looking and enduring results. Begin by applying the filler paste with a small trowel or putty knife. Pack the paste into indentations and depressions. Generally, areas less than ¼ of an inch wide and deep can usually be patched with one application. Deeper or wider areas are best filled in layers. Allow several hours drying time before applying a second layer. Keep in mind that a thick coating of filler will have a tendency to chip or crumble in time. It is always best to apply only enough filler paste to do the job. Outside corners are always vulnerable to damage in use so it makes sense not to build up much in the way of filler on these surfaces. After the filler paste has dried hard, it must be sanded smooth (Fig. 4-28). This requires a special approach.

When sanding filled edges on plywood furniture, it is important that you strive to create edge surfaces that blend in with the rest of the project. Basically, there are two types of edge treatments: flat or square, and rounded. In either case, you will not want to see any type of seam or joint so you must sand to remove any feathering of these filled edges.

It is usually best to work with a fine grade of abrasive paper when smoothing filled edges on a plywood furniture project. A 220 grit is a good choice because this grade will not leave scratches on the surface as a more coarse grade will. Sand with a light touch to achieve the results that are most pleasing to the eye. You will also find it helpful to use some type of sanding block for this work. If the abrasive paper becomes clogged with filler material, change to a fresh sheet.

If you are planning to apply a natural finish to your plywood furniture project, you will not be satisfied with filled edges. There are several alternate methods of finishing off exposed plywood edges. Generally natural edge treatments involve applying a new face—of a similar wood veneer—to the edge of the plywood (Fig. 4-29). This edge covering can be a thin hardwood strip attached to the face, a veneered face, or a hardwood inset. These types of edge treatments range in difficulty

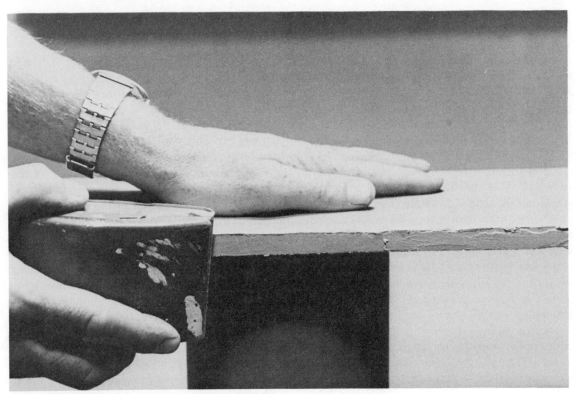

Fig. 4-28. After the filler dries, edges must be sanded flat.

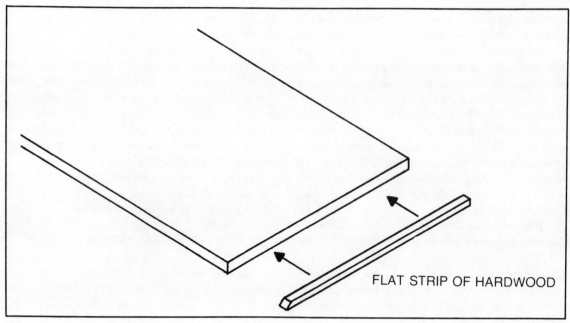

Fig. 4-29. Hardwood strip edge treatment.

from fairly simple for the face strip to rather advanced in the case of hardwood insets.

The simplest of all plywood furniture exposed edge treatment involves attaching strips of hardwood (the same or similar to the face veneer on the plywood) to all edges of the project. Strips can be from ¼ to ½ inch thick and must be the same width as the plywood used for the project.

Strips can be easily obtained by ripping a hardwood board, into the required dimensions, on a table saw. This stationary power tool will enable you to cut the strips accurately. The strips can be attached with thin wire brads, adhesive, or a combination of the two. This edge covering lends itself to a number of joints where the strips meet on the face of the project. The possibilities include simple butt joints, mitered joints or, if you have the skills required, some type of intricate joint such as dovetailed joint.

Covering the exposed edges of a plywood furniture project results in an attractive finish for the project. This is fairly easy to accomplish with common woodworking tools. In addition, if the existing

edges were not cut precisely, the strips of hardwood tend to mask this fault very well.

Similar edge treatment uses ½ or ¾ round wooden molding over all exposed edges on the project. Softwood molding of this type is widely available in a variety of widths. Hardwood ½ and ¾ moldings are sometimes a bit difficult to find, but they are probably worth the extra effort because they tend to look better when finished properly. Molding is attached in the same manner as the hardwood strips described earlier—wire brads, adhesive, or a combination of the two. See Fig. 4-30.

Moving up in difficulty, the next type of exposed edge treatment involves attaching strips of hardwood veneer to the edges of the plywood furniture project. Hardwood veneer is available in strip form. It measures from 1 to about 4 inches in width. Strip veneer is designed for finishing off the edges of plywood and is applied in a manner that is similar to the tape. The existing edges must be flat and square for best results. Don't expect to cover any cutting errors with this material. It is a common practice to use contact cement for attaching the strips of veneer to the edges of the project.

Once the strips have been secured in this manner, they are trimmed to blend in well. This can be done with a hand veneer saw, X-Acto knife or special veneer trimmer bit in a hand-held router. Because all veneer work requires a lot of conscientious effort, this is not generally a good method of edge treatment for the casual woodworker. Nevertheless, when done correctly, veneering is an excellent way to finish off the edges of a plywood furniture project and is used widely in the furniture industry. See Fig. 4-31.

Probably the most difficult of all edged treatments for a plywood furniture project involves insetting a strip of hardwood in such a manner that it appears to be part of the wood rather than a piece that was added. In many cases, this type of edge treatment is used on the more expensive commercially made furniture.

As you can see in Fig. 4-32, there are a number of ways of insetting hardwood strips into the edges of a plywood furniture project. The simpliest of these begins by making a bevel cut on the edge of

the plywood—before the project is assembled— and making a similar cut on a strip of hardwood. In most cases, it is easier to finish off the edges of the pieces of plywood before the project is assembled. This type of cutting can be easily accomplished on a good table saw. The beveled strip is attached to the beveled edge of the plywood with a good liquid adhesive—such as Elmer's Professional Carpenter's Glue. Clamps should be used to hold the strip in place until the glue sets up or fine wire brads can be used.

The angle cut to the edge of a piece of plywood is also possible on a table saw. You must plan and measure carefully if you want to make this edge come out properly. When this edge treatment is done with enough care (in both planning and cutting), it will be almost impossible to see the joint between the strip and the plywood.

Probably the most difficult of all plywood furniture edge treatments is the tongue-and-groove insert. This is a good exercise in the use of power tools; all cuts must be made with precision. The cuts can be made on a table saw or with a router. Some type of guidance system must be used.

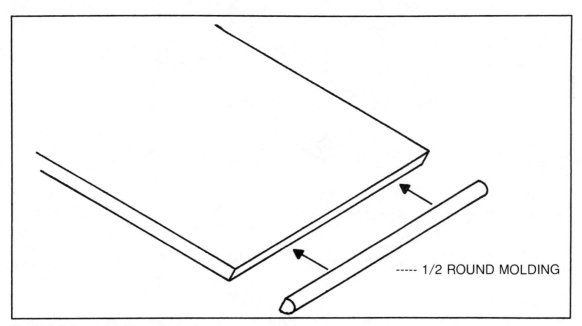

----- 1/2 ROUND MOLDING

Fig. 4-30. Half-round molding edge treatment.

Fig. 4-31. Veneer-edge treatment.

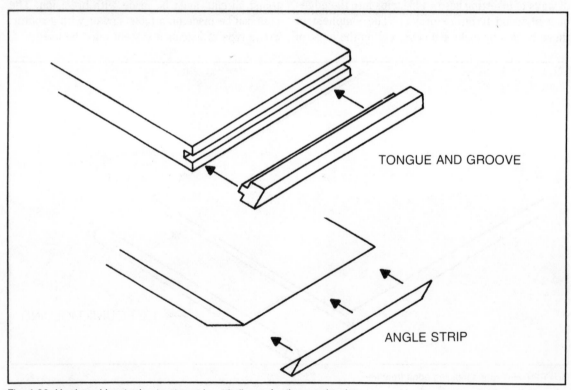

TONGUE AND GROOVE

ANGLE STRIP

Fig. 4-32. Hardwood inset edge treatment is a challenge for the woodworker.

Hardwood edging on plywood furniture is distinctive and will add a special custom look to the piece. Often the entire piece of furniture is stained then given several coats of a clear finish. Polyurethane is a popular choice because it stands up very well to wear and actually seems to add a bit of overall strength to the project.

SURFACE PREPARATION

Before you even think about applying a finish coating to your plywood furniture project, there are a number of things that must be done to ensure that the surface is in good shape. Because the project has been constructed with new materials, most of the surface preparation will involve sanding the surfaces after they have been filled, sealed, and received some type of edge treatment. The amount of energy you expend in preparing the surface will directly effect how the finished project looks and endures.

Something must be done with all exposed edges on a plywood furniture project. In addition, the entire project must be sanded so that it is smooth and ready to accept an application of stain, followed by several light coatings of a clear finish. If the project will be painted, you will also probably want to use a paste-type filler for both edge treat-

ment and overall uniformity. All areas that have had such a treatment must, of course, be sanded so the filler will not be visible after painting. Dents and scratches on the surface veneer of the plywood can also be patched or filled in this manner. If you are planning to apply a stain to the project, you can reasonably expect this to mask small patches, providing that the area has been sanded well.

Another part of surface preparation is the removal of any glue that has oozed out during the assembly stage. As a rule, you should not sand off excess glue because this will force the glue into the pores of the wood. This would have a sealing effect on the wood. Once wood has been sealed, it will not take a stain. Instead it will remain the original color or tone of the wood. Remember, sealers are applied after the wood has been stained. The best technique for removing excess glue on the surface of a plywood furniture project is to use a sharp knife or wood chisel (Fig. 4-33).

Surely the best time to remove excess glue is during the construction phase of the project. If you fail to do this, then you must remove the excess glue before a stain or clear coating is applied. When working with a sharp tool, you must be careful only to remove the hardened glue and not any of the face veneer. Usually this is a simple task, but you must

Fig. 4-33. Excess hardened glue is removed with a chisel and then sanded.

nevertheless work carefully so as not to damage the project. After the glue has been removed, you should also lightly sand the area to make it blend in well with the rest of the piece of furniture.

The next step in surface preparation is to sand, sand, sand. In addition to edges and joints, you will also have to sand all other surfaces of the piece of plywood furniture. Your goal should be to achieve as flat and smooth a surface as possible. You will be able to do this by sanding with the grain and working with finer grades of sandpaper until you are working with extra-fine paper. A sanding block works well for small areas, but you will find the work to go much quicker if you use an electric sander. In any event, the last sanding should be done by hand with a paper of about 220 grit. When all of the sanding has been completed, vacuum the surface to remove all traces of the dust created by the sanding.

Before painting you might want to cover certain areas of the project such as a plastic laminate top. Masking tape and newspaper are handy for this type of masking.

Apply a filler, sealer or primer as discussed previously in this chapter. A filler is used for surface veneer with large pores, sealer is used for closed-pore woods, and a primer is used for all bare wood surfaces that will later receive a coat of paint.

If you are planning to apply a stain to the furniture, this should be done after the filler, but before the sealer has been applied. As an alternative, consider using a combination stain/sealer. These are generally available, they will save a lot of time, and the overall results are about the same as if you applied a stain and then applied a sealer.

If you have built a plywood cabinet, the interior should be primed and painted before you start on the exterior of the unit. Interiors can be painted almost any color, but white, semigloss enamel is one of the better choices. This light color will help to provide reflected light inside the cabinet and make finding things easier.

Before actually applying the finish coating on your plywood furniture project, there are several things you should be certain about. If you are applying a solid-color paint, you should first apply some type of primer, fill all edges, nail holes, and

dents, and the primer must be dry. All surfaces should be flat and level and there should be no excess primer (this usually shows up as running globs). If the piece of furniture has any areas that are not in this condition, now is the time to correct them. In most cases, a sanding with a fine-grit sandpaper will be all that is necessary.

You should make certain that the surface is free from dust, moisture and, anything else that would have an effect on the finish coat. You may find a tack cloth helpful for cleaning the surface just prior to applying a final finish coating of either paint or clear finish. A tack cloth is a specially treated cloth, sold at all paint and hardware stores, which when wiped across the surface will pick up dust or loose dirt particles.

You can very easily make your own tack cloth in a few minutes. A tack cloth is simply a piece of cotton cloth about 1 × 2 feet in size. Half of an old pillow case is ideal, but it must be clean to begin with. To make a tack cloth, start off by washing the material in soap and water. Rinse the cloth, making sure to remove all soap residue, and then wring it out until it is almost dry. Next, pour about two ounces of turpentine into the cloth and work in until it is evenly distributed. Wring it dry once again. Pour about the same amount of varnish into the cloth and work it in thoroughly. The tack cloth is ready for use when it has an overall yellowish cast. See Fig. 4-34.

As the name implies, a tack cloth must remain tacky during use. If it should become dry as you use it to pick up dust, you can easily rejuvenate it by adding small amounts of turpentine and water to keep it damp. If the cloth is too damp, hang it to dry slightly. A tack cloth will last for a long time if you store it in a sealed glass container when not in use (Fig. 4-35).

After you have wiped the surface of your plywood furniture project with a tack cloth, it will be ready for a coating of either paint or clear finish. Solid-color paint should be applied to your project with a clean brush (Fig. 4-36). Begin working on the verticle surfaces first. Brush the paint out evenly and not too thickly. Next, all horizontal surfaces are coated in the same manner. Begin working at the

Fig. 4-34. Pour a small amount of turpentine into a clean cloth to make a tack cloth.

Fig. 4-35. A tack cloth can be stored in a glass jar.

Fig. 4-36. Apply all paints and clear coatings from the top down (courtesy American Plywood Association).

high point and brush downward. This painting action will tend to minimize runs as well as help you to apply the paint uniformly.

Brush work is important while painting. You must paint with even pressure and always with the grain of the wood. Do not try to get the job done with one heavy coat but, instead plan to give the project several light coats. This will enable the paint to dry properly and assure that the coverage is uniform.

Varnish and other clear coatings (Fig. 4-37) are a little more difficult to apply than solid-color paints. Surface preparation is basically the same. The first coat of varnish should be applied directly from the can (after stirring the contents well). It is never a good practice to shake clear coatings before

use as this action tends to create air bubbles in the finish.

Applying varnish from the middle of the surface toward the sides and from one side toward another are just two techniques that generally give good results. Your best bet is to start in one area and brush varnish out in slow, even strokes. The brush itself should hold a sufficient amount of varnish to cover an area before dipping it into the can of varnish again. Never pour varnish or any other clear coating onto the surface and brush out. This practice always leads to areas that have a greater layer of varnish than others. See Fig. 4-38.

It is important to brush out varnish so it covers the surface uniformly. Most professionals will tell

Fig. 4-37. Always stir clear coatings. Never shake them or you will create air bubbles in the thick liquid.

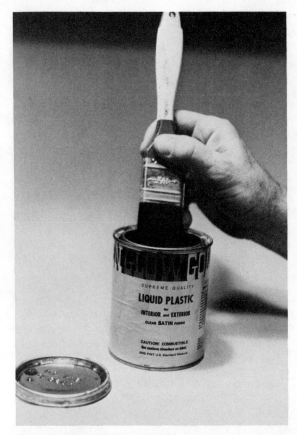

Fig. 4-38. Dip brush into varnish.

length of wooden dowel with a sharply pointed end.

Brush control is very important when applying clear coatings. Some experts suggest that only the bottom third of the brush should be used for applying the coating and stroking pressure should be light. Brush smoothly and slowly to reduce the chances of producing air bubbles in the finish. Sometimes air bubbles will break and not be a problem. More often than not, the bubbles will not break until the varnish has started to harden. This causes depressions and craters on the surface of the finish. These must be sanded before the next coating is applied.

Edges that are perpendicular to a surface, such as the edges of a table, present a bit of a problem that must be taken into consideration when applying a clear coating or a solid-color paint. If you were to brush from the center of the surface out to the edges, and then lift the brush or bring the brush past the edge, you would create an excess of the coating along this edge. If this excess is allowed to dry, the surface coating would be thicker around the edges than in the middle. This type of coating buildup must be avoided or corrected if it is present.

The recommended technique for avoiding excess coating buildup around the edges of a piece of furniture is to brush the coating close to the edge—say within 2 inches. Then while still brushing, lift the brush upward so there is almost no pressure on the bristles. This action will not deposit an excess of the coating around the edge of the piece of furniture. Keep an eye out for this potential buildup problem. Correct it by brushing the excess coating with a dry brush. This will remove the buildup along the edge as will brushing the coating back toward the middle of the surface. See Fig. 4-39.

Once you have completely covered the plywood furniture piece with paint or clear coating, check the work to make sure everything is right and then leave the area. This is the best way to prevent you from disturbing the coating or from getting dust or other airborne material on the surface. While there might be some areas that have problems—such as air bubbles or other coating imperfections—it is usually best to leave these things

you that varnish is easiest to apply on a horizontal surface. You should work in this manner even if it means tipping the piece of furniture on end so that the surface you are working on is in the horizontal position. This will give the best results. Working on verticle surfaces always lends itself to running varnish and thinner coverage at the top than at the bottom.

Once a surface has been coated with varnish, stop and look over the work. You will almost always find areas that did not receive good coverage. You can easily spot these by looking at the surface from different angles. Touch up these areas when you spot them. You should also look for specks of dust or bristles that have fallen out of your brush. You can usually pick these surface floaters off with the tips of your paint brush or you can try using a pointed stick. A pointed stick need be nothing more than a until you can correct the problems with sandpaper after the coating has dried. Because a light sanding is usually required between coats, especially for clear coatings and enamel paints, you can correct problems at that time. It is always a good practice to let the coating dry undisturbed for a few hours to minimize dust in the area.

Before a second coating is applied, all enamels and varnishes should be sanded lightly. The reasons for this are to correct any mistakes in the first coating and to rough up the surface slightly so the second coat will have a good adhesion base.

You will achieve the best sanding results by using a sanding block and very fine abrasive paper (220 grit) when sanding between coats of enamel or varnish. As you move the block over the surface, it is important to remove all peaks that are caused by dust specks. Depressions that are the result of air bubbles must also be leveled, and this requires a little pressure on the sanding block (Fig. 4-40). It is important to check the abrasive paper often. If it becomes clogged, replace it with new paper.

After you have completely sanded all surfaces on your plywood furniture project, you must remove all of the dust created by the sanding. A vacuum cleaner and tack cloth will help with this task. It is important to remove all traces of dust or it will end up in the next coating. The second coating is applied with the same caution and technique used for the first coat.

After the second coating has dried, you can either consider the plywood furniture project complete or sand and apply a third coat. In most cases, two coatings will be sufficient, but three coats will offer greater protection. More than three coats of most clear finishes will tend to hide the natural look of the wood underneath.

A selection (Fig. 4-41) of quality paint brushes, 1-inch, 2-inch, and 4-inch brushes, to be used only for interior painting projects is a good investment for the do-it-yourselfer. In your paint box you should have both natural-bristle and synthetic-fiber brushes. The former are required for varnish and other clear coatings and the latter are required for latex based paints.

If you plan on doing much furniture painting,

Fig. 4-39. Lift the brush as you near the edge of the project.

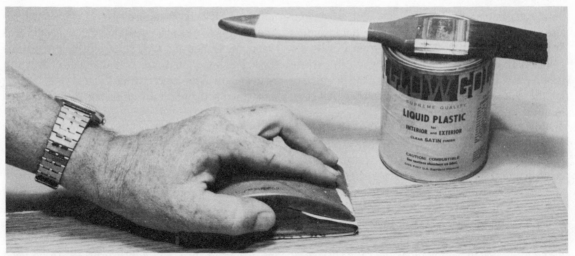

Fig. 4-40. Sand lightly between coats to create a base with some tooth.

Fig. 4-41. A selection of good brushes is essential for good finish work.

Fig. 4-42. Punch holes in rim of the can so excess can drip back into can. This will also make it easy to get the lid back on the container.

try to designate one area of your workshop as a painting area. Such a place should be kept as free of dust as possible. You should also provide plenty of lighting so you can clearly see during a painting task.

Try to wear synthetic clothing when painting because it is less prone to give off dust and lint. Wool clothing is probably the worst choice of clothing to wear when painting because it has a tendency to pick up foreign matter and deposit it at random over the area you are painting.

To reduce the glossy effect—which some people find offensive—of enamels and varnish, apply a good paste wax to the surface. Apply several coatings of the wax—buffing between. The wax will add a soft cast to the coating and make it more pleasing to look at. Wax can be applied over any type of paint or clear topcoat.

When you first open a can of varnish or paint, the first thing you should do before actually starting to paint is to punch holes around the rim of the can with a hammer and nail (Fig. 4-42). This small act will enable you to wipe the edge of your brush off—after dipping in the coating—without fear of filling up the rim of the can. The holes enable this liquid to drip back into the can. Also, you will be able to replace the lid with little problem.

Aside from these tips the only other thing that will help you to apply paint and clear coatings is experience. Once you become familiar with a paint brush and paints in general you will have a better understanding of how much pressure is required on a brush, how to cover a surface properly, and how to achieve professional-looking results.

When a clear finish or solid-paint coating is applied properly, your plywood furniture project will look good. In all cases, you must exercise a lot of care because many a seemingly perfect piece of furniture has been almost ruined by a shoddy finish. Take the time to finish your plywood furniture project properly and you will truly have something you can be proud of.

Chapter 5

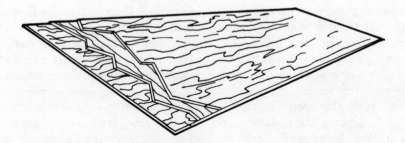

Adhesives, Joints, Fasteners, and Hardware

PLYWOOD FURNITURE CAN BE ASSEMBLED with adhesives, nails, screws, and special wood joints or a combination of these. The type of plywood project, its function, size, ultimate use, and your ability to work with woodworking tools will all have a bearing on the way you assemble your plywood furniture. Some projects lend themselves to simple joints while others require a special (and very strong) joint for long-lasting success.

This chapter includes descriptions of the major woodworking joints that are commonly used for plywood furniture. There is also a look at several construction techniques, adhesives, clamps and other fasteners. This information will help you choose the construction methods or combination of methods that are right for your plywood projects.

ADHESIVES

A quick glance at the shelves stacked with different types of adhesives in a lumber yard or home improvement center is easily enough to confuse even an experienced woodworker. There are white

glues, different resin glues, hot-melt glue, super-strength glue, panel adhesive, epoxy, mastic, and contact cement. To add to the overall confusion, glue is sold in powder, paste, or liquid forms, and in tubes that resemble caulking. As you might have guessed, many of these adhesives are designed for special joining tasks and cannot be considered, in any way, all-purpose glues. See Fig. 5-1. Descriptions of the most common and useful adhesives for plywood furniture construction follow.

Polyvinyl Resin

Polyvinyl resin, commonly known as white glue, is one of the most popular adhesives around the workshop and home. It is ideal for general-purpose wood joining. It is available in a variety of sizes from 1-ounce squeeze tubes to 5-gallon bulk packs. White glue can be applied over a wide range of temperatures with success. It usually sets up in about two hours. It is a poor choice, however, if the project will be exposed to moisture or if great strength is required.

Fig. 5-1. There are several suitable adhesives for plywood furniture projects.

Aliphatic Resin

Aliphatic resin is one of the strongest and probably the best choice for an adhesive for a plywood furniture project, providing that the project will not be exposed to high moisture levels. Aliphatic resin is excellent for projects with less than perfect joints because it has very good gap-filling capabilities. It is easy to work with because it does not set up very fast and it can be used at temperatures as low as 45 degrees Fahrenheit. Mating surfaces should be given a light coat of this adhesive, fitted, and then clamped until the glue sets up—usually in about two hours. Once hardened, excess glue can be easily sanded off. Aliphatic resin is nonstaining.

Plastic Resin

If the plywood furniture project you are constructing requires a water-resistant adhesive, a plastic resin is a good choice. This adhesive is more dif-ficult to work with than aliphatic resin, but it has some desirable features nevertheless. This is a good general-purpose adhesive for use in the woodworking shop, providing the project has tight-fitting joints. It is difficult to work with because it requires an ambient temperature of at least 70 degrees Fahrenheit. The glued project must also sit undisturbed for around 16 hours for best results. Clamping is also usually required during this period.

Resorcinol Glue

If your plywood furniture project requires a water-proof glue, this is the best choice. This is an extremely strong resin-type adhesive that is fully waterproof and ideal for plywood furniture projects. It has very good gap-filling capability. Less than perfect joints can benefit from its use. It must be used at temperatures of at least 70 degrees

Fahrenheit both during application and setup, which takes about 16 hours. Resorcinol resin is only available in powdered form and it must be mixed just prior to use. Pot life—the amount of time the mixed adhesive will remain workable and usable—is approximately 4 hours. To use this excellent adhesive, mating surfaces are given a light coating, fitted, and then clamped until the adhesive sets up.

Hide Glue

Hide glue is one of the oldest adhesives known to man. As the name suggests, it is made from animal hides, hooves, horns, and bones. Hide glue has been used for hundreds of years for making cabinetry, furniture, and even bamboo fishing rods. It is very strong (although not as strong as some of the resin adhesives), it has excellent gap-filling capabilities, and it does not become brittle.

Hide glue will fail if it is exposed to moisture. Therefore it is a poor choice for those projects having water resistance as a requirement. It is commonly applied in liquid form (usually a con-

tainer of hide glue is set in a pan of warm water) to both surfaces and allowed to dry to the tacky stage before assembly. Setup time is around 4 hours. During that time the project should be clamped.

Casin Glue

This is a strong, general-purpose glue that is made from milk. It is reasonably water-resistant adhesive with good gap-filling properties. It can be used at any temperature above freezing. Available only in powdered form, casin glue must be mixed just prior to use. It is always best to mix up only enough of this glue to take care of your immediate needs because the pot life is rather short. Setup time is less than 4 hours under moderated temperatures. Clamping is necessary during this period.

Hot-Melt Glue

Generally, hot-melt glues are ideal for small projects where the pieces can be assembled quickly. As soon as the hot glue is applied, it starts to cool and harden (Fig. 5-2). It has good gap-filling cap-

Fig. 5-2. Hot melt glue has limited application for plywood furniture.

abilities, but it is not generally as strong as other types of glue. As a rule, hot melt glues are not a good choice for plywood furniture projects.

Contact Cement

Contact cement is used for attaching plastic laminate and true wood veneer to plywood furniture. Contact cement is available in water-base (Fig. 5-3) and solvent-base formulations. It is important to check the container label because some contact cement is highly flammable, others are toxic, and still others are very safe to use. Because all contact cements tend to be about the same, most experts seem to agree that the nontoxic, water-base varieties are the safest for the home woodworker to use.

Panel Adhesive

Panel adhesives are commonly sold in caulking gun tubes. They are designed for attaching wall paneling to interior walls. Generally, this type of adhesive and the stronger construction adhesives that are also sold in tubes are not suitable for plywood furniture projects.

Super-Strength Glue

Super-strength adhesives are very expensive and they are designed for small, precise gluing tasks. As a rule, the high cost of this adhesive makes it unsuitable for use during the construction phase of a plywood furniture project. It is probably safe to say that the real value of super-strength glues lies in making small repairs on both porous and nonporous materials.

WOOD JOINTS

There are several types of wood joints that are generally used in the construction of plywood furniture. Some are very simple, but effective, while others are complex and an exercise in working with power and hand tools. As a rule, the more involved a woodworking joint the stronger it tends to be.

Butt Joint

The simpliest of all woodworking joints is the *butt joint*. Butt joints are made by placing two ends of plywood together (Fig. 5-4) and fastening them with glue and nails or screws. While this is certainly not the strongest of all wood joints, it is a good choice for many types of plywood furniture. Some of the real advantages of the butt joint are that it is very easy to make, it is reasonably strong, and if the joining pieces are cut true, it is almost foolproof. A butt joint need not necessarily be used only on the

Fig. 5-3. Contact cement is the best choice for attaching plastic laminate.

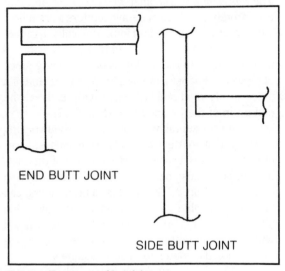

END BUTT JOINT

SIDE BUTT JOINT

Fig. 5-4. Two types of butt joints.

end of a plywood furniture project. For example, internal shelving can be attached with the butt joint.

Success in making the simple butt joint is largely dependent on having true edges on the mating surfaces of the pieces. A table saw or hand-held circular saw—used with some type of guidance system—will help you to achieve square and true edges on pieces of plywood that are used for the butt joint. Also keep in mind that a few drops of adhesive along both mating surfaces will add strength to this joint. Most butt joints are also nailed or screwed to keep the pieces aligned as the adhesive sets and to add strength.

If you plan to use either nails or screws when making a butt joint, remember that the heads of these fasteners must be concealed. Generally, this can be accomplished by countersinking the nail or screw head, and then filling the depression with a suitable paste-type filler material. One alternative to this type of fastener-head concealment is to use filler plugs of wooden dowel. These plugs are given a light coat of glue, inserted in the hole over the fastener head and then, after the glue has set up, they are sanded flush with the face of the plywood. See Figs 5-5 through 5-10.

Rabbet Joint

The *rabbet joint* is a popular woodworking joint that is relatively simple to make and it offers a great deal more strength than the butt joint. Basically, a rabbet joint is constructed by removing a section of plywood equal to the thickness of the joining piece of plywood. Rabbet joints are made on one end of a piece of plywood and will effectively conceal the end grain of the joining piece (Fig. 5-11).

A successful rabbet joint (or any woodworking joint for that matter) depends on having square-ended pieces. Because a section of one of the mating surfaces must be removed, great accuracy in cutting is required. The section to be removed can be cut on a table saw or a radial-arm saw. One alternative to this is to use a hand-held router fitted with a straight cutter. Use some type of guidance system for the router to ensure accuracy.

Rabbet joints are always glued and sometimes nailed or screwed. If glue alone is used, the joint

must be clamped until the glue sets up. If nails or screws are used, they should be driven through an edge that will be concealed or the exposed heads should be countersunk, filled, and sanded flush with the face of the project.

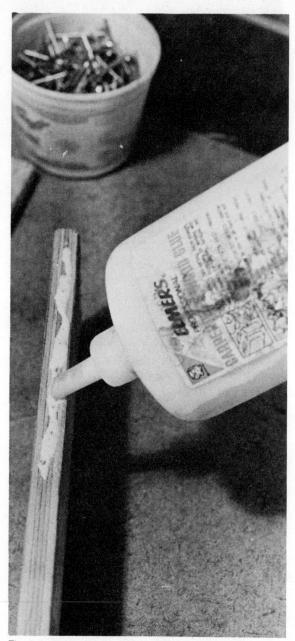

Fig. 5-5. Apply glue to mating surfaces of butt joint.

Fig. 5-6. Nails are added to butt joint.

The *edge rabbet joint* is a very good joint for concealing one edge of a plywood furniture project (Fig. 5-12). This is a very strong joint. To make this joint, mating edges of a project are cut along the entire mating surface to a depth of approximately one-half of their thickness. Usually both edges are rabbet cut before the project is assembled. When the pieces are assembled, one of the edges will be completely concealed from sight. This long joint requires more than a casual approach for success. A table or radial-arm saw is a real aid for this joint.

The *double rabbet joint* is similiar to the edge joint except that it is made on the edges of the project rather than on the long sides (Fig. 5-13). It is a very strong woodworking joint that offers concealment of one entire edge of the two mating surfaces.

The *back panel rabbet joint* is used when a back panel will be installed on a plywood furniture project. An example is the back of a bookcase. To make this joint, a rabbet cut is made all the way around the interior edges of a project—a box for example. The depth of the cut is equal to the thickness of the back panel. In most cases, it is ¼ of an inch.

Not only must great care be exercised in making this cut, but the panel itself must be cut out precisely. It is common practice to make the rabbet

Fig. 5-7. Countersink nail heads.

Fig. 5-8. Nail holes are filled.

Fig. 5-9. Filled nail holes are sanded flush.

Fig. 5-10. Small pieces of dowel can also be used for filling nail and screw holes.

cut on all pieces of the project before it is assembled, rather than attempt cutting after the pieces have been fastened together. The back panel rabbet joint is probably the best choice for adding a concealed back panel to a plywood furniture project.

Dado Joint

Dado joints are similiar to rabbet joints, but they are not made on the edge of a project. Dado joints are used commonly for internal shelving where the shelves themselves are in a permanent position (Fig. 5-15). The simple dado joint consists of a groove that is commonly cut out of the vertical members of the unit and a shelf that has not received any type of treatment other than being cut square and precise. As you might have guessed, dado joints add great strength to a project. They

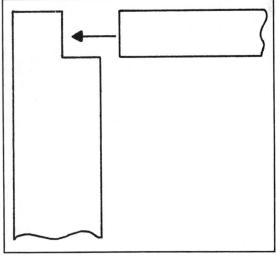

Fig. 5-11. Rabbet joint.

159

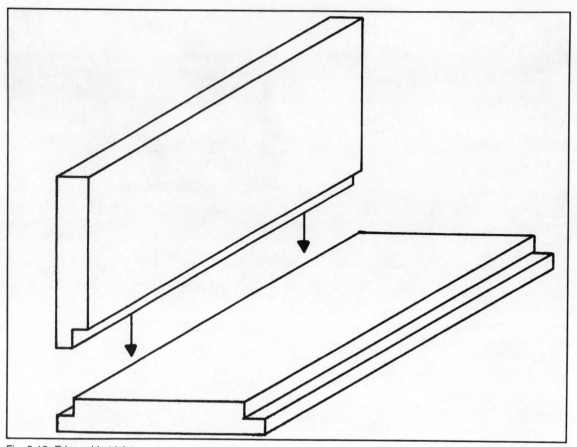

Fig. 5-12. Edge rabbet joint.

also add a professional-looking touch to book-shelves and cabinets.

Many so-called woodworking experts suggest that the table saw is probably the best way to make a dado cut, providing that a special dado blade is used for the task. I have found that a router with a straight cutter does the job a lot quicker (Fig. 5-16). In addition, if you are working with large sections of plywood, it is far easier to work on top of the piece, as with a router, than to try to maneuver the sheet on a table saw. Still another point in favor of a router is that the straight bit costs only a few dollars, even with a carbide tip, while a quality dado blade costs in the neighborhood of $50.

In addition to the basic dado joint, there are two other variations that might be of use to you. These are the *dado/rabbet* and the *stop dado joint*.

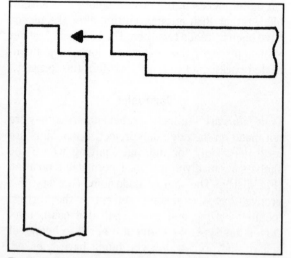

Fig. 5-13. Double rabbet joint.

Fig. 5-14. Back panel rabbet joint.

Fig. 5-15. Dado joints are strong.

Fig. 5-16. A router can be used to make a dado joint.

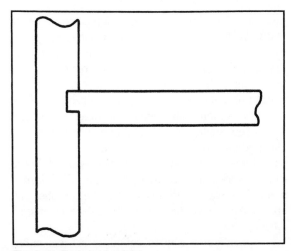

Fig. 5-17. Dado/rabbet joint.

Both of these joints require a bit of extra work, but they also offer a more professional-looking joint in the bargain.

The dado/rabbet joint (Fig. 5-17) is a combination of the dado and rabbet woodworking joints.

Perhaps an example will help to describe this joint. Assume that you are building a bookcase with internal shelves. After you have determined the spacing for each shelf, you will make a dado cut on the vertical sides of the bookcase, but only to a thickness of one-half of the thickness of the shelf. Then you will make a rabbet cut on both ends of each shelf equal to the thickness of the dado cut made previously. This should also be one-half the thickness of the shelf.

The stop dado (Fig. 5-18) woodworking joint also requires working on both the shelf and vertical sides of a bookcase, but it results in a concealed edge joint for the shelf. To make this woodworking joint, a dado is cut from the back edge of the workpiece and stops at least 1 inch from the forward edge. Next, the shelf is notched to fit exactly inside the dado. When the shelf is inserted into the dado cut (from the rear), the joint between the shelf and the vertical upright of the bookcase will not be visible. It is usually necessary to do a little chisel work to the inside of the dado cut to make it square.

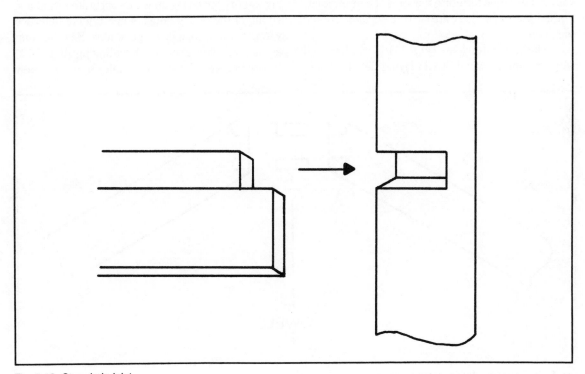

Fig. 5-18. Stop dado joint.

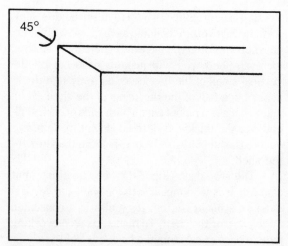

Fig. 5-19. Flat miter joint.

Or you can use a router to make the inside of the dado front edge square.

Miter Joints

Another useful woodworking joint for the do-it-yourself plywood furniture maker is the miter joint. For our purposes, there are two types: *flat miter* and *edge miter*.

The flat miter joint (Fig. 5-19) can be used when joining plywood that is laying flat. Probably the best example of this joint is a picture frame. If you were making doors for a plywood cabinet, for example, this is one possible woodworking joint that you could use. While the flat miter joint looks very simple, it requires very accurate layout and cutting to make it look and perform properly. In a typical miter joint, the edges to be joined are cut at a 45-degree angle, and then commonly glued and clamped until the adhesive sets up. Generally, the basic miter joint is not a strong one by itself, but it can be made stronger by some type of reinforcement. One way to do this is to make a rabbet cut around the inside edges of the workpiece and install a backpanel.

Still another way to reinforce a basic miter joint is to drill holes in the joint and install wooden dowels. The use of dowels in the basic miter joint assumes that the plywood stock you are working with is of a thickness that will accommodate dowels. In most cases, this means that the plywood must be at least three-fourths of an inch thick. Because the success of the doweled miter joint (Fig. 5-20) depends so much on accurate layout and drilling of the dowel holes, some type of guidance system is more than just a good idea. Several companies now offer a special doweling jig (Fig. 5-21) for this purpose. They are simple to use and they

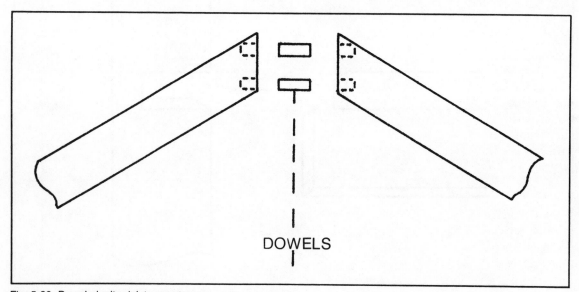

DOWELS

Fig. 5-20. Doweled miter joints are strong.

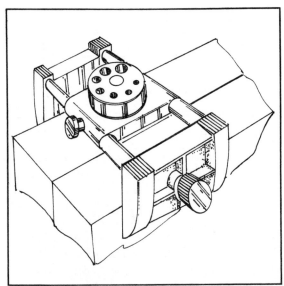

Fig. 5-21. A doweling jig is a real aid for making doweled joints.

equal parts of plywood from the mating surfaces of a project. When the two pieces are then fitted together, the resulting thickness will be equal to one of the pieces. Success in making a lap joint depends a great deal on planning, accurate layout, and precise cutting. It is important that the mating pieces fit together snuggly for appearance and strength. Stationary power tools such as table saw or radial-arm saw will help you make accurate cuts in plywood. A hand-held router, fitted with a straight cutter and used with some type of guidance system, can also be used for making lap joints.

will enable you to make perfect doweled miter joints everytime.

The edge miter joint (Fig. 5-22) is used for joining the edges of a piece of plywood furniture. This joint is relatively strong and effectively conceals the edges of the plywood. Basically, all an edge miter requires is careful cutting of the edges of mating surfaces. This is best accomplished on a good table saw. This is a good edge joint to use for the cube, box, and cabinet projects described in the following chapters.

There are a number of other more complex miter joints that are used in woodworking, but as a rule these are not generally suitable for working with plywood. The main reason that many of these miter joints are not suitable is that they require wood stock of at least 1 inch thick to be made properly.

Lap Joints

Generally, *lap joints* are not used often when constructing plywood furniture but, there are a few instances where this simple joint comes in very handy. An example is when you must fit several components of functional plywood furniture.

A lap joint (Fig. 5-23) is made by removing

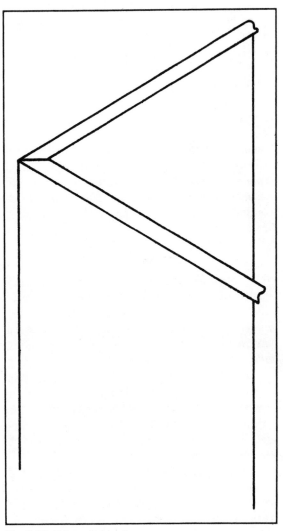

Fig. 5-22. Edge miter joint.

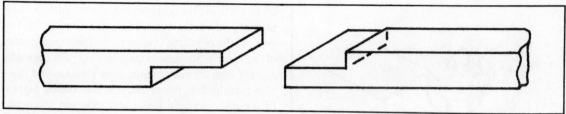

Fig. 5-23. Lap joint.

One lap joint that is useful in plywood furniture making, particularly bookcases and shelves, is the *edge cross lap joint*. With this lap joint, equal parts are removed from two pieces to be joined. Then the pieces are fitted together for a very strong and attractive joint (Fig. 5-24).

PLYWOOD FASTENERS

Although all plywood furniture projects use adhesive during the assembly stage, it is also usually desirable to use some type of metal fastener as well. Some of these fasteners are rather specialized in application. Others such as screws and nails can easily be used for a wide variety of joining tasks. As a rule, some type of fastener is used to add strength to a plywood furniture project because some woodworking joints do not offer a great deal of strength when simply glued.

Nails

While not all nails are suitable for plywood furniture construction, there are a few types that can be used with success. These include *casing* and *finish nails, thin-wire nails* (often called *wire brads*) and, special purpose nails such as *ring-shank* or *annular-shank nails*.

The casing nail (Fig. 5-25) is used for finish work in general carpentry. The head of this nail is commonly countersunk. The head of a casing nail is small, it has tapered sides and it has a flat face. It is used where light weight is required along with maximum strength.

The finishing nail (Fig. 5-26) is similiar to the casing nail, but it is made from thinner wire and has a rather rounded-appearing head. Finishing nails are used in finish carpentry work to attach moldings and trim on interior surfaces. Exterior finishing

nails are also available in a galvanized version.

Casing and finish nails are available in a wide range of sizes from about 1 inch in length (#4) to over four inches long (#10 and #12). Bright steel nails of either type are used for interior applications where rust is not a consideration. For exterior projects or where moisture might be present at times, hot-dipped galvanized casing or finish nails are a better choice.

Casing and finish nails are commonly countersunk when used on plywood furniture. The head of

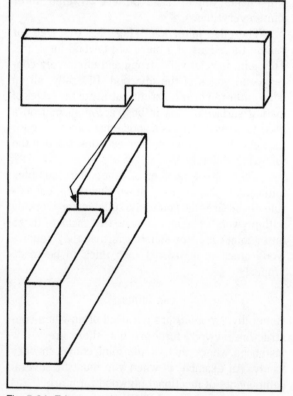

Fig. 5-24. Edge cross lap joint.

Fig. 5-25. Casing nail.

the nail is driven below the surface, with a nail set (Fig. 5-27), and the resulting depression is filled with putty. Then the filler is sanded flush with the surface of the project and finished in the preferred manner using stain and clear finish or a solid-paint coating.

Wire brads (Fig. 5-28) are also used often in plywood furniture construction, largely for attaching the back to a cabinet or bookcase. Wire brads are actually a mini version of a casing or finish nail, having a small head which can be easily countersunk. Wire brads tend to be difficult to work with because of their size. Often this type of nailing can be made easier if the brad is held with a pair of needle nose pliers to start.

Many innovative do-it-yourselfers now use

Fig. 5-26. Finish nails.

Fig. 5-27. A nail set and hammer are the tools used for countersinking nail heads.

Fig. 5-28. Wire brads.

Fig. 5-29. A staple gun is useful for attaching the back to the cabinet.

staples in place of conventional wire brads. With a good staple gun (Fig. 5-29), it is entirely possible to substitute wire staples for wire brads. Wire staples are easier to use and actually hold better than a single wire brad. You could use wire staples for attaching the back to a cabinet or bookcase.

Ring or *annular shank nails* (Fig. 5-30) have become popular with woodworkers and professional carpenters over the past 10 years or so. A large part of this attraction is because these special nails have a holding power that is far greater than a conventional nail of the same shank diameter and length. This superior holding power can be put to good use when you are concerned about strength in your plywood furniture project.

One problem with using these strong nails is that, to my knowledge, they are not available with casing or finish nail heads. Instead. all annular or ring shank nails have a common or box head that can be difficult to countersink. In most cases, however, these wide nail heads can be countersunk with a large punch and then filled.

If you are working on a plywood furniture project that will be finished by painting with a solid-color paint, this approach should prove quite suitable. If you are planning to finish off the project with a stain and clear coating, you might not be totally satisfied with the large filled nail holes. In this case, it would probably be better to use either casing or finish nails as fasteners.

Screws

As a rule, screws have much greater holding power than nails. A possible exception is annular or ring-shanked nails. Screws are probably the best fastener choice when you are building plywood furniture that will be subjected to a lot of stress and strain. A plywood chair is one example. Another good reason for using screws is that the piece of furniture can be disassembled—providing that no glue was used during construction—for ease of moving.

The use of screws in a plywood furniture project means a bit more work for the do-it-yourselfer. Screw holes must be located and drilled on the project, the screws must each be carefully screwed into place (and commonly countersunk), and then the hole that results must be filled, sanded flush, and either stained and covered with a clear coating or painted with a solid-color paint. These extra operations can add considerable time to the project, and especially if a large number of screws are required.

Because wood screws are commonly countersunk (Fig. 5-31), you can save a considerable amount of time by drilling all of your screw holes with a special countersink drill bit rather than drilling two holes: one for the screw shank and another for the wider screw head.

The better countersink drill bits (Fig. 5-32) are available in a range of sizes that will enable you to

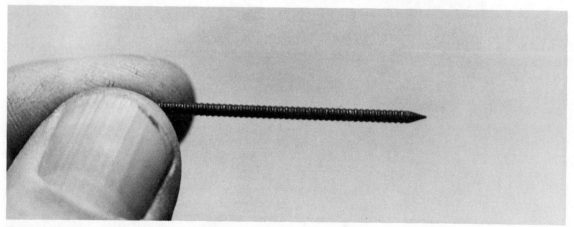

Fig. 5-30. Ring or annular shank nails have extreme holding power.

Fig. 5-31. Countersink head wood screws (courtesy American Plywood Association).

accomplish two operations at one time. They are a good investment for the home woodworker. A complete set of countersink drill bits can be purchased for approximately $5 and will easily take care of all your countersinking operations.

It is no secret that the most time-consuming part of using woodworking screws on any project is the actual screwing that must be done by hand for each and every screw (Fig. 5-33). It will usually take about 1½ to 2 minutes to turn each screw down tight. On a small woodworking project, this can amount to about one-half hour of turning screws. This task offers little joy and usually a blister in the palm of your hand.

Mechanical screwdrivers and the screw gun are handy tools that will help you take a lot of the drudgery out of large tasks. The proper size and type tip (standard or Phillips) is inserted in the end of a driver, the unit is switched to screw or un-

screw, and the screwdriver is then used in a manner not unlike a ratchet to drive or withdraw the screw. Because most mechanical screwdrivers tend to be long, their use is limited to projects that offer plenty of room to work. Speed and efficiency are both possible with a mechanical screwdriver. Generally, a mechanical screwdriver can really speed up operations. Two and in some case three screws can be driven in place with a mechanical screwdriver in the time it would take to drive only one screw with a conventional screwdriver.

Some mechanical screwdrivers have ball handles while others have more conventional-looking wooden handles with a long shank. There is even one relatively new model that has a shank that resembles a bit and brace. A good mechanical screwdriver like the one shown in Fig. 5-34 can be purchased for approximately $15.

Screw guns are another way of quickly driving

Fig. 5-32. Countersink drill bit.

wood screws into place on your plywood furniture projects. These are much faster than a mechanical screwdriver and they are widely used in industry. The most common version is simply a conventional, variable-speed electric drill (Fig. 5-35) that has been fitted with a special attachment that allows the user to control the speed and torque of the bit. It is probably safe to say that a 2-inch long wood screw can be driven into place in about 10 seconds. This same work would probably take about 2 minutes with a conventional screwdriver.

You should also be able to find a screw gun attachment that can be used on your variable-speed electric drill. It is also possible to use a conventional screwdriver (with the handle removed) in an electric drill (Fig. 5-36). While this arrangement leaves a bit to be desired, it is nonetheless one good way to drive a large number of screws quickly.

While there are probably over 100 different screw designs in existence today, there are really only a few that are suitable for use on plywood furniture projects (Fig. 5-37). These are the *flathead wood screw* and the *oval-head wood screw*.

The flathead wood screw has a tapered shank that is threaded only part way and is probably the best choice of a screw for plywood furniture projects. These screws have a flat head and chamfered

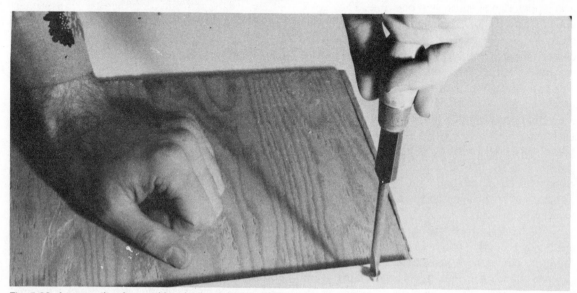

Fig. 5-33. A conventional screwdriver is slow but dependable.

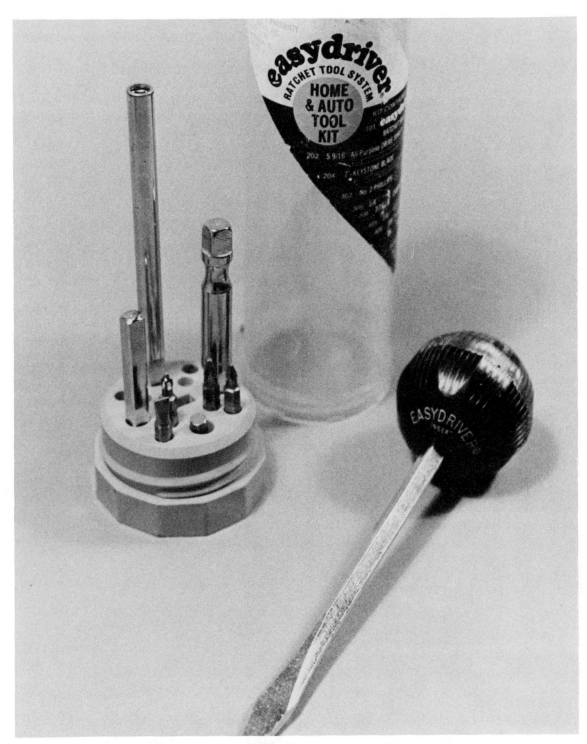

Fig. 5-34. Ratchet-type screwdrivers can speed up the task.

Fig. 5-35. An electric screw gun is very handy when you have a lot of screws to drive.

sides that lend themselves quite well to countersinking. The most common flathead wood screw will have a slot across the head that will accommodate a standard screwdriver. Phillips-head wood screws are also available.

The oval-head wood screw (Fig. 5-38) is the type of screw that is commonly sold with builders hardware, and it is usually chrome plated. As a rule, oval-head wood screws are used for attaching decorative hardware to plywood furniture projects and the flathead wood screw is designed to be countersunk.

Both types of screws are available in bright steel. This is a perfect choice of fastener where moisture will not be a problem. If moisture is present, a different type of metal should be used. These include brass, aluminum, stainless steel, and galvanized screws. If you are constructing an outdoor plywood furniture project or an interior piece that may come in contact with moisture, you should use one of these types of wood screws.

Screw length and size are both important considerations when choosing wood screws for a plywood furniture project. The recommended

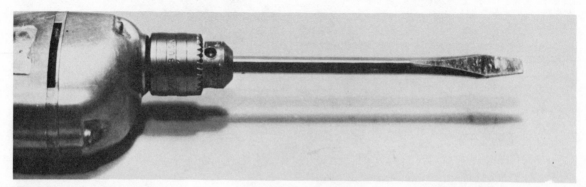

Fig. 5-36. A screwdriver shaft, chucked into a variable speed drill, will make short work out of large tasks.

174

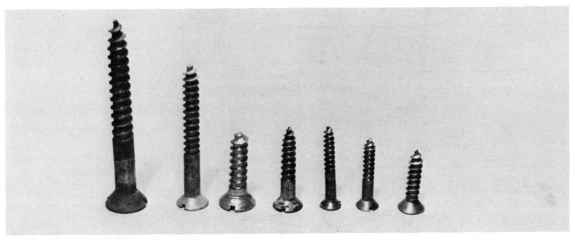

Fig. 5-37. Flat head wood screws can be countersunk easily.

screw sizes and lengths for various thickness of plywood are given in Table 5-1. These recommendations are for use when you are joining plywood through the face of one piece and into the edge of another. If you are joining two pieces face to face, a shorter-length screw must be used to prevent a break through on the bottom piece.

Flathead screws and oval-head screws are available in small packages containing about six screws to boxes of 500 screws. It has been my experience that those little plastic packages, available in any variety store in the country, tend to be of poor quality. These inexpensive and seemingly worthwhile screws often will not stand up to being turned with a screwdriver. Often the head will break off before you have even countersunk it properly. I am sure that a large part of the failure of these inexpensive wood screws is due to the poor quality steel used in manufacturing the screws. The do-it-yourselfer would be much better off finding a source of good-quality steel (or nonferrous metal such as brass) screws rather than buying these poor-quality screws. The effort you expend in finding a source of quality wood screws will be worth your time.

Specialty Fasteners

Corrugated fasteners (Fig. 5-39) are actually a form of nail. They are driven in place with a few blows of a hammer. These specialty nails are simply a piece of corrugated steel with a sharpened bottom edge. They are commonly used by professional cabinet-makers, but they have a limited application when building plywood furniture. They are available in a variety of sizes and lengths. Their real value comes

Fig. 5-38. Round head wood screws are used for attaching hardware.

Table 5-1. Wood Screw Lengths and Sizes.

Plywood Thickness	Screw Size	Screw Length
¼″	4	¾″
⅜	6	1″
½	6	1¼″
⅝	8	1¼″
¾	8	1½″
1	10	2″

into play when edge joining two pieces of plywood and for strengthening miter joints.

These fasteners should not be used where appearance is a factor. They can be used quite effectively when countersunk and filled or when the joint area will be covered with plastic laminate or true wood veneer. Whenever corrugated fasteners are used, it is important to choose the right size and length. It is obviously undesirable to use too large or too long of a fastener.

There are a number of fasteners that are designed for attaching a plywood furniture project to a wall or ceiling. Probably the two most common of these specialty fasteners are *expansion fasteners* and *toggle bolts*. Expansion fasteners (commonly called *molly fasteners*) and toggle bolts are used in a slightly different manner.

Expansion fasteners (Fig. 5-40) can be driven into a wall or pushed through a drilled hole. After installation, however, all expansion fasteners work in the same manner. After the sleeve is inserted

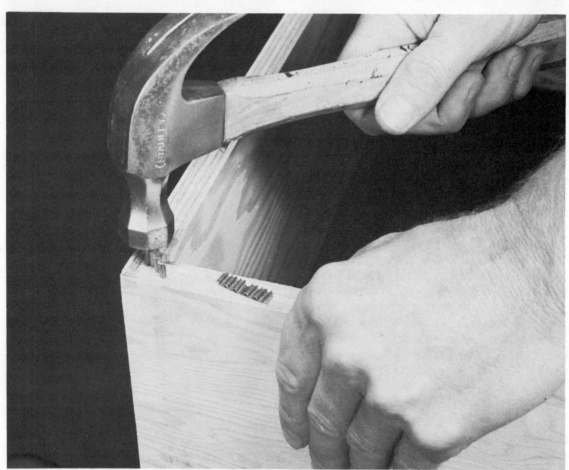

Fig. 5-39. Corrugated fastener.

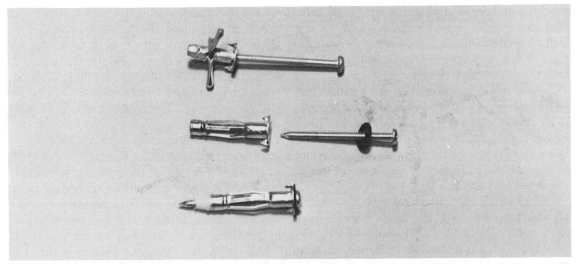

Fig. 5-40. Molly fasteners are used for securing light projects to a wall.

into the wall, the screw is turned until you feel some resistance. At this point, the expansion sleeve is mushrooming against the back side of the wall. Continue screwing until you feel that the fastener has totally expanded; then remove the screw. The next step is to push the screw through the plywood furniture piece and start it into the unit already in the wall. Then drive the screw through the furniture piece and into the sleeve until the piece is secure. Expansion fasteners are available in a wide range of sizes and holding power, but they do not offer as much strength as toggle bolts.

A toggle bolt is simply a long bolt with a pair of foldable wings that encase the nut (Fig. 5-41). To use a toggle bolt you must first drill a hole in the wall that is large enough to accommodate the folded wings of the bolt. Next, the toggle bolt is separated and the bolt itself is passed through the back of the plywood furniture project. Then the toggle bolt is assembled once again and then the folded wings are pushed through the hole in the wall. As the toggle bolt wings pass into the open wall cavity, they open and cannot be removed. The next step is to turn the bolt until the project is secured against the wall. It is

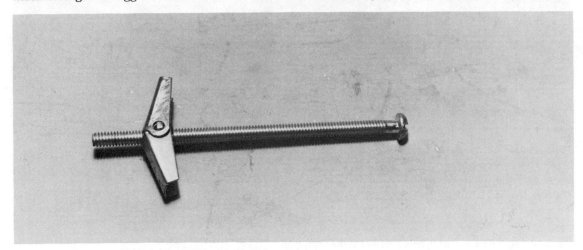

Fig. 5-41. Toggle bolts are used for heavy-duty fastening projects.

important to keep in mind that, while toggle bolts offer the strongest means for attaching a cabinet to a wall, they are also meant for permanent installations. Where they are used, holes will be covered entirely by the cabinet itself.

As a rule, expansion fasteners are used for attaching relatively light plywood furniture projects to an interior wall and toggle bolts should be used for heavy projects. It is important to keep in mind that neither expansion fasteners or toggle bolts can be expected to hold a project against a wall that is not in sound condition.

Another means that can be used to secure a plywood furniture project to a wall is to use *lag bolts* (Fig. 5-42). These heavy-duty bolts—which resemble large wood screws—are inserted in a hole in the cabinet back, through the interior wall covering, and into a wall stud. Lag bolts must be long enough to pass through all of these surfaces and into the wall studs. A length of 2 inches is about the smallest you should use.

Lag bolts can also be used effectively for holding a project to the floor (providing, of course, it is

wood). If you are planning to attach your plywood furniture project to the wooden floor in your home—a kitchen island or work table, for examples—you must first locate the flooring joists beneath the finish flooring. Then, drill suitable size holes through all layers of flooring subflooring and into the floor joists. This approach will result in the strongest attachment.

Some homes have concrete, cinder block or brick walls with no wood framing or wall studs whatsoever. For walls of this type, you will have to use special masonry fasteners for holding a plywood project in place. The only possible exception is a wall that is constructed of cinder or cement blocks. In this case, you can use toggle bolts.

Probably the strongest masonry fastener is called a lead anchor (Fig. 5-43) and these are available at almost any home improvement center or lumber yard. To install a lead anchor, you must first mark the location and, then drill a hole in the masonry wall. The hole can be easily bored with a carbide-tipped drill bit in an electric drill. The hole should be just slightly larger than the lead anchor

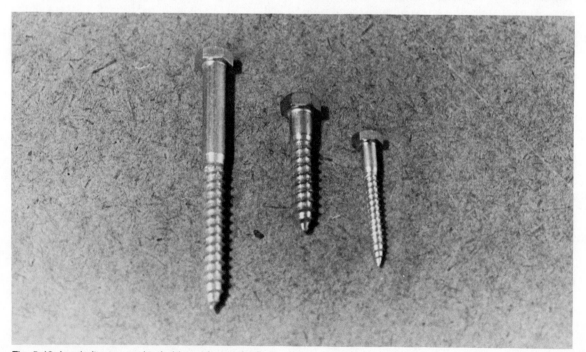

Fig. 5-42. Lag bolts are used to hold a project to the floor.

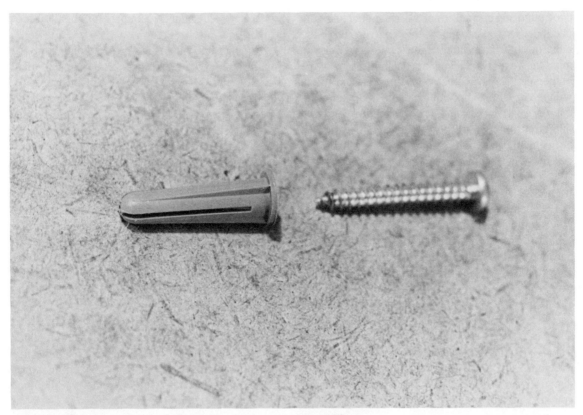

Fig. 5-43. Lead anchors are used in concrete and masonry walls and floors.

diameter and deeper than the lead anchor is long. While drilling the lead anchor holes, you must keep the drill and carbide-tipped drill bit at a 90-degree angle to the face of the wall or the hole will be at the wrong angle. You should also wear some type of eye protection when drilling masonry because the dust, which is cement powder, is an eye irritant.

After you have drilled the required number of holes in your masonry wall, insert the lead wall anchors. Next, push the bolts through the back of the project and into the wall anchors already in the wall. The last step is to screw the bolts tight. This will cause the lead wall anchors to expand in the wall and thus securely hold the cabinet in place.

HARDWARE

There are five basic types of hinges that fall into the category of cabinet hardware. These include: *butt, offset, flush, invisible,* and *pivot.* The type of hinge

you choose will, at least in part, depend on the type of doors you are planning to have on your plywood cabinet. Flush doors, for example, can use a few different types of hinges while lapped doors are limited to offset hinges.

Butt hinges (Fig. 5-44) are probably the most widely used type of hinges. Butt hinges come in all shapes, sizes, styles, and finishes. They can be mounted on flush fitting doors so that only the hinge pin is visible or, if a decorative style is chosen, they can be mounted on the face of the door and the cabinet frame.

If you build a plywood cabinet with flush-fitting doors, you might decide that you do not want to have the face of the cabinet cluttered with hinge hardware. In this case, you can install butt hinges between the cabinet frame and the door edge.

There are several ways of doing this. You can mortise the thickness of one hinge leaf onto both the door edge and cabinet frame. You can mortise only one side. Or you can mount the hinge on top of the edge of both the cabinet frame and door. Keep in mind, however, that if you mortise both sides of the hinge seat, the space between the door and frame will be very thin. This will make the door appear as if it were part of the cabinet. If you simply mount the hinge on the edge of the door and frame, the gap between the door and cabinet frame will be the thickness of the hinge. In other words, the mortise reduces the gap between the door and cabinet frame.

To install butt hinges in a flush-mounted door, you should begin by putting the door into the cabinet. You will have to prop the door in place because at this time there is nothing holding the door in place. You should leave a small gap all the way around the door so it will be easy to open and close after the hinges have been installed. The easiest way to accomplish this is to insert paper matches, or the equivalent, between the door and frame. Next, mark the location of the hinges on both the door edge and cabinet frame edge. Next, the door is removed and the hinge mortise is cut. Of course, you will be installing two hinges per door

that are spaced about 2 feet apart for standard-size cabinet doors.

Cabinet butt hinges are most commonly made from brass and the leaves are quite thin. The mortise cuts can be made with a sharp utility knife. Begin by outlining the location of the hinge with the knife and then removing the waste wood with a sharp chisel. Work carefully because the edges of plywood have a tendency to splinter easily. After the mortise cut has been made, slip one leaf into the slot and check for fit. The face of the hinge should be flush with the edge of the door. Next, the cabinet frame receives a mortise cut in the same fashion.

After both the door edge and cabinet frame edge have been mortised and you are satisfied with the fit of the hinge, attach it with the screws that came with it to the door. Then lift the door into its proper position and screw the other half of the hinge into its place on the cabinet frame edge.

Generally, all concealed butt hinges will be installed in the same manner, but some are easier than others. Loose-pin butt hinges, for example, are installed as described in the preceding paragraph except that one leaf is installed on the door and the other half on the cabinet frame. Then the

Fig. 5-44. Butt hinge.

Fig. 5-45. Loose-pin butt hinges are easy to work with.

door is lifted into place, the hinges are meshed, and the pin is dropped into place. Loose-pin butt hinges (Fig. 5-45) are very easy to install, especially for large doors, because you do not have to hold the door while attaching the other hinge leaf to the cabinet frame.

Butt hinges can also be installed on the face of flush fitting cabinet doors. For this type of application, however, you will want to use decorative butt hinges, and there are easily thousands of different designs. These butt hinges are very simple to install. Generally, all that is required is to position the door in the cabinet, mark the location of the hinges, drill screw holes, and attach the hinges.

Offset hinges (Fig. 5-46) are very similar to butt hinges and are available in almost as wide of a selection. These can be installed in the semiconcealed or surface-mounted styles. Offset hinges find the greatest use when doors of a cabinet are cut

larger than the opening in the cabinet. This means, of course, that the doors overlap the cabinet frame and a special hinge is required—the offset hinge.

Generally, there is nothing difficult about installing offset hinges providing that you purchase the proper size. The amount of offset on the hinge must be equal to the thickness of the doors you are installing. Offset hinges are available in almost any standard size; ½ inch and ¾ inch are probably the most popular sizes.

Flush-mounted hinges (Fig. 5-47) are still another type of butt hinge variation. These are intended not only to do the job of a hinge, but also to decorate the cabinet as well. Flush-mounted hinges are installed to both the face of the cabinet door and the face of the cabinet frame—in a flush door configuration. They are very simple to install. About the only problem you will encounter with flush-mounted hinges is choosing a style of hinge. There

Fig. 5-46. Offset hinge.

are easily thousands of different styles, shapes, and finishes available.

Pivot hinges are available for flush-mounted and overlapping cabinet doors and there are three basic designs: those that attach to both the top and bottom edges of the door; those that attach to the vertical edge of the door and, "knife" hinges that attach to the top and bottom of the door edge. Probably the most appealing feature of pivot hinges is that only the small pivot part of the hinge is visible when the door is closed. While pivot hinges require careful planning during installation, they are worth the effort. This is especially true for finer plywood furniture projects such as a china cabinet.

Invisible hinges require the most work to in-stall. These are the most expensive of the five basic hinges. When installed properly, this hinge will not be visible when the cabinet door is closed. They are available for both flush-mount and overlapped doors. Detailed instructions and a template for placement of the hinges are always included in the packaging.

In addition to hinges, the plywood cabinet will also require a few other pieces of hardware. These include knobs or handles so the cabinet can be easily opened and a catch of some sort to keep the cabinet closed. A catch can be eliminated if a spring-loaded hinge is used. This device will keep the door closed by applying an inward pressure on the hinge.

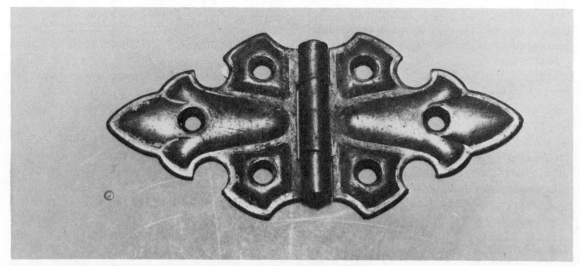

Fig. 5-47. Decorative flush mounted hinges are used for face-mounted doors.

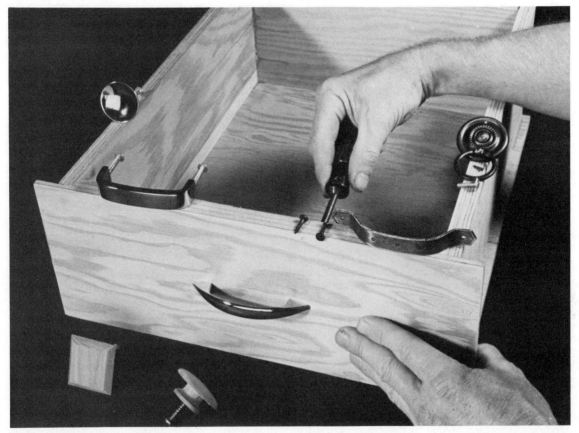

Fig. 5-48. Examples of knobs and pulls.

Knobs and handles (Fig. 5-48) are used in cabinets to make it easier to open and close doors and draws. Another requirement is that the knob or handle must add something to the door (or at least not be offensive) and this accounts for the thou-sands of different knobs and handles currently available. A quick glance down the isle of any store that sells hardware will reveal knobs and hardware made from porcelain, wood, plastic, aluminum, stainless steel, embossed steel, iron, and other

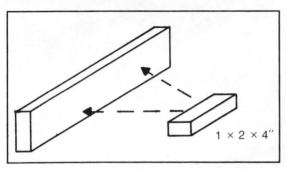

Fig. 5-49. A drawer pull made from hardwood.

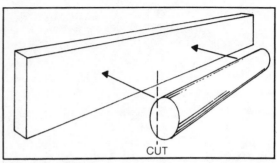

Fig. 5-50. A drawer or door pull made from a 2-inch wooden dowel.

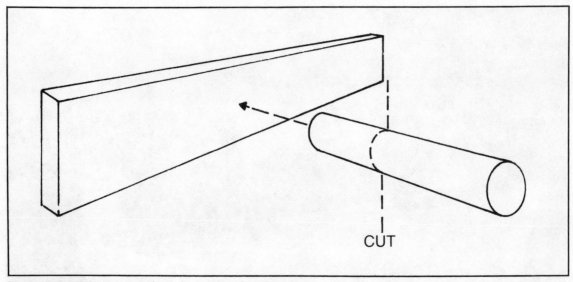

Fig. 5-51. Knobs can be made from short pieces of wooden dowel.

materials. About the only problem you will encounter with knobs and handles is finding a style, material, and color that will look good on your project.

After looking over the selection of knobs and handles available, if you are not satisfied you can make your own custom knobs and handles in your woodworking shop. Some of the possibilities include a block of hardwood 1 × 2 inches by 4 inches long, with one edge bevel cut. Screw this handle onto the face of the cabinet (or draw) face from the inside. See Fig. 5-49.

A 4-inch-long piece of 2-inch wooden dowel with one edge cut flat can be screwed horizontally on a drawer face (from the inside) for an effective handle. A shorter length of the same dowel can be attached vertically on a door for a simple handle (Fig. 5-50).

Another possibility using a 2-inch wooden dowel is to cut 2-inch pieces, round the edges, and

Fig. 5-52. A knobless drawer pull (courtesy American Plywood Association).

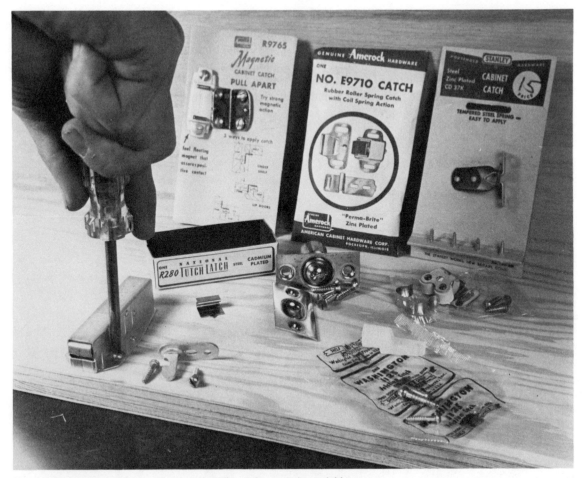

Fig. 5-53. Magnetic catches are easy to install and they are dependable.

attach it to a door or drawer face. If you sand one end of such a knob, you can make it quite attractive. See Fig. 5-51.

Alternatives to conventional or homemade knobs and handles are pulls and handles that are actually part of the door or drawer face. I like to call these no-pulls. See Fig. 5-52.

Whether you decide to buy or make knobs for your plywood furniture, you should not attach them until the project has been finished. Not only will this make finishing the project easier to accomplish, but you will also not run the risk of getting any of the finish on the knob.

It is a common practice to have some type of catch system (Fig. 5-53) on cabinet doors to keep the door closed. While there are a number of different types—*roller, friction* and *magnetic*—they are all installed in about the same manner. The holding mechanism is installed inside the cabinet and the strike plate or finger is attached to the inside of the door. Careful layout is required.

Undoubtedly, the most popular type of catch is the magnetic version. These are very easy to install, they do the job of keeping the door closed quite well, and they last almost forever. In addition, magnetic catches can be mounted almost anywhere inside the cabinet as long as the catch can make contact with the strike plate. Generally, one small magnetic catch should do the job of keeping your cabinet door closed. If small children are in the home, consider using a larger magnetic catch or a childproof catch. There are several types of childproof catches currently available.

For overlapped cabinet doors, you might want to add a piece or two of felt—either on the cabinet frame or on the backside of the door—to soften the shock of closing the door. The felt will also prevent any marring of the two surfaces.

Cabinet hardware performs a dual function. It is important to plan and shop around for the most attractive and functional hardware for your plywood furniture project.

Chapter 6

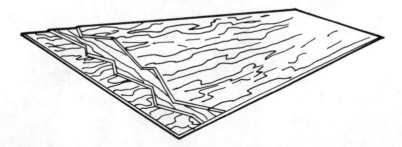

Shelves and Storage Systems

THIS CHAPTER CONTAINS 15 PLYWOOD PROJ-
ects primarily designed for use as storage sys-
tems or display tables. Each project has a materials
list and directions for building the unit. There are
easy-to-build projects and some designed for the
advanced woodworker.

MODULAR STORAGE SYSTEM

This clean-lined modular storage unit (Fig. 6-1A) is
easy to build and versatile for a variety of applications. Side by side or stacked, they are functional
and well designed. Build a wall, a bench, or end
tables. Each unit is simple to construct.

Materials

For six boxes, as in Fig. 6-1B.
1 sheet (4 × 8 feet) ¾-inch exterior, A-A grade.
Filler paste.
1 pound #8d finishing nails.
Sandpaper.
2 quarts primer.
3 quarts semigloss enamel.

12 1½-inch-long hex bolts with nuts.
24 washers to fit bolts; 2 each.

Directions

Begin by cutting plywood into strips each measuring 10 × 48 inches. A table saw is quite handy for
this type of cutting. After all plywood has been cut
in this manner, you will have nine strips. Now cut
six of the strips in half. This will give you 12 pieces
each measuring 10 × 24 inches. Then cut the remaining three strips into 12-inch lengths. This will
give you 12 pieces, each measuring 10 × 12 inches.
Now you are ready to start constructing your modular shelf system.

Each box in this storage system is composed of
four pieces. Two measure 10 × 24 inches (the top
and bottom) and the other two measure 10 × 12
inches (the sides). Assemble your boxes using
white glue and finishing nails so that both the top
and bottom pieces extend 3 inches past the sides.

It is important that each box be constructed in
the same manner so that, when you have finished

Fig. 6-1A. Modular storage system (courtesy Georgia-Pacific).

building, each box is identical to the others in the system. Now you must drill countersunk bolt holes (8 per cube) on both the top and underside of each cube.

The next step is to finish off each of the cubes before bolting them together. Begin by filling all nail holes and exposed edges. After the filler paste dries hard, sand everything smooth and apply a coat of primer. Once the primer has dried, apply two coats of semigloss enamel, sanding between coats. The last part of this project is to bolt the cubes together.

ROOM DIVIDER

Add a room, make a hall, section off a room—the options are limitless with this sturdy room divider (Fig. 6-2A). Each unit is very simple to build and is a great place to store everything from books to

knickknacks. The plans given will enable you to build one unit. If you want more than one, simply double or triple the materials list. The unit goes together so quickly that you will surely want to build several.

Materials

For each unit, you will need the following.
8 1-×-4-inch-by-7-feet-long lumber.
½ sheet (2 × 8 feet) ¾-inch-exterior plywood, A-B grade
½ pound #8d finishing nails
Filler paste.
Sandpaper.
White glue.
1 quart primer.
2 quarts semigloss enamel.

Directions

Begin by cutting the plywood into pieces measuring 10 × 24 inches. You will need six of these for shelves. Next, attach these shelves to the 1-×-4 inch lumber as shown in Fig. 6-2B. Use white glue and finishing nails for this. After all of the shelves have been secured, the unit is ready for finishing.

To finish, begin by filling all exposed edges and nail holes. After the filler paste has dried hard, sand everything smooth and apply a coat of primer to the bookcase. When the primer has dried, sand lightly and apply two coats of semigloss enamel, sanding between coats. The bookcase is ready for use.

STEREO DISPLAY UNIT

This distinctive stereo display unit offers protection and organization for even the most elaborate component stereo system (Fig. 6-3A). Capable of being built in just a few evenings, the assembly procedures are simple to accomplish even if you are not a master woodworker. This stereo display case will look great in your living room or family room and you will surely get compliments about the craftsmanship.

Materials

1 sheet (4 × 8 feet) ¾ inch, exterior, A-A grade.
1 pound #8d finishing nails.
White glue.
Wood filler paste.
Sandpaper.
2 pieces aluminum channel ½ × ¾ × 24 inches.
6⅝-inch long #6 Phillips-head wood screws.
1⅜-inch wooden dowel, 6 feet long.
1 quart primer.
2 quarts semigloss enamel.

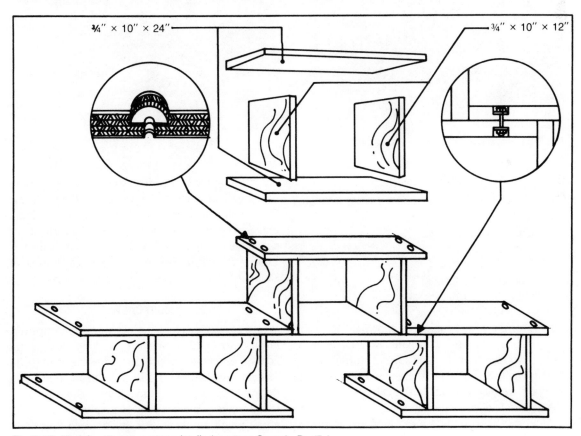

Fig. 6-1B. Modular storage system details (courtesy Georgia-Pacific).

Fig. 6-2A. Room divider (courtesy Georgia-Pacific).

Directions

Begin by cutting the plywood into the following pieces:

    Two 8-×-27 inches.
    Two 3-×-24 inches.
    Six 8-×-24 inches.
    One 16-×-24 inches.
    One 13-×-24 inches.
    Two 12-×-36 inches.

Assemble the stereo cabinet as shown in Fig. 6-3B. Use white glue and finishing nails. Note the location of the wooden dowels used for separating LP albums. Drill the holes for these dowels before the shelves are installed inside the cabinet. Also note the position of the aluminum channel inside the cabinet and the 16-×-24-inch shelf that is placed inside the channel. Do not fasten this shelf in place; it is designed to be a slider. After the entire cabinet has been constructed, you can begin the finishing.

To finish, begin by filling all nail holes and exposed edges. After the filler paste has dried hard, sand everything smooth and apply a coat of primer. Follow this with two coats of semigloss enamel, sanding between coats.

BOOKCASE

With a power saw, this distinctive piece of furniture is easy to build. Using the modular design, the adjustable bookcase provides a variety of setup possibilities (Fig. 6-4). Much depends on how you decide to put it to use. Stack them six high for a wall unit or change them around to give you more living area as well as a new look. In any case, this bookcase will provide plenty of storage space for such items as books, stereo, sculptures, and other things around your home.

Materials

2 sheets (4 × 8 feet) ¾ inch, exterior, A-A grade.
White glue.
Wood filler paste.
2 pound #6d finishing nails.
Sandpaper.
2 quarts of primer.
1 gallon of semigloss enamel.
Molly bolts, if required.

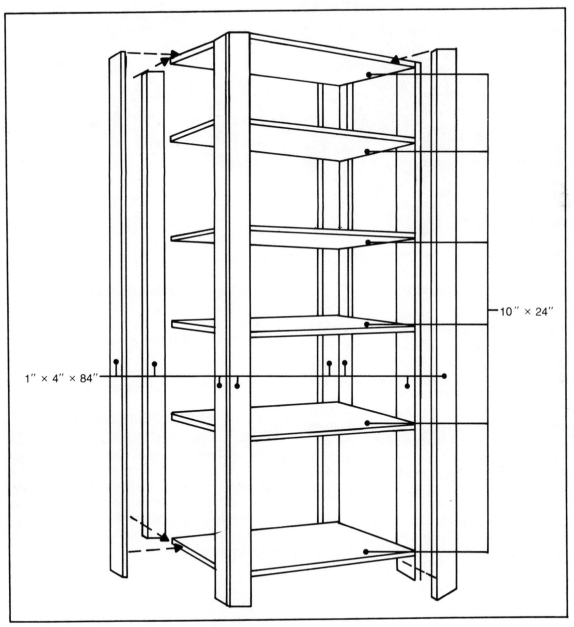

1″ × 4″ × 84″

10″ × 24″

Fig. 6-2B. Room divider details (courtesy Georgia-Pacific).

191

Fig. 6-3A. Stereo unit (courtesy Georgia-Pacific).

Directions

Begin by ripping the plywood panels into strips measuring 12 inches wide by 8 feet long. After this has been completed, you must cut five of these strips into lengths 12 × 34½ inches. Next, cut six pieces measuring 12 × 30½ inches and 12 pieces measuring 12 × 14¼ inches. Now, cut a ¼ × ¾ inch rabbet 3 inches down from the edge on all of the 12 pieces (which measure 12 × 14¼ inches—the ends). Then take eight of these end pieces and cut slots measuring 3¾ × ¾ inches 1½ inches in from the edge. Refer to Fig. 6-4 and slot four of the end pieces accordingly.

For the back, slot the five boards to be used 2¼ × ¾ inches and 1½ inches in from the edge. Next, using your hand-held sabre saw, round off the corners with a 1½-inch radius. Now each of the six bookcase sections are ready to be put together. Do this with white glue and finishing nails.

The next step is to finish off the bookcase. Begin by filling all nail holes and exposed edges on the project. After the filler paste dries hard, sand everything smooth and apply a coat of primer. When dry, apply two coats of semigloss enamel, sanding between coats.

Now the bookcase is ready to be pressed into service. If you are planning to add many heavy objects to the bookcase, it is a good idea to anchor the top shelf to an interior wall with molly bolts.

BOOKCASE/ROOM DIVIDER

Here is a workshop project from the Hardwood Plywood Manufacturer's Association that has every characteristic of a fine furniture piece, and yet it is easy to build. A "peninsular bookcase" by itself, this unit can also serve as a room divider. The fine-furniture look comes from using quality hardwood plywood. It is the same material that many quality furniture manufacturers use.

Materials

2 sheets (4 × 8 feet) ¾-inch-thick, hardwood-faced plywood, A-A grade.
White glue.

1 pound #8d finishing nails.
Wood filler paste.
Sandpaper.
1 pint wood stain for species of hardwood used.
1 quart clear finish.

Directions

Begin by cutting all parts from the plywood panels as indicated in Fig. 6-5. Next, assemble the pieces using white glue and finishing nails. After the basics of the project have been built, you can begin applying the finishing touches.

To finish, begin by filling all nail holes and exposed edges on the project. After the filler paste has dried hard, sand smooth and apply a coat of wood stain. Follow this with two coats of clear finish, sanding between coats, and then put the bookcase/room divider to good use.

MOVABLE TV STAND

Roll this handy TV stand into the bedroom, the den,

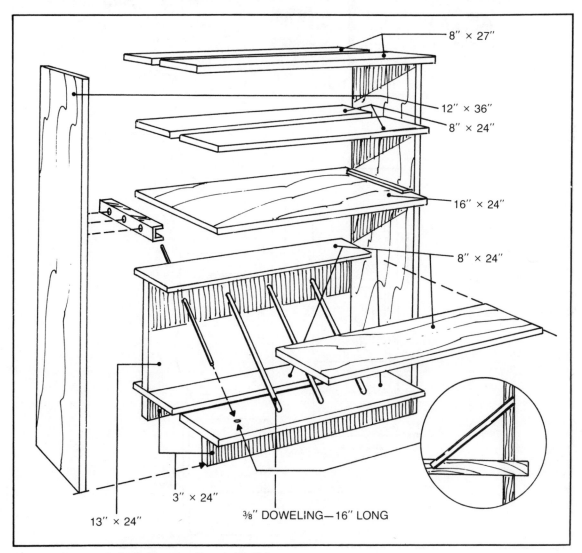

Fig. 6-3B. Stereo unit details (courtesy Georgia-Pacific).

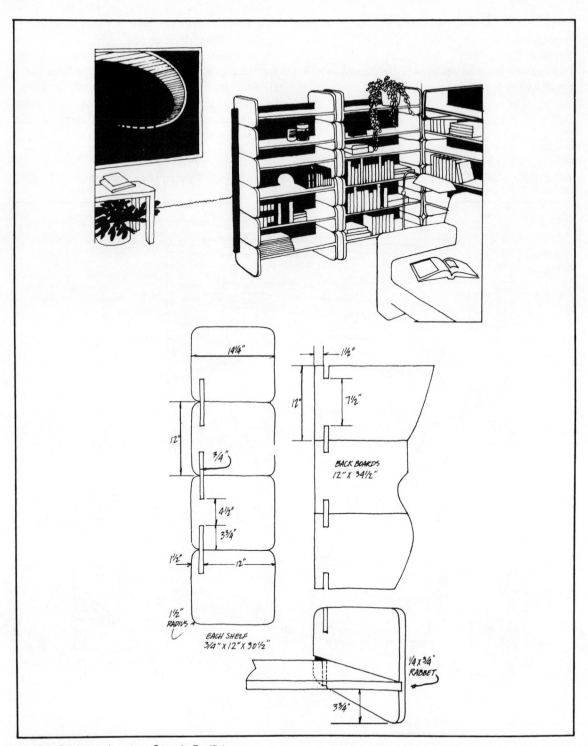

Fig. 6-4. Bookcase (courtesy Georgia-Pacific).

or the family room. This TV stand is attractive enough to sit in your living room and be very functional at the same time. A recessed shelf holds the television in place and storage compartments below can be used for games, magazines, books or knickknacks. This is a very inexpensive project to make. It requires only one sheet of plywood and a few hours of your time.

Materials

1 sheet (4 × 8 feet) ¾-inch-thick, exterior plywood, A-B grade.
White glue.
1 pound #6d finishing nails.
Wood filler paste.
Sandpaper.
1 quart primer.
2 quarts semigloss enamel.
4 spherical caster wheels with mounting screws.

Directions

Begin by measuring, marking, and cutting the plywood according to Fig. 6-6. Work carefully and use a hand-held sabre saw for plunge cutting the openings. Start building by attaching the blocking to the bottom of the stand. Attach the caster wheels to the underside. Next, glue/nail the middle shelf to the divider piece and attach the divider to the base. Finally, glue/nail the remaining pieces into place with a careful eye on the diagram. Now that the TV stand is entirely built, it is time for finishing.

To finish, begin by filling all nail holes and

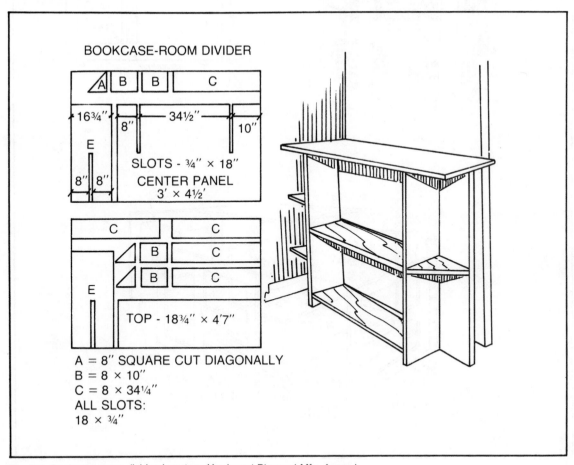

Fig. 6-5. Bookcase room divider (courtesy Hardwood Plywood Mfg. Assoc.).

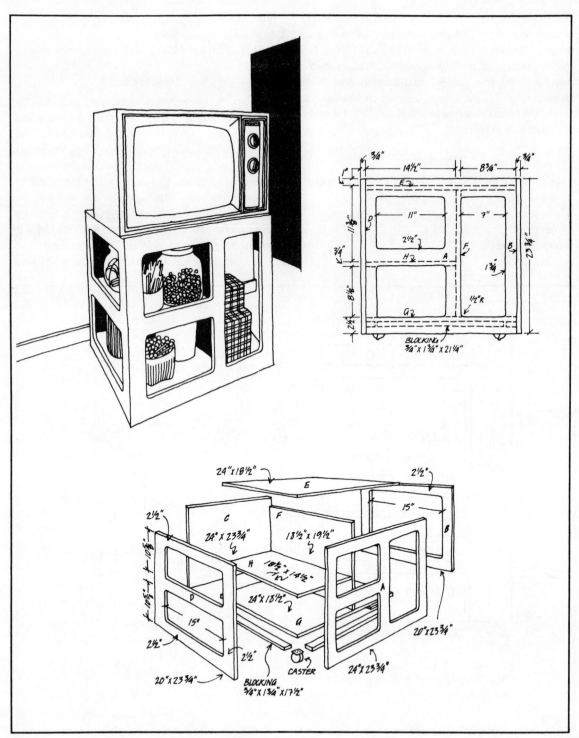

Fig. 6-6. Movable TV stand (courtesy Georgia-Pacific).

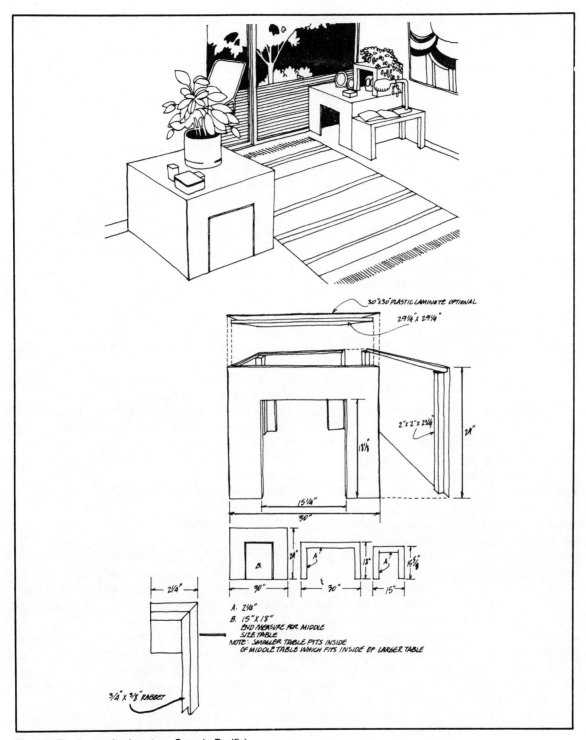

30"X30" PLASTIC LAMINATE OPTIONAL

29¼" X 29¼"

2"X 2"X 23¾"

24"

18¼"

15¼"

30"

24"

B.

18"

15⅝"

30"

30"

15"

2¼"

3/4" X 3/8" RABBET

A. 2¼"

B. 15" X 18"
END MEASURE FOR MIDDLE
SIZE TABLE

NOTE: SMALLER TABLE FITS INSIDE
OF MIDDLE TABLE WHICH FITS INSIDE OF LARGER TABLE

Fig. 6-7. Furniture cube (courtesy Georgia-Pacific).

197

exposed edges on the project. After the filler paste has dried hard, sand smooth and apply one coat of primer. Next, apply two coats of semigloss enamel, sanding between coats, and the project is ready for service.

FURNITURE CUBE

Now you see it . . . now you don't. Turn one table into three with an easy-to-build furniture cube (Fig. 6-7). Display your prized collectables, photographs, or plants. If you find that one table is not enough, this cube separates into three tables for stacking or stepping. You can use these furniture cubes indoors or out; they will look great almost anywhere.

Materials

2 sheets (4 × 8 feet) ¾-inch exterior plywood, A-B grade.
2 2-×-2 inch lumber, 10 feet long.
White glue.
Wood filler paste.
2 pounds #8d finishing nails.
Sandpaper.
1 quart primer.
2 quarts semigloss enamel.

Directions

Allowing for your saw cut and using the ¾-inch-thick plywood, cut four pieces measuring 24 × 30 inches and one piece measuring 29¼ inches square. These five pieces comprise the first table. For a professional-finished look, miter all 24-×-30-inch pieces on the 24-inch side and cut a ¾-inch rabbet along one remaining side. With the rabbeted sides facing up, the table top will sit flush.

Next, mark two 24-×-30-inch pieces for the openings, measuring 15¼ inches from the bottom by 18⅛ inches. Drill a ¼-inch hole in the two inside corners and start cutting or make a plunge cut. After all pieces have been cut, it is time to assemble the project. Glue and nail the 2 × 2 inch pieces to the side pieces along the inside of the mitered edges and set aside to allow the glue to dry. Once the glue has set, glue and nail the four side pieces together. Make sure the two opening pieces are opposite one another. Clamp and allow the glue to dry. The next step is to finish off the project.

To finish, begin by filling all nail holes and exposed edges. When the filler paste has hardened, sand smooth and apply a coat of primer. Follow this with two coats of semigloss enamel, sanding between coats.

SPINDLE BOOKCASE

Here is a simple-to-construct bookcase (Fig. 6-8) that can easily be adapted to any room in the house. These plans call for shelves that measure 12 × 36 inches, but they can, of course, be modified (8 × 24 inches, for example) to fit your particular needs. In any event, this bookcase is easy and fun to build and offers plenty of storage space.

Materials

½ sheet (4 × 4 feet) ¾-inch exterior plywood, A-B grade.
16 hardwood spindles, each 12 inches long, with metal-threaded ends.
Two 1-×-4-×-36-inch lumber; base.
Two 1-×-4-×-10 ¾-inch lumber; base.
Two ¾ round molding, 10¾ inches long; base.
Two ¾ round molding, 36 inches long; base.
Wood filler paste.
White glue.
Sandpaper.
1 pound #6d finishing nails.
1 quart wood stain.
2 quarts clear coating.

Directions

Begin by cutting the plywood panel into 5 pieces, each measuring 12 × 36 inches, and then drill four holes in each. Holes should be ¼ inch in diameter and located 1 inch in and 1 inch down from each corner. Next, assemble the base of the unit with the 1-×-4 inch lumber. Use white glue and finishing nails for this. Then attach the hardwood spindles to the base (four, one at each corner) from below. Then attach the first shelf by placing it over the threaded metal rod in the first row of spindles. Add four more spindles and another shelf. Continue in

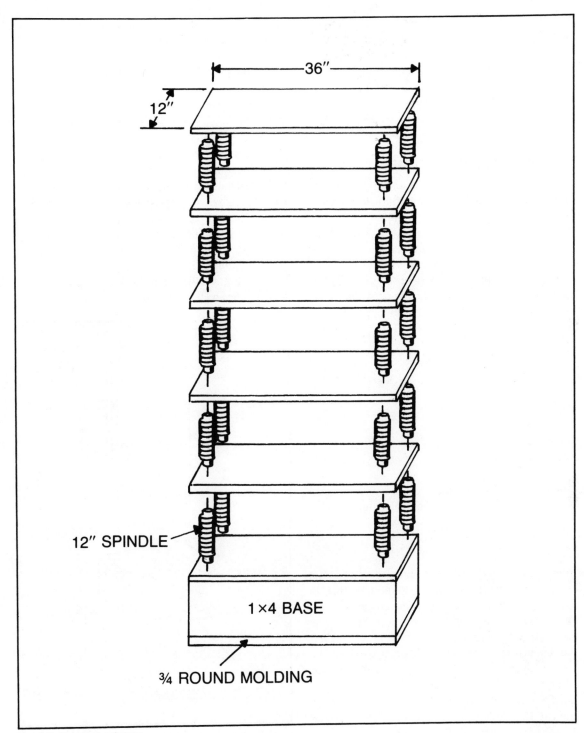

Fig. 6-8. Spindle bookcase.

this fashion until the shelf is constructed. Then you can begin the finishing.

To finish, begin by filling all nail holes (in the base) and all exposed edges on the shelving. After the filler paste dries hard, sand smooth and apply a coat of stain. Follow this with two coats of clear finish, sanding between coats. When the final coat dries, the bookcase is ready for use.

OPEN CUBE STORAGE

Here is a very simple project that offers almost unlimited storage potential (Fig. 6-9). These cubes are inexpensive to make; each requires four pieces of plywood and a length of wooden dowel. Eight cubes can be made from a single sheet of plywood. While the original design calls for ¾-inch-thick plywood, you could possibly save several dollars by substituting particle board for the plywood. In any case, these are attractive and quite functional as well.

Materials

1 sheet (4 × 8 feet) ¾-inch-thick exterior, A-B grade.
White glue.
2 pounds #6d finishing nails.
Wood filler paste.
Sandpaper.
1 quart primer.
2 quarts semigloss enamel.
Eight 12-inch long hardwood dowels ¾ of an inch in diameter.

Directions

Begin by cutting the sheet of plywood into 8 strips each measuring 12 × 48 inches. Remember that the saw blade width will take up some space. You will end up with eight strips that measure 11⅞ inches each rather than a full 12 inches. Next, cut each of the 48-inch-long strips into 12-inch pieces. This will result in 32 square pieces 12 inches on a side. After a careful look at Fig. 6-9, assemble the cubes. Each will be composed of four 12-×-12 inch pieces and one 12-inch-long wooden dowel. Use white glue and finishing nails for all fastening.

To finish, begin by filling all nail holes and exposed edges. After the filler paste has dried hard, sand everything smooth. Apply one coat of primer and two coats of semigloss enamel; Sand between coats. Then you can stack your cubes for use.

SPEAKER CABINET

If you have looked at the price of stereo speakers lately, you have probably been amazed at the cost. Almost anyone can build a good speaker cabinet for under ten dollars; it is the speakers themselves that are expensive. It is possible to build your own stereo speaker cabinets for a fraction of the retail cost even if you install the best speaker units available. The directions for this project will give you enough information to build your own speaker cabinet (Fig. 6-10). From there talk to some qualified people and find out about what type of speakers

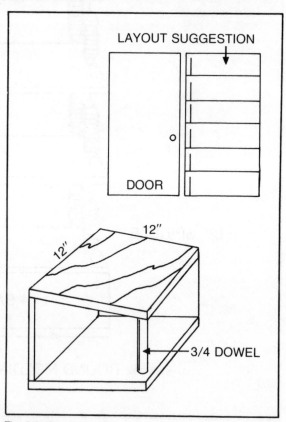

LAYOUT SUGGESTION

DOOR

12"

12"

12"

3/4 DOWEL

Fig. 6-9. Open cube storage.

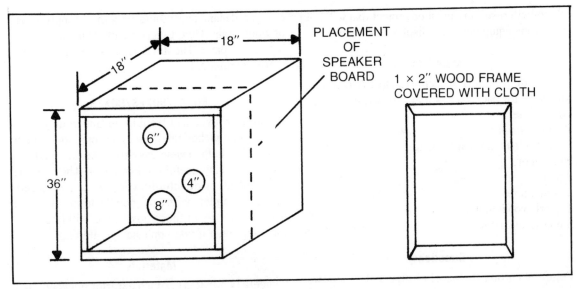

PLACEMENT
OF
SPEAKER
BOARD

1 × 2″ WOOD FRAME
COVERED WITH CLOTH

Fig. 6-10. Speaker cabinet.

to install inside. Because you will probably want to build two speaker cabinets, the material list includes enough for two units.

Materials

2 sheets (4 × 8 feet) ½-inch interior, A-D grade.
½ sheet (4 × 4 feet) ¼-inch Masonite (for backs); 20 feet 1-×-2-inch lumber.
2 pounds #6d finishing nails.
White glue.
Sandpaper.
1 quart wood stain.
2 quarts clear coating.
Fabric for front covers.

Directions

Begin by cutting the plywood into six strips, each measuring 18 × 48 inches. From the remaining plywood, cut two strips measuring 17 × 35 inches. These are the speaker boards and they must have holes cut for mounting the speakers before they are placed inside the speaker cabinets. Next, working with the 18-×-48-inch strips cut the following:
Four 18-×-18 pieces; tops and bottoms.
Four 36-×-36 pieces; sides.
Assemble these pieces to form two basic speaker

cabinets. Next, cut the Masonite and fit one piece to each speaker back.

Now it is time to make the front of the cabinet. This is done using the 1-×-2 inch lumber. Make a wooden frame the exact size as the front of the cabinet (36 × 18 inches) and over which a piece of fabric will be stretched to form a cover that will allow sounds to pass freely. The frame can have mitered or butt end joints. After building it, cover the frame with fabric. This cover can then be lightly tacked to the front of the speaker cabinet after the speaker board has been installed and the cabinet exterior has been finished to your satisfaction.

To finish off each cabinet, begin by filling all nail holes and exposed edges. After the filler dries hard, sand everything smooth and apply a coat of wood stain. Follow this with two coats of clear finish. When the final coat dries, attach the front cover, hook up your wires, and you are ready to hear some good sounds.

STEREO CABINET

This project is one sure solution to the common problem of what to do with a pile of stereo equipment; amplifier, turntable, tape deck, LP albums and tapes. The plans (Fig. 6-11) for this stereo

201

cabinet will result in a finished project that will hold all of your equipment and display it as well.

Materials

1 sheet (4 × 8 feet) ¾-inch exterior, A-B grade.
Masonite for back; 2 × 4 feet, ¼-inch thick.
White glue.
Wood filler paste.
2 pounds #8d finishing nails.
Sandpaper.
2 pairs of door hinges.
2 door knobs.
1 quart wood stain.
2 quarts clear finish.

Directions

Begin by cutting the panel of plywood as follows:
Two 18-×-18-inch pieces; top & bottom.
Two 18-×-16 ½-inch pieces; two shelves.
Two 18 × 48-inch pieces; sides.
Two 24 × 9-inch pieces; doors.
Next, assemble the cabinet (less doors) using white glue and finishing nails. See Fig. 6-11. Then install the doors to the front of the unit. Next, attach the back of the cabinet, cutting it to fit exactly. Now the cabinet is ready for finishing.

To finish, begin by filling all nail holes and exposed edges on the project. After the filler paste dries hard, sand everything smooth and apply a coat of wood stain. Give two coats of clear finish; sand between coats. The final step is to install your stereo equipment.

BOXES/BOXES/BOXES

If you have ever had trouble getting your youngster's room picked up, here is a project that might be of some help. These easy-to-make box modules will form many useful combinations. They can be open ended, made into drawers, made two-tiered, or made complete with a door on the front. After you have made a set of these boxes, you will find a use for them even if you don't have children.

Materials

2 sheets (4 × 8 feet) ½-inch exterior plywood, A-A grade.
½ sheet (4 × 4 feet) ½-inch exterior plywood, A-A grade.
White glue.
Wood filler paste.
5 pounds #6d finishing nails.
Sandpaper.
3 quarts primer.
1 gallon enamel paint.

Directions

Begin by cutting up all of the plywood into 10-×-48-inch strips. Cut each of the strips into three piece (each 18 × 18 inches). Next, cut each of these pieces to resemble those shown in Fig. 6-12. Now you can begin assembling each of the cubes.

To finish, begin by filling all nail holes and exposed edges. After the filler has dried hard, sand everything smooth and apply a coat of primer. Follow this with two coats of enamel paint, sanding lightly between coats. When the paint dries, stack these boxes for use.

HI-FI AND BAR UNIT

For the deluxe rumpus room here is a deluxe woodworking project (Fig. 6-13). It includes drop and piano hinges, sliding doors, turntable carrier (which slides out for easy use), and a built-in

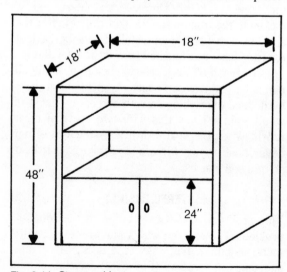

Fig. 6-11. Stereo cabinet.

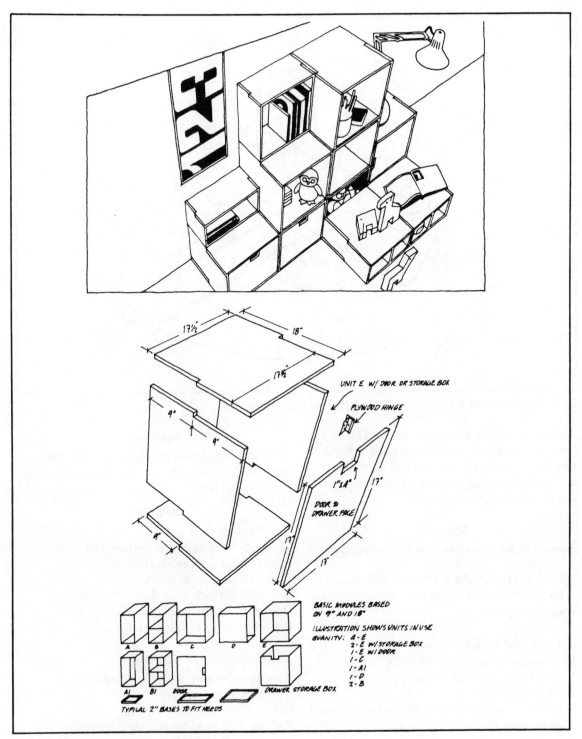

Fig. 6-12. Boxes (courtesy Georgia-Pacific).

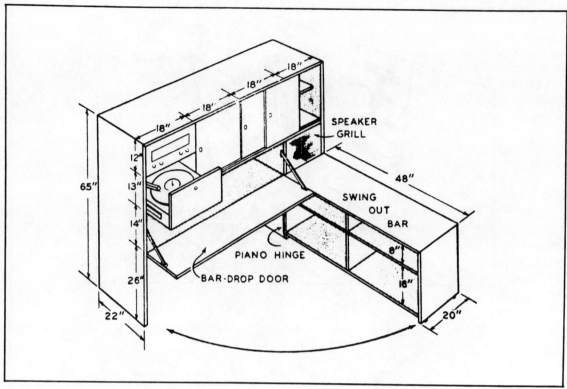

Fig. 6-13. Hi-Fi and bar unit (courtesy Hardwood Plywood Mfg. Assoc.).

speaker grill. This unit will easily hold all of your stereo gear and it has a side bar. It is a woodworking project that is meant for advanced students. With quality hardwood plywood, it will turn out looking professionally done.

Materials

8 sheets (4 × 8) ¾-inch interior hardwood plywood, A-A grade.
1½ sheets (4 × 8 and 4 × 4 feet) ¼-inch Masonite, for backs. Wood filler paste.
Wood filler paste.
Sandpaper.
5 pounds 26d finishing nails.
1 drawer slider hardware, 20 inches long.
1 piano hinge, 60 inches long.
2 bar drop hinges.
1 quart wood stain; to match hardwood veneer used.
2 quarts clear finish.
White glue.

Directions

This stereo unit is composed of two parts: the main unit and the side unit. Cut the plywood and Masonite as follows.

Main Unit

Two 65 × 22-inch; sides.
Three 22 × 72 inch; top, bottom, and shelf.
One 22 × 54 inch; internal shelf.
Three 18 × 25 inch; doors.
One 14 × 60 inch; drop door.
One 14 × 22 inch; speaker wall.
One 65 × 72 inch; Masonite back.

Side Unit

Two 48 × 20 inch; top and bottom.
One 46½ × 20 inch; shelf.
One 8 × 20 inch; shelf support.
One 16 × 20 inch; bottom shelf support.
One 48 × 20 inch; Masonite back.

Cut out all of the pieces for both units and then begin constructing the larger of the two. Use white glue and finishing nails for all fastening. Make sure you look over the diagram carefully before beginning as well as during construction. After both cabinets have been built to your satisfaction, you can begin finishing off the project.

To finish, begin by filling all nail holes and exposed edges on the project. After the filler paste has dried hard, sand everything smooth and apply a coat of wood stain. Next, apply two coats of clear finish, sanding between coats.

WINDOW PLANTER

Figure 6-14 shows a window planter design from the Hardwood Plywood Manufacturer's Association. It is simple to build and it offers an attractive way to organize a planting in front of a low window. The shelf to the right of the planter box can be used as a bookcase or room for potted plants.

Materials

1 sheet (4 × 8 feet) ½-inch exterior, A-D grade. White glue.
Edge filler paste.
1 pound #8d finishing nails.
1 plastic liner for planter 8 × 24 × 12 inches deep.
2 wooden dowel ¾ of an inch thick, 23½ inches long.
Sandpaper.
1 pint primer.
1 quart semigloss enamel.

Directions

Begin by cutting the sheet of plywood into the following pieces:
One 18 × 60 inch; top.
One 18 × 36 inch; bottom.
Two 18 × 23 inch; ends.
Two 35 × 23 inch; sides.

Assemble the pieces using white glue and finishing nails. Consult Fig. 6-14 to see how the

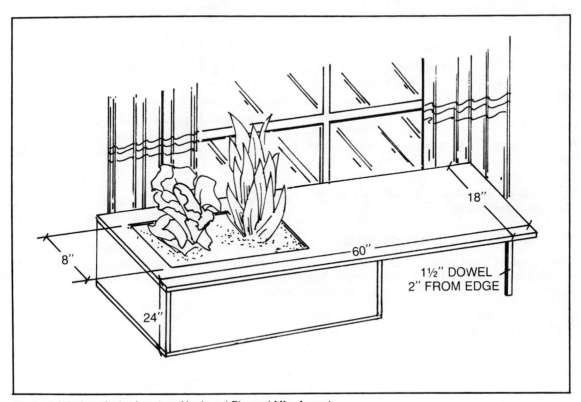

Fig. 6-14. Window planter (courtesy Hardwood Plywood Mfg. Assoc.).

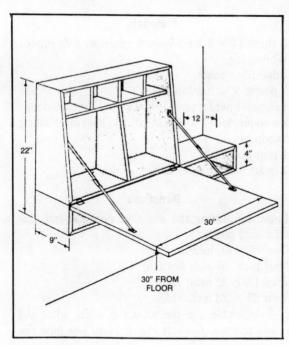

Fig. 6-15. Wall mounted desk (courtesy Hardwood Plywood Mfg. Assoc.).

pieces go together. After the unit is built, you must make a cutout for the planter box. Once this has been completed, you can begin finishing the project.

To finish, first fill all nail holes and exposed edges. After the filler paste has hardened, sand everything smooth and apply a coat of primer. Next, apply two coats of semigloss enamel, sanding lightly between coats. Install the plastic liner inside the plunge cut planter hole and fill with top soil. Then add a few plants.

HOMEMAKER'S WALL-MOUNTED DESK

Here is a great little project that will give you a suitable place to store all kinds of paperwork. The project is simple to make and will prove to be very handy in use. Position it close to the telephone for added value. See Fig. 6-15.

Materials

1 sheet (4 × 8 feet) ¾-inch exterior, A-A grade hardwood plywood.
Two 24-inch long drop-leaf hinges.
Two butt hinges.
Wood filler paste.
Sandpaper.
2 pounds #8d finishing nails.
4 molly bolts.
White glue.
1 quart primer.
2 quarts semigloss enamel.

Directions

Begin by cutting the plywood into the following pieces:
Two 9 × 22 inches; sides.
One 9 × 30 inches; top.
One 30 × 22 inches; door.
Two 9 × 42 inches; bottom and shelf.
Five 4 × 9 inches; separators.
One 9 × 30 inches; upper shelf.
One 9 × 21 ½ inches; long separator.
One 30 × 31 inches; back.

Assemble all parts with white glue and finishing nails. Consult Fig. 6-15 to see how the pieces go together. After the unit has been built, you should finish it before hanging it on the wall.

To finish the piece, begin by first filling all nail holes and exposed edges. After the filler has dried hard, sand everything smooth and apply a coat of primer. Next, apply two coats of semigloss enamel, sanding between coats. When the paint dries, attach this unit to a kitchen wall, near the phone, about 30 inches off the floor. Use molly bolts for this attachment.

Chapter 7

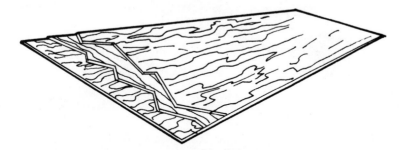

Chairs and Couches

THIS CHAPTER CONTAINS 11 PLYWOOD CHAIR OR couch projects. Each piece of furniture is designed to be comfortable and stylish. Each project has a materials list and directions for building the unit. You should find all of these plans easy to follow.

OCCASIONAL FURNITURE

Here is a simple project to build, and one that you will be proud to display in your home. The chair and sofa are comfortable and stylish. The complete set—chair and sofa—can be built from just two sheets of ¾-inch thick plywood. This set is very affordable.

Materials

2 panels (4 × 8 feet) ¾-inch thick exterior grade plywood, A-A grade.
Sixteen 2-×-2-×-⅛-inch metal angle brackets.
Sixteen ¼-×-½-inch carriage bolts.
Sixteen ⅝-inch, #6 roundhead screws (for angle brackets).

Sixteen 1½-inch, #8 flathead wood screws (for front strip).
Two 2-inch butt hinges with screws.
Eight foam slabs 2 × 2 feet by 3 inches thick.
Upholstery fabric and zippers.
Wood filler.
Sandpaper.
1 quart of primer.
2 quarts of semigloss enamel.

Directions

Mark full sheets of plywood, for cutting according to Fig. 7-1, rounding edges of side and back pieces you prefer. Drill ¼-inch holes in the sides for bolts. Screw angle brackets to the backs and seats as shown; then bolt them to the sides. For greater strength, the back of the sofa should be connected to the seat with two butt hinges, placed about 2 feet from each end. This will keep the back from bending in the center when two or three people are leaning against it.

Attach the plywood front strip with counter-

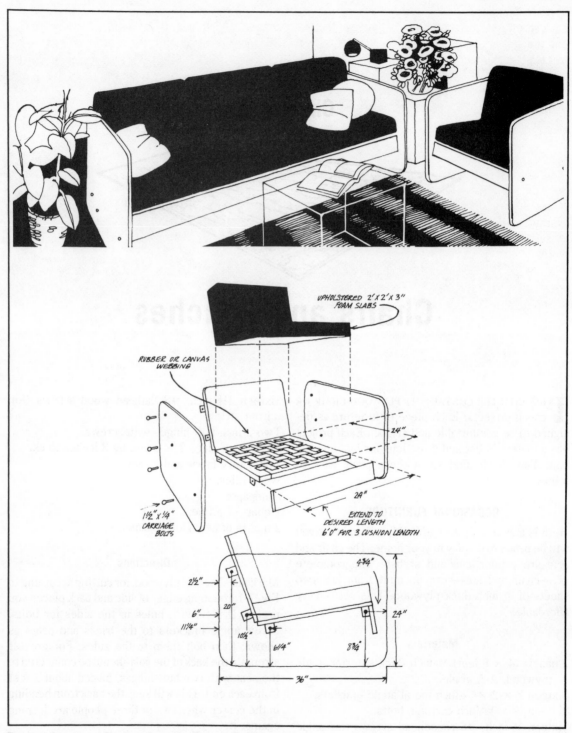

UPHOLSTERED 2' X 2' X 3" FOAM SLABS

RUBBER OR CANVAS WEBBING

24"

24"

EXTEND TO DESIRED LENGTH 6'0" FOR 3 CUSHION LENGTH

1½" X ¼" CARRIAGE BOLTS

2½"

4¾"

20"

6"

11¼"

10½"

6¼"

8¾"

24"

36"

Fig. 7-1. Occasional Furniture (courtesy Georgia-Pacific).

sunk screws through both the front edge of the seat and the sides. Upholstery firms will cut and cover the foam cushions to size or you can just buy the foam and cover it yourself. Sand and fill all exposed edges. Apply a primer coat, sand after dry, and apply two coats of semigloss enamel (sanding between coats.)

SOFA

This sofa is easy to construct, good looking, and very durable. It's all here in a unit designed to give years of comfort. The loose-cushion look adds warmth and style to family and living rooms alike. Assembly is easy and the results look terrific (Fig. 7-2A).

Materials

Two ½ sheets (4 × 8 feet) ¾-inch thick exterior grade plywood A-B grade.

Sixty 1½-inch-long, flat-head wood screws (#8).
Two foam cushions for back (24 × 36 × 3 inch).
One foam cushion for seat (24 × 72 × 3 inch).
Fabric and zippers for cushions.
Filler for screw holes and edges.
1 quart of primer.
2 quarts of semigloss enamel.
Optional finish; stain and clear coating.

Directions

Cut plywood into following size pieces:
Three 8 × 30 ¾ inches.
Two 8 × 31 ½ inches.
Two 8 × 33 ¾ inches.
Two 8 × 36 inches.
Two 8 × 18 ¾ inches.
Nine 8 × 72 inches

After cutting component parts, assemble ac-

Fig. 7-2A. Plywood Sofa (courtesy Georgia-Pacific).

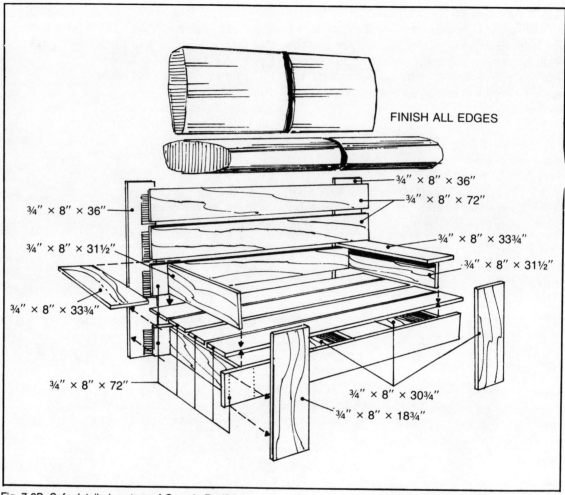

FINISH ALL EDGES

¾" × 8" × 36"

¾" × 8" × 72"

¾" × 8" × 36"

¾" × 8" × 33¾"

¾" × 8" × 31½"

¾" × 8" × 31½"

¾" × 8" × 33¾"

¾" × 8" × 72"

¾" × 8" × 30¾"

¾" × 8" × 18¾"

Fig. 7-2B. Sofa details (courtesy of Georgia-Pacific).

cording to Fig. 7-2B. Countersink all screw holes. After assembly, fill all exposed edges and screw holes. Sand, apply primer, and when dry sand again before applying finish coatings. Two coats should do it. Cushions can be easily made on a home sewing machine or you can have them custom made at an upholstery shop.

MODERN CHAIR

This modern chair is functional, comfortable, and very inexpensive to build. In addition, it is very simple to build because you will require only a sabre saw and electric drill as power tools.

Materials

One sheet (4 × 8 feet) ¾-inch thick exterior plywood, A-A grade.

Three hardwood dowels, 28 inches long.

Canvas: 24 inches wide, 10 feet long (available at almost any fabric shop).

Six #8 finishing nails.

Sandpaper.

1 pint primer.

1 quart semigloss enamel.

Directions

Cut two sides from a full sheet of plywood (there

will be some excess). Next, drill three holes in each side panel as indicated in Fig. 7-3. Assemble pieces allowing wooden dowels to extend approximately 1 inch. Pin these at this location with #8 finishing nails. Fill all edges and sand the entire project smooth. Apply one coat of primer and two coats of semigloss enamel (sanding between coats) before attaching the canvas sling.

UNDER-WINDOW SEAT

This window seat might not be for everyone, but it is a good project for those of you who have the space. The dimensions of this project are variable according to your personal requirements. If you have the room, you should extend the edges of the seat at least 4 inches past the windows (on either side). The standard width of this project is 24 inches. If your space requirements are limited, you can construct this project narrower and make a plant stand. A good width for such a project is 12 inches.

Materials

One full sheet (4 × 8 feet) ¾-inch exterior, A-C grade (for plant stand, only ½ sheet (2 × 8 feet) is required).
Thirty #8 flathead wood screws.
One 2-×-4-inch lumber, 72 inches long.
Six #16d nails for attaching the 2 × 4 under windows.

1 quart of primer.
2 quarts of semigloss enamel.
Optional finish #1:
    Plastic laminate material, 4 × 8 feet.
    Contact cement for attaching plastic laminate.
Optional Finish #2:
    1 quart of stain.
    2 quarts of clear finish.

Directions

Begin by first determining if the space in front of your windows is compatible with the plans shown in Fig. 7-4 (approximately 6 feet of window length). Make any necessary adjustments. Cut out front and sides of project as shown in Fig. 7-4. The back brace is a length of 2 × 4 inch lumber. Attach the 2 × 4 to the wall below the window. Then assemble other parts of the project using wood screws. Countersink all heads and fill holes.

Fill all exposed edges and sand. Apply primer, sand when dry, and then apply two coats of semigloss enamel (sanding lightly between coats). Cushions or throw pillows can be added. If either optional methods of finishing are used (plastic laminate or stain and clear coating), consult the appropriate chapters for more information.

STORAGE COUCH

This handy couch can serve as a guest bed and

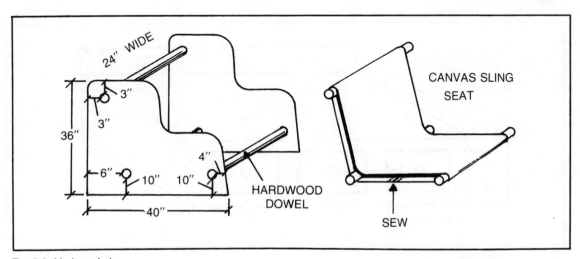

Fig. 7-3. Modern chair.

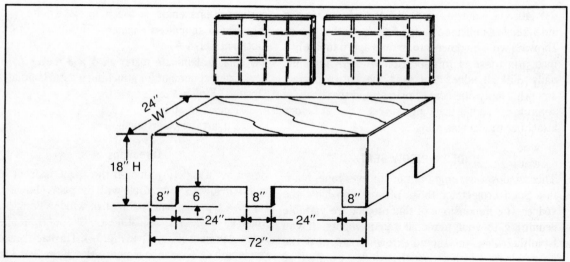

Fig. 7-4. Under-window seat.

storage compartment. The ample size can easily accommodate two sleeping guests, and the full-size drawers will offer plenty of storage.

Materials

Two sheets (4 × 8 feet) ¾-inch plywood, exterior A-D grade.

One-half sheet (4 × 4) ½-inch plywood, exterior A-D grade (for drawers).

Three sets of drawer hardware (sliding mechanisms).

Three drawer pulls.

Two pounds of #8 finishing nails.

White glue.

Filler material.

Sandpaper.

1 quart of primer.

2 quarts of semigloss enamel.

One foam cushion (40 × 72 × 4 inches).

Fabric to cover the cushion.

Directions

Cut the couch pieces from ¾-inch-thick plywood as follows:

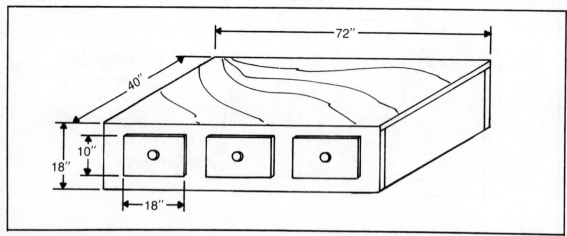

Fig. 7-5. Storage couch.

One 40 × 72 inches (top).

Two 18 × 72 inches (front and back).

Two 38½ × 18 inches (ends).

In addition, make drawer cut-outs on the face of the front (9½ × 17½ inches).

Assemble the couch with finish nails and white glue, making certain that all edges are square. Next, cut and assemble drawers from ½-inch-thick plywood. Install the drawer mechanisms and drawer pulls (to drawer faces) and fit the drawers in place.

Sand the entire project and prime. Sand lightly and then apply two coats of semigloss enamel (sanding between coats). Construct the cushion by simply covering it with fabric.

CANVAS SLING CHAIR

This distinctive chair is easy to build. It requires only an electric drill and sabre saw for all cuts. The style suggests a modern touch, and it is quite comfortable to sit in. This plywood furniture project goes together quickly, and it will endure the test of time.

Materials

One sheet (4 × 8 feet) ¾-inch thick exterior plywood, A-A grade.

Three hardwood dowels ¾-inch in diameter, 28 inches long.

Canvas; 24 inches wide, 10 feet long.

#8 finish nails.

Stain and clear coating.

Sandpaper.

Edge filler material.

Directions

Cut two sides from a full sheet of plywood, as indicated in Fig. 7-6, and then cut out centers of

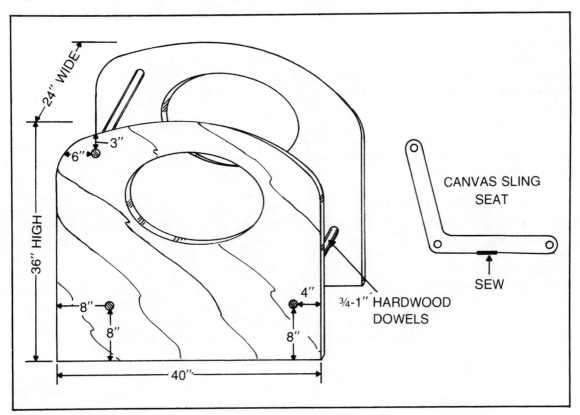

Fig. 7-6. Canvas sling chair.

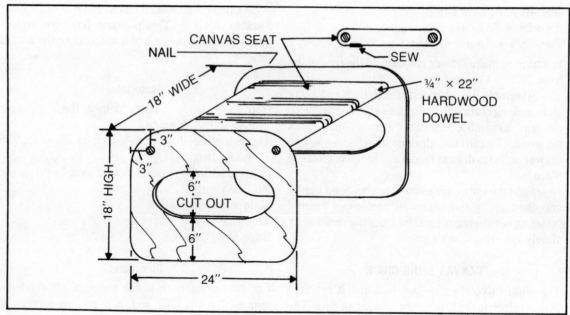

Fig. 7-7. Canvas sling-foot stool.

each. Drill ¾-inch holes in sides as shown. Assemble pieces allowing hardwood dowels to extend approximately 1 inch past sides. Pin dowels at this point with #8 finishing nails. Fill in exposed edges of project with filler material, sanding smooth when dry. Sand entire project smooth. Apply stain and then two coats of clear coating (sanding between coats). After project is constructed and finished, attach canvas seat/back.

CANVAS SLING-FOOT STOOL

This stool (Fig. 7-7) can be used with the canvas sling chair (Fig. 7-6) or by itself. It is simple to build and quite functional. It will look best in a modern setting. Bright canvas material seems to lend itself well to this design.

Materials

½ sheet (4 × 4 foot) ¾-inch thick exterior plywood, A-A grade.
Two hardwood dowels, ¾-inch in diameter, 22 inches long.
Canvas for the sling; 18 × 48 inches.
Four #8 finishing nails.

Sandpaper.
Edge filler material.
1 pint of stain.
1 quart of clear finish.

Directions

Cut two sides of stool from a half sheet of plywood; then cut out the centers of both pieces. Next, drill two ¾-inch diameter holes at the top two corners. Locate holes approximately 3 inches down and 3 inches in from top corner. As an aid, drill holes through two pieces at the same time. Assemble by placing hardwood dowels in place. Allow about 1 inch of dowel extension. Pin dowels in place by driving #8 finish nails down from top.

Finish by filling all edges, sanding smooth, and then applying stain. When dry, apply two coats of clear finish (sanding between coats). After finishing, attach sling seat (sewing from below).

PLYWOOD CHAIR

This modern-looking chair (Fig. 7-8) is easy and quick to build. Because almost all of the cuts are straight (except for the front edge of the arms), they are best made on a table saw. If you don't have such a saw, ask about custom cutting when you purchase the plywood.

Materials

One sheet (4 × 8 feet) exterior plywood, ¾-inch thick, A-A grade. There will be excess plywood (approximately 2 × 4 feet) after cutting.
Twelve flathead wood screws, 2 inches long (#8).
White glue.
Sandpaper.
Edge filler paste.
1 pint of stain.
1 quart of clear coating.

Directions

Cut pieces as follows:
Two 30-×-27-×-¾-inch pieces for sides, with one corner rounded for the front edge.
One 24-×-18-×-¾-inch piece for the seat.
One 18-×-30-×-¾-inch for the back.

Assemble pieces and drill holes through sides and into the back and seat of the chair (drill countersink drill holes). Sand all pieces before assembly. Attach the sides to the seat and back using glue and countersunk screws. Fill all exposed edges, sand smooth, and apply stain. Apply two coats of clear coating (sanding between coats). Foam pillows are an optional addition that can add a little softness to the seat.

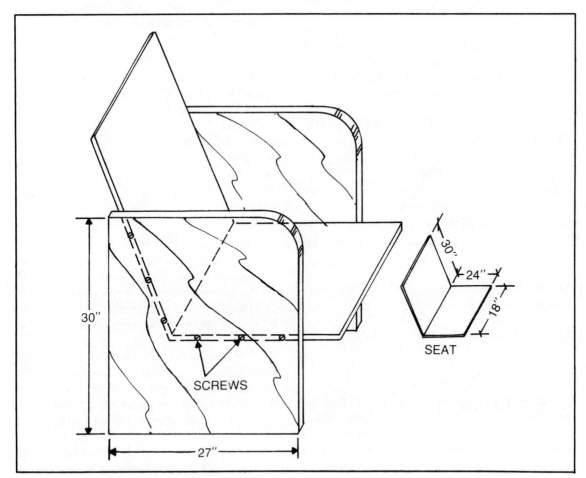

Fig. 7-8. Plywood chair.

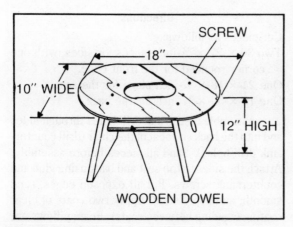

SCREW

|← 18" →|

10" WIDE

12" HIGH

WOODEN DOWEL

Fig. 7-9. Small stool.

SMALL STOOL

This is a good project for small scrap pieces of plywood as long as the scrap is ¾ of an inch thick and of a good grade such as A-A or A-B. The top for this project is sort of a free-form design—in this case oval. You can vary this design if you like. One feature you will want to keep, however, is the hole in the top. This hole makes for easy picking up of the stool with one hand. See Fig. 7-9.

Materials

One piece of ¾-inch plywood measuring 4 feet long by 18 inches wide, A-A grade.
One hardwood dowel, ¾ of an inch in diameter by 16 inches in length.
Edge filler paste.
White glue.
#10 finishing nails.
Sandpaper.
½ pint of primer.
1 pint of semigloss enamel; bright colors look best here.

Directions

Cut the freeform shape for the top of stool. Then cut the hand hole in the center. Next, cut two legs (each measuring 12 inches high and 8 inches wide). Drill ¾ inch in diameter 2 inches up from bottom of each leg (centered). Position the legs under the top and drill countersink screw holes down from top and

into each leg. Three screws per leg are required. Secure the top to the legs with screws. Insert hardwood dowel and pin in place with #10 finishing nails and glue. Fill all exposed edges and countersunk screw holes. Sand the entire project. Apply primer, sand, and then apply finish coating (two coats). Remember to sand between coats.

THREE-PLY CHAIR

This chair is easy to build when all of the pieces have been cut exactly the same. Although the three-ply lamination adds to the overall cost of this chair, the design is well worth the extra cost. In addition, the three-ply chair is very strong. Notice that the plans (Fig. 7-10) do not call for any type of cushions. You can add your own made from 3-inch thick foam and covered with a bright fabric.

Materials

Two ½ sheets (4 × 8 feet) ¾-inch-thick exterior plywood, A-C or A-D grade.
Twenty-two 3-inch-long #8 countersunk wood screws.
Four 2-inch-long #8 countersunk wood screws.
White glue.
Sandpaper.
Stain (optional).
Clear coating for finish.

Directions

Cut all pieces of chair from plywood. A table saw will help you to make long, straight cuts for this project. Laminate the sides (three pieces 24 × 30 inches) together using white glue and clamps. Do the same for the two back pieces (30½ × 30 inches high).

After the glue hardens, assemble the pieces by attaching the seat, the bottom member, and the back with long wood screws and more white glue wherever two or more pieces of the chair come together. The original plans call for finishing with clear finish only and leaving all plywood edges exposed (although coated with clear finish). If you find this type of finish objectionable, you could fill all exposed edges of the plywood and then stain before

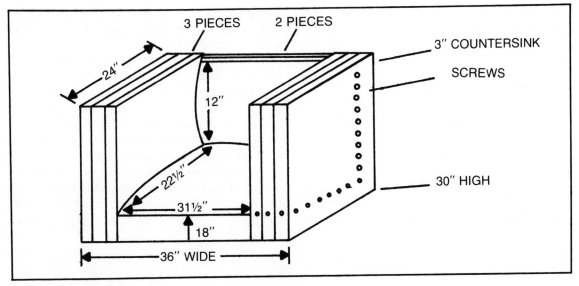

Fig. 7-10. Three-ply chair.

coating with clear finish. Still another alternative is to prime and paint the three-ply chair.

THREE-PLY COUCH

This couch (Fig. 7-11) can be used by itself or as a mate to the three-ply chair (Fig. 7-10). The set will provide you with plenty of comfortable seating in your living room or playroom. You will notice that there are no pillows shown in Fig. 7-12, but you can add some for more comfort.

Materials

Six sheets (4 × 8 feet) ¾-inch-thick exterior plywood, A-D grade.

Twenty-six flathead wood screws, 3 inches long (#8).

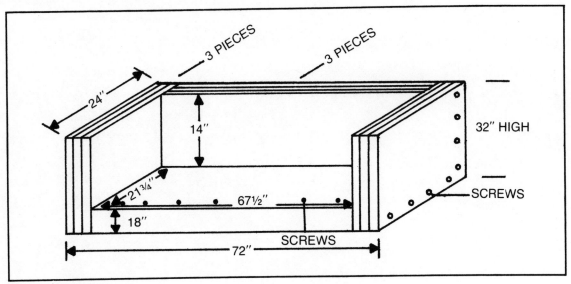

Fig. 7-11. Three-ply couch.

White glue.

Sandpaper.

2 quarts of clear finish.

Optional finish #1:

    1 quart of stain.

    2 quarts of clear finish.

Optional finish #2:

    Edge filler paste.

1 quart of primer.

2 quarts of semigloss enamel.

Directions

Cut all pieces according to Fig. 7-11. Use a table saw for best results. Laminate three side pieces (two groups of 24-×-32 inch pieces) with white glue and clamps. Do the same for the three back pieces (67½ × 32 inches).

After the glue has hardened (it is usually best to wait 24 hours), assemble the sides and back of couch. Use long wood screws and white glue for this. Next, attach the seat and front of the couch using white glue and long wood screws. The original design calls for sanding and then coating with a clear finish—leaving all edges exposed. If you prefer, all edges can be filled, project stained, and then coated with a clear finish. One other way to finish the piece is to fill all edges and screw holes, prime, and paint.

Chapter 8

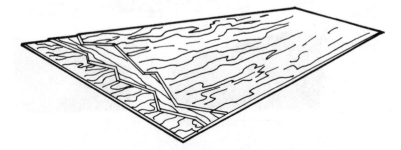

Tables and Stands

THERE ARE 21 PLYWOOD TABLE AND STAND projects in this chapter. Each furniture piece is designed to provide workspace and some have storage space. All of the projects have materials lists and step-by-step directions for constructing the units. The projects range from very simple to advanced designs.

PARSONS' COFFEE TABLE

The traditional parsons' table has the strong, simple lines of modern furniture. It makes a beautiful coffee table for the living room or an occasional table for almost any room. As shown in Fig. 8-1, construction is fairly simple. It is so easy, in fact, that you may want to make several parsons tables—in different sizes—for your home.

Materials

1 sheet (4 × 8 feet) ¾-inch-thick exterior plywood, A-C grade.
Two 1-×-2-×-40-inch sections of lumber (for ledgers).

Two 1-×-2-×-34½-inch sections of lumber (for ledgers).
½ pound of #4d finishing nails.
White glue.
Filler paste.
1 quart of primer.
2 quarts of semigloss enamel (white is recommended).
Sandpaper.

Directions

Cut out pieces as indicated in Fig. 8-1. Glue/nail the two 34½-inch ledgers to the inside of the leg pieces ¾ of an inch below the upper edge. The top of the table will rest there. Assemble the leg pieces (A,B,C) and inset pieces (D) using nails and glue. Fit 40-inch ledgers between the plywood legs as shown. Glue/nail ledgers ¾ of an inch below the upper edge of the table. Next, glue/nail 34½-×-46½-inch table top into the assembled frame. Now the table is ready for finishing.

To finish, begin by filling all exposed edges and

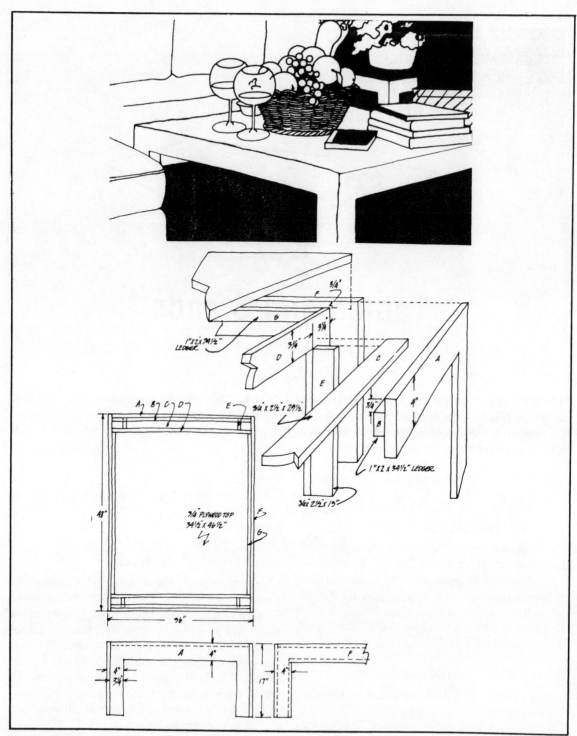

Fig. 8-1. Parson's table (courtesy Georgia-Pacific).

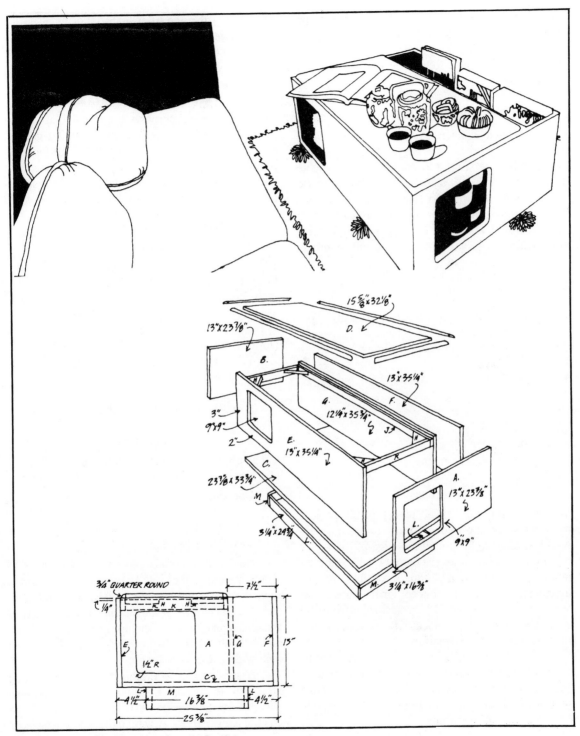

15 5/8" x 32 1/8"

13" x 23 7/8"

B.

13" x 35 1/4"

F.

3"

9" x 9"

2"

G.
12 1/4" x 35 3/4"

J.

E.
15" x 35 1/4"

C.

23 7/8" x 33 3/4"

A.
13" x 23 7/8"

M

9" x 9"

L.

3 1/4" x 29 3/4"

M   3 1/4" x 16 3/8"

D.

3/4" QUARTER ROUND

7 1/2"

1/4"

R   N   K   H

E

A

G

F

15"

1/2" R

C

L   M   L

4 1/2"   16 3/8"   4 1/2"

25 3/8"

Fig. 8-2. Coffee table (courtesy Georgia-Pacific).

221

nail holes with the paste filler material. When the filler has dried hard, sand to make the entire table smooth and flat. Prime the project. Apply two coats of semigloss enamel. Remember to sand lightly between coats.

COFFEE TABLE

If you've been wondering where to store some magazines that are a little ragged but still useful, this coffee table (Fig. 8-2) could be what you've been looking for. Built in, beneath the tabletop, are two storage areas for just that purpose. For your current reading material, this easy-to-make coffee table sports an attractive bin as a built-in feature. Once again, it's easy to build and you will never run out of places to use it.

Materials

1 sheet (4 × 8 feet) ¾-inch-thick exterior plywood, A-C grade.
10 feet ¾-inch, quarter-round molding.
Forty #8 wood screws.
1 pound of #8d finishing nails.
White glue.
Sandpaper.
Wood filler paste.
1 quart of primer.
2 quarts of semigloss enamel.

Directions

Measure, mark, and cut all pieces of the project from the sheet of plywood. Next, cut the quarter-round molding to fit around the edge of the table-top. Remember to miter the corners. Glue/nail the molding around the tabletop. Assemble the remaining pieces together (except for the base L, M, and C). Attach the top (D) by screwing from the underside of the corner blocks (H). Next, it is time to assemble the raised platform and attach the unit to the base section (C, L, and M). It is important to use both while glue and finishing nails or white glue and screws for all fastening tasks. Once the base section has been secured to the raised platform, it is time to finish off the project.

To finish, begin by filling all exposed edges and

nail holes. After the filler material dries, sand the entire project smooth. Prime and apply two coats of semigloss enamel, remembering to sand lightly between all coats.

ALL-PURPOSE WORKTABLE

This is a general-purpose worktable that can be pressed into service in the home workshop, garage, or hobby and crafts room. The plans call for CDX plywood. This plywood is not especially attractive, but it is strong. If you want a table that is cosmetically more attractive, use a better-grade plywood such as A-D.

Materials

1 sheet (4 × 8 feet) ¾-inch-thick CDX plywood.
Four 4-×-4-inch lumber (cedar looks good) 28¾ inches long.
Twenty-four 2-inch-long #8 wood screws.
½ pound of #8d finishing nails.
Optional Finish
  Filler material paste.
  Sandpaper.
  1 quart of primer.
  2 quarts of semigloss enamel.

Directions

Cut all plywood parts of the table from the full sheet of plywood as indicated in Fig. 8-3 and listed below:

  One 24 × 48; top.
  One 19 × 43; shelf.
  Two 3 × 48; front and back edge.
  Two 3 × 22½; ends.

Notch out the ends and middle of the 4-×-4-inch lumber as indicated. These notches in the leg tops should be on two sides and they should measure ¾ of an inch deep and 3 inches wide. Notch out the middle of each leg (8 inches up from the bottom) for the shelf. These shelf notches should be ¾ of an inch wide and 1 inch deep.

Assemble the worktable top first, and then attach this to the legs. Install the shelf. Use screws and glue for the top and top to legs. Use white glue and finishing nails for attaching the shelf to the legs. The original plan does not call for any type of finish,

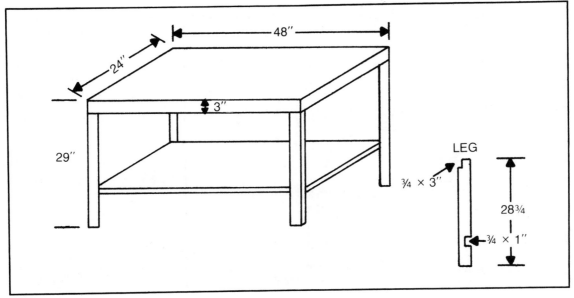

Fig. 8-3. All-purpose work table.

but you can fill all edges, screw holes, and nail holes. Sand everything smooth and apply primer and two coats of semigloss enamel.

KIDNEY-SHAPED COFFEE TABLE

This coffee table is more or less a freeform design that you can modify to suit your personal needs. Basically, the top of this table is cut from a double thickness of ¾-inch-thick plywood—laminated together with white glue—before cutting. The two leg units are made from the other half of a full sheet. Because only one side of the plywood will show on the finished project, it is possible to realize a considerable savings by using A-D grade plywood. Just remember to laminate the "D" sides together.

Materials

1 sheet (4 × 8 feet) ¾-inch-thick, exterior A-D plywood.
White glue.
Six 1½-inch-long #8 wood screws.
¼ pound of #6d finishing nails.
Edge filler paste.
1 quart of primer.
2 quarts of semigloss enamel.
Sandpaper.

Directions

Begin by cutting two 2-×-4 foot sections out of the full sheet of plywood. Laminate these together using clamps and white glue so that you will end up with a double thickness sheet of plywood measuring 2 × 4 feet. Remember to place the two "D" sides together.

After the glue hardens (24 hours) draw a kidney shape (or other design) and cut it out with a sabre saw. Next, construct the two leg supports leaving the bottom of each open. Use white glue and finishing nails for this. After the legs are built, attach them from below to the underside of the coffee table and then the table is ready for finishing.

To finish this kidney-shaped coffee table, begin by filling the edges around the top of the table and on the legs. At this time, also fill any nail holes on the legs. Sand smooth, prime, and apply two coats of semigloss enamel.

WALL-MOUNTED KITCHEN WORKTABLE

Every kitchen can use a little extra workspace and this project (Fig. 8-5) will provide you with plenty. In addition, the small shelf support area can also provide storage space for canned goods, spices, or other small items. The original plans call for cov-

223

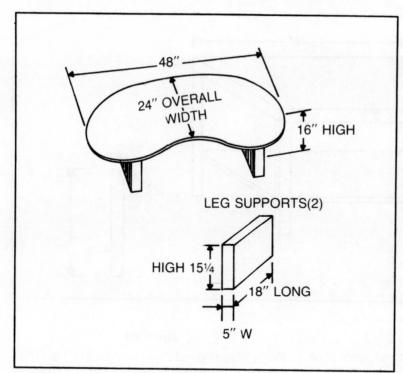

Fig. 8-4. Kidney-shaped coffee table.

ering the work table with plastic laminate. Be sure to choose a color or design that will blend in well with your existing kitchen.

Materials

1 sheet (4 × 8 feet) ¾-inch, CDX plywood (table-top).
16 feet 1-×-4 inch lumber - support shelf.
½ pound of #6d finishing nails.
2 molly bolts - for attaching top to wall.
Three 1½-inch-long #8 wood screws for attaching the shelf to the top.
Wood filler paste.
Sandpaper.
½ sheet (26 × 50 inches) plastic laminate material.
1 quart of contact cement.
1 quart of primer.
1 quart of semigloss enamel.

Directions

Begin by cutting the tabletop from the full sheet of plywood. Next, cut the edge strips for the table (two 3-×-24-inch and two 3-×-34½-inch strips). Attach the edges around the tabletop using white glue and finishing nails. Make certain that all edges and joints are square and flush or you will have a problem with the plastic laminate.

When all is right, attach the plastic laminate—edges first then the top (for more information see Chapter 4). Next, build the shelf support according to Fig. 8-5. It is a good idea to finish this shelf—fill all nail holes, sand, prime, and paint—before attaching it to the tabletop.

Attach the shelf support approximately 4 inches from the front edge of the tabletop (screw from below). Then attach the unit to the wall with molly bolts so the overall height is 29 inches from the floor.

COFFEE TABLE: WITH STORAGE

This easy-to-build project (Fig. 8-6) not only looks good, but it will serve as a storage area for reading materials. This coffee table can also be used as an end table or lamp stand with storage. Because the entire construction takes only about one hour (less finishing) you may want to make two.

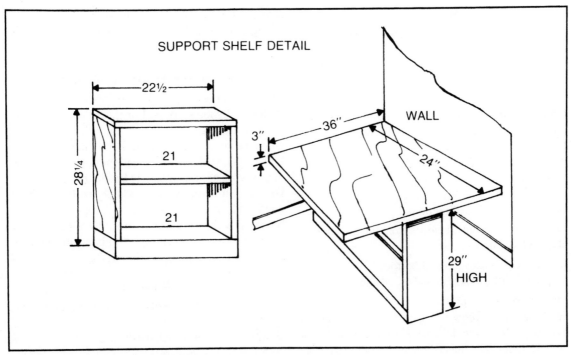

Fig. 8-5. Wall-mounted kitchen work table.

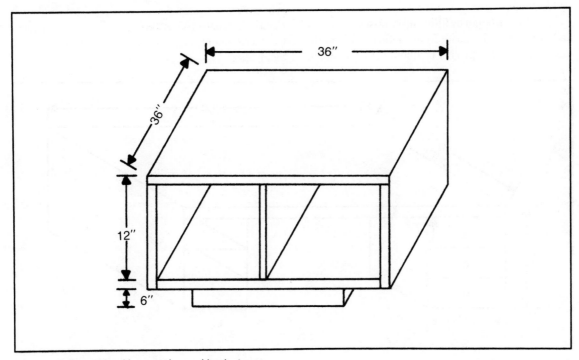

Fig. 8-6. Coffee table with magazine and book storage.

Materials

1 sheet (4 × 8 feet) ¾-inch thick, exterior plywood, A-B grade.
One 10-foot length of 2 × 6 lumber (for the base).
Wood filler paste.
Sandpaper.
1 quart of primer.
2 quarts semigloss enamel (for the top).
1 pint of flat, black enamel for the base.
2 pounds of #8d finishing nails.
White glue.

Directions

Begin by cutting out all pieces from the full sheet of plywood as follows:

Two 36 × 36; top and bottom.
Three 10½ × 36; two sides and center support.

Then assemble all parts using white glue and #8d finishing nails. Allow the glue to dry and harden overnight. Next, build the base of the unit using the 2-×-6 lumber. The finish dimensions of the base are 30 × 30 inches. Attach the base to the top of this coffee table.

To finish, begin by filling all exposed edges and nail holes with the paste filler material. When this dries, sand so the project is smooth. Prime all surfaces. After sanding, paint the entire project with semigloss enamel (except for the base which is painted flat black). Sand between coats.

SEWING TABLE: WITH WORK AREA

This is a large project that requires accurate and straight cuts for success. For this reason, it is best to make all cuts on a table saw or with some type of guidance system if you must use a hand-held circular saw. The original plans call for covering the top of this work area with plastic laminate material, but you can cut some costs by simply building with a good grade of plywood—such as A-A plywood—and finishing with primer and paint. Most people will agree, however, that the plastic laminate top provides the best type of work surface.

Materials

Two ½ sheets (4 × 8 feet) ½-inch exterior plywood, A-B grade.
3 sets of drawer slider hardware.
3 drawer pulls.
3 pounds of #8d finishing nails.
White glue.
Plastic laminate (65 × 38).
Contact cement.
Sandpaper.

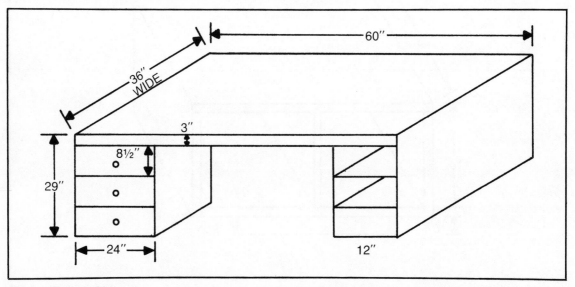

Fig. 8-7. Sewing table.

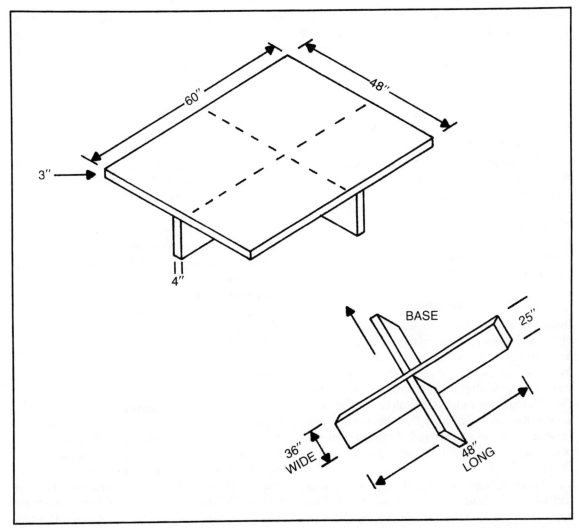

Fig. 8-8. Dining table.

Edge filler paste.
1 quart of primer.
2 quarts of semigloss enamel.

Directions

Begin by cutting all parts from the plywood. The shelf unit on the right of the diagram in Fig. 8-7 will measure 12 inches wide and be 28¼ inches high. The drawered support on the other side will have a finished dimension of 24 inches wide and will also be 28¼ inches high. After building these two support units, attach the top. Be sure to use white glue

and finishing nails for all building steps. After the top is securely in place, cover it with plastic laminate. Next, finish off the support units with edge filler applied to all edges and nail holes. Prime and apply two coats of semigloss enamel (remembering to sand between coats.

DINING TABLE

Here is an attractive dining room table (Fig. 8-8) that is relatively simple to build with common woodworking tools. When finished according to the original plan, this table is very sturdy and will easily seat six people. In a pinch, you can squeeze eight people around this table. The plans call for covering the top with plastic laminate material. Be sure to choose the color or design pattern with care so that the table will grace your dining room.

Materials

2 sheets (4 × 8 feet) ¾-inch-thick exterior plywood, A-D grade.
Plastic laminate material (60 × 72 inches).
White glue.
1 quart of contact cement.
2 pounds of #8d finishing nails.
Wood filler paste.
1 quart of stain.
2 quarts of clear finish.
Sandpaper.

Directions

Begin by cutting out all parts from the full sheets of plywood. Because the base of this table requires the most work, you should assemble it first making sure to use white glue and #8d finishing nails for all fastening tasks. After the base has been built, attach the tabletop (with 3-inch edging all the way around). Secure the top to the base from above with #8d finishing nails and apply a bead of white glue on top of the base as well. Next, the project is ready to be finished.

To finish, begin by filling all exposed edges and nail holes in the base of the table. Sand and when dry apply stain and two coats of clear coating. After the

base has been finished to your satisfaction, attach plastic laminate material to the top. First attach the sides of the project and then the top. Consult Chapter 4 for more information about how to best attach plastic laminate material to plywood.

SMALL TABLE

This is a good project for beginners. It requires only a few hours for building and finishing. The modern lines of this table will go nicely in many different types of surroundings. This small table makes an attractive end table or lamp stand as well. See Fig. 8-9.

Materials

¾ sheet (4 × 6 feet) ¾-inch-thick exterior plywood, A-B grade.
White glue.
½ pound of #6d finishing nails.
Edge filler paste.
1 pint of primer.
1 quart of semigloss enamel.
Sandpaper.

Directions

Begin by cutting the sheet of plywood into three pieces, each measuring 24 × 48 inches. Hold two of the pieces together with clamps and cut out the two leg pieces. By clamping before cutting, you are almost certain of achieving two identical pieces for the legs. Cut the third piece to a final measurement of 24 × 32 inches. Assemble the pieces with white

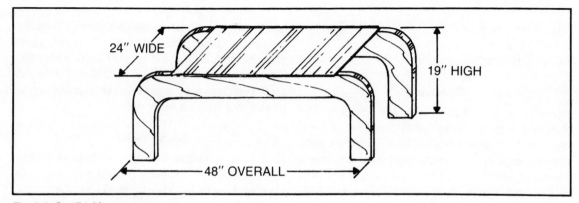

Fig. 8-9. Small table.

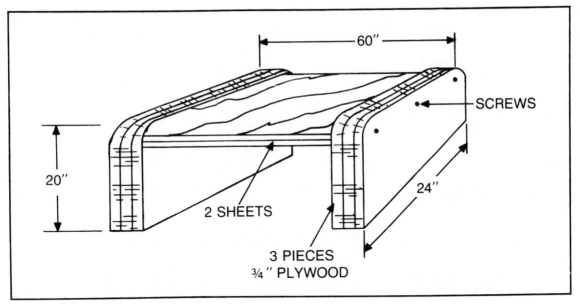

Fig. 8-10. Layered coffee table.

glue and finishing nails. The project is ready to be finished.

To finish, begin by filling all nail holes and exposed edges. When the filler material is dry and hard, sand everything smooth. Next, apply primer and two coats of semigloss enamel—sanding between coats.

LAYERED COFFEE TABLE

This is an interesting modernistic design that can be used with similar designs found in Chapter 7. The finished piece is extremely sturdy and distinctive looking. It is simple to construct; the entire project requires only a few hours. The original design calls for a finish of only two coats of clear finish—such as varnish. If you find the exposed edges of plywood objectionable, you can fill all edges and then stain or prime and paint with a good-quality semigloss enamel.

Materials

2 sheets (4 × 8 feet) ¾-inch-thick exterior plywood, A-D grade.
White glue.
Eight 4-inch-long, #8 wood screws (brass screws will also look good).
Sandpaper.
2 quarts of clear coating.

Directions

Begin by cutting six pieces for the legs and two pieces for the tabletop. See Fig. 8-10. Before bounding the top corners of the legs, laminate three pieces together (for each of the two legs). Use plenty of white glue and clamps. Make sure that the "A" side of the plywood faces outward and that the bottom edges are all square. Laminate the two top pieces together with white glue and clamps. Make sure that the two "D" faces are inboard.

After the glue has hardened (overnight is best), round off the top corners of the legs with a sabre saw. Attach the legs to the top of the table with the brass wood screws. Countersink the heads of the screws so they are just below the surface. Sand the entire project smooth and apply two coats of clear coating (sanding between coats).

PLASTIC LAMINATE COFFEE TABLE

This coffee table (Fig. 8-11) will look good in almost any decor. It is simple to build and very sturdy. If you like the basic design, you can build smaller versions to serve as end tables. Most people find the combination of white plastic laminate and natural oak a very appealing combination.

Materials

½ sheet (4 × 4 feet) ¾-inch-thick CDX plywood.
8 pieces 4 × 15 inch white oak.
Plastic laminate, white, 4 × 4 feet.
1 pint of oak stain.
1 quart of clear finish.
Sixteen roundhead brass wood screws, 2 inches long.
½ pound of #6d finish nails.
White glue.
1 quart of contact cement.
Sandpaper.

Directions

Begin by cutting the top and sides of the table out of the sheet of plywood. Attach the sides to the top of the table using white glue and finishing nails. Next, attach the plastic laminate material to the tabletop. Remember to attach the sides first and then the top. Consult Chapter 4 for more information on how to go about this if you are unsure.

The next step is to make the legs for this table. Each leg is composed of two pieces that have been cut to resemble an upside down letter L. See Fig. 8-11. Fasten the two leg parts together with white glue and finishing nails. Attach the legs, one set to each corner, with the brass wood screws. Do not attempt to countersink the screw heads. The last step is to finish the legs with oak stain and two coats of clear coating—sanding between coats.

HEX STAND

This design produces a sturdy base for plants or a lamp (Fig. 8-12). The plans call for a round plywood top, but you can use another material such as clear glass or even slate. Because all edges of the base are cut to a 60-degree bevel, it is best to make all cuts with the aid of a table or radial-arm saw.

Materials

1 sheet (4 × 8 feet) ¾-inch-thick exterior plywood, A-D grade.
White glue.
Edge filler paste.
1 pound of #6d finishing nails.
1 pint of stain.
1 quart of clear coating.
Sandpaper.

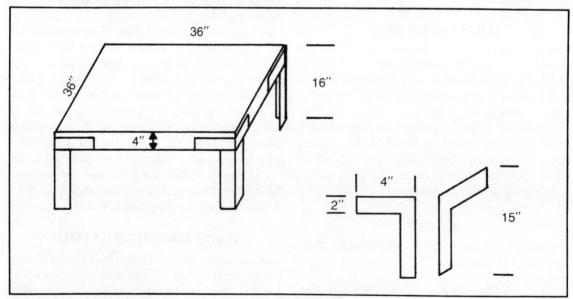

Fig. 8-11. Plastic laminate table.

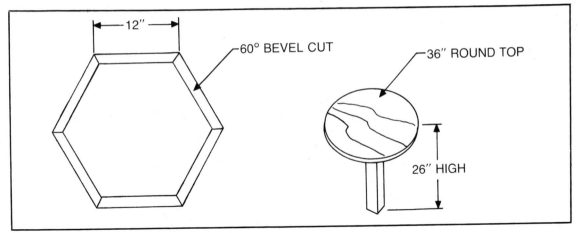

Fig. 8-12. Hex stand.

Directions

Begin by cutting six 12-inch-wide by 26-inch-long pieces of plywood for the base. Run these through your table saw to cut a 60-degree bevel edge on both sides of each strip. Make sure that the "A" side will face outward after the bevel cut has been made. Next, cut out the 36-inch diameter round top for the base. Build the base by attaching the beveled edges with white glue and finishing nails. Attach the top to the base.

To finish this project, begin by filling all nail holes in the base (there will be no exposed edges) and the edge of the round top. When the filler has dried and hardened, sand everything smooth and apply a coat of stain. Next, apply two coats of clear coating—sanding between coats.

BEDSIDE NIGHTSTAND

This easy-to-build stand is ideal for a bedside lamp. In addition, the storage space underneath is a handy place to keep reading materials. With the optional drawer, this bedside nightstand is a project that you will want to build as soon as possible.

Materials

½ sheet (4 × 4 feet) ¾-inch-thick exterior plywood, A-B grade.
White glue.
1 pound of #6d finishing nails.
Sandpaper.
1 pint of wood stain.
1 quart of clear coating.
Edge filler paste.
Optional drawer:
    Drawer hardware; knob and sliding mechanism.

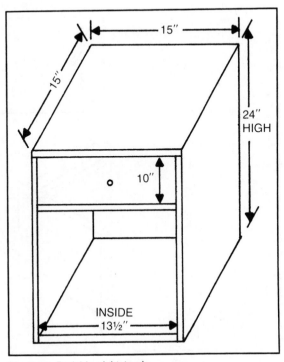

Fig. 8-13. Bedside nightstand.

231

Directions

Begin by cutting all pieces from the sheet of plywood. Assemble the nightstand using white glue and finishing nails. See Fig. 8-13. If you are including a drawer, build it before finishing the project. See Chapter 5 for information about how to build drawers and install a sliding mechanism.

To finish the project, begin by filling all nail holes and all exposed edges. When the filler has dried hard, sand everything smooth and apply a coat of stain. The last step is to apply two coats of clear finish, sanding between coats.

GLASS-TOP COFFEE TABLE #1

This is a very simple plywood furniture project (Fig. 8-14) to build and one that you can turn out in

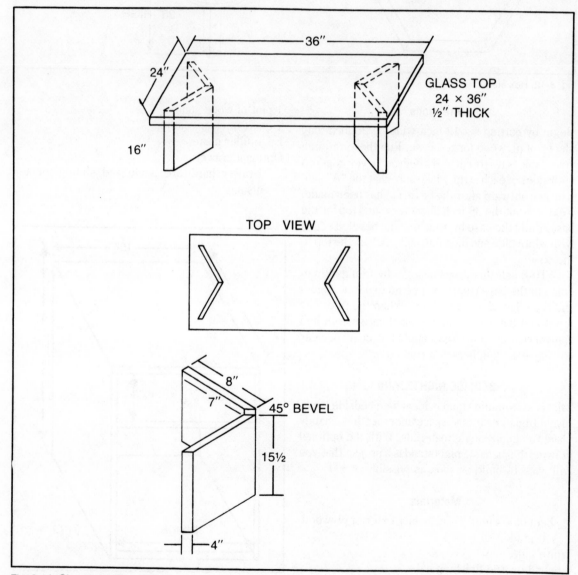

Fig. 8-14. Glass-top coffee table #1.

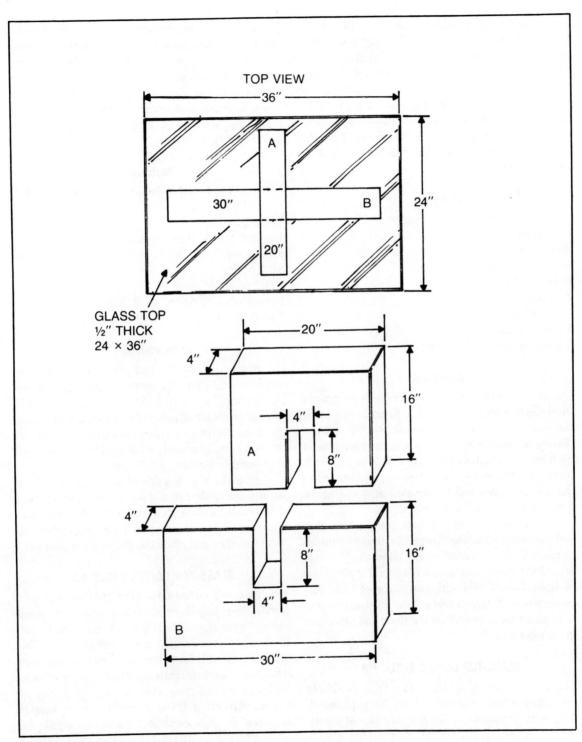

TOP VIEW

36"

A

30"   B

24"

20"

GLASS TOP
½" THICK
24 × 36"

20"

4"

16"

4"

A   8"

4"

16"

8"

4"

B

30"

Fig. 8-15. Glass-top coffee table #2.

just a few hours—start to finish. There are a number of variations to this basic design. An example is covering the leg supports with plastic laminate material. The basic design calls for finishing with stain and clear coating. You will have to buy thick glass—at least ½ inch is best—for this table. That generally means going to a store that specializes in selling glass. It is a good idea to have the edges of the glass beveled or at least polished for looks as well as safety.

Materials

½ sheet (4 × 4 feet) ½-inch-thick exterior plywood, A-D grade.
White glue.
1 pound of #4d finishing nails.
Filler paste.
Sandpaper.
1 pint of stain.
1 quart of clear coating.
1 piece of ½-inch thick glass, 24 × 36 inches.

Directions

Cut all of the pieces necessary for the leg supports from the half sheet of plywood. Keep in mind that the inside of the legs measure 7 × 15½ and the outside measure 8 × 15½. Each support leg (one at each end of the table) will have two 7-×-15½-inch pieces and two 8-×-15½-inch pieces. Additionally, the joining edges will be beveled at a 45-degree angle to form a "V" when joined.

Assemble the leg supports using white glue and finishing nails. When complete, finish by filling all nail holes and exposed edges. When the filler has dried hard, sand everything smooth and apply a coat of stain. Follow this with two coats of clear finish—sanding between coats. Now all that remains is to place the supports on the floor and place the glass top on them.

GLASS-TOP COFFEE TABLE #2

The base for this glass-top coffee table is simply two interlocking rectangles built from plywood. The two parts shown in Fig. 8-15 are almost identical except that one is 20 inches long and the other is 30 inches long. In addition, the "A" support has a notch (that measures 4 inches wide and 8 inches long) removed from the bottom while the other support ("B") has an identical section removed from the top. A careful look over the plans will aid you in constructing these supports. When buying the glass for the top, use only safety glass with a thickness of at least ½ of an inch.

Materials

½ sheet (4 × 4 feet) ¾-inch-thick exterior plywood, A-D grade.
White glue.
1 pound of #6d finishing nails.
Filler paste.
Sandpaper.
1 pint of stain.
1 quart of clear finish.
1 piece of glass, ½ inch thick, 24 × 36 inches.

Directions

Cut all pieces from the half sheet of plywood. Be careful to make straight and accurate cuts. Assemble one section at a time. Use white glue and #6d finishing nails for all joints. After building the piece, check that the pieces will interlock tightly. With the two sections separated, finish by filling all exposed edges and nail holes.

After the filler has dried hard, sand everything smooth and apply a coat of stain. Apply two coats of clear finish, sanding between coats. After both sections have been finished to your satisfaction, fit them together and place the glass top in position.

GLASS-TOP COFFEE TABLE #3

This glass-top coffee table (Fig. 8-16) is a project worth attempting if you have average woodworking skills. The coffee table is not difficult to build, but the finished project looks professionally done. The original plan calls for covering all exposed surfaces with plastic laminate material (white), but you could realize a considerable cost savings by filling all joints and painting. If you do this, however, keep in mind that the finished project will not have quite the same effect. As with the other glass-topped coffee tables described in this chapter, it is best to use tempered glass of at least ½ of an inch thickness and that has polished or beveled edges.

Materials

½ sheet (4 × 4 feet) CDX plywood, ¾-inch thick.
Four 2-×-2-×15-inch lumber (for legs).
White glue.
Contact cement.

Plastic laminate material (white):
  1 piece 30 × 30 inches; top.
  4 pieces 15 × 30 inches; sides.
  8 pieces 2 × 7½ inches; insides of legs.
  4 pieces 2 × 2 inches for tops of legs.
  1 piece of glass ½ × 30 × 30 inches.

Directions

Begin by cutting 1 top piece (A) and sides (four,

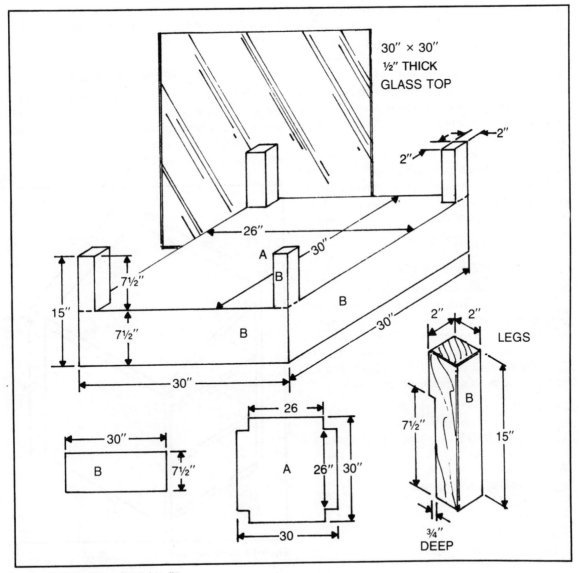

Fig. 8-16. Glass-top coffee table #3.

"B") from the half sheet of plywood. See Fig. 8-16. Next, notch out each of the four legs. Note that each notch is 7½ inches high and ¾ of an inch deep on two sides of each leg (the outsides). With the legs notched in this manner, the plywood sides will fit flush. Next, assemble the sides and legs of the table with white glue and finishing nails, but do not install the top until it has been covered with plastic laminate material.

Begin attaching the plastic laminate material to the top of the coffee table. Once this has been done, slip the covered top into place inside the table and fasten with white glue and nails from the outside. Next, cover the inside of the legs with plastic laminate. Then cover the outsides with plastic laminate and trim. The last thing to do is to cover the tops of the legs with a square of plastic laminate material and trim. Finally, place the glass top in place.

You might find the addition of small cork squares (½ × ½ inch each) to the top center of each leg will prevent the glass from moving. Before positioning the glass, make certain that all joints are tight and flush. Clean them up with a file if necessary.

TELEPHONE STAND

Every home should have one of these handy little telephone stands. This project is simple and inexpensive to build, and it is an ideal place for storing telephone-related materials such as telephone directories and address books. In addition, this basic design lends itself very well to modifications such as the inclusion of a drawer or two doors.

Materials

1 sheet (4 × 8 feet) ½-inch-thick exterior plywood, A-B grade.
White glue.
1 pound of #6d finishing nails.
Filler paste.
Sandpaper.
1 quart of primer.
2 quarts of semigloss enamel.

Directions

Begin by cutting the following pieces:

One 24 × 16 inch; top.
Three 24 × 14½ inch; 2 shelves and bottom.
Two 24 × 28¼ inch; 2 sides.
One 16 × 29 inch; back.

Assemble the parts, according to Fig. 8-17, using white glue and finishing nails. To finish, begin by filling all exposed edges and nail holes. When the filler paste hardens, sand everything flat and apply primer and two coats of semigloss enamel—sanding between coats.

BUTCHER BLOCK TABLE

This is a good project if you have a table saw and a lot of scrap pieces of plywood. The finished table is strong and very distinctive looking as well as functional. The easiest way to hold the table up is to purchase a metal base. Such a base is commonly

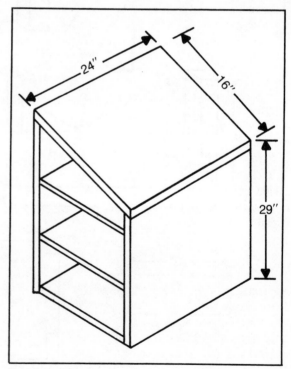

Fig. 8-17. Telephone stand.

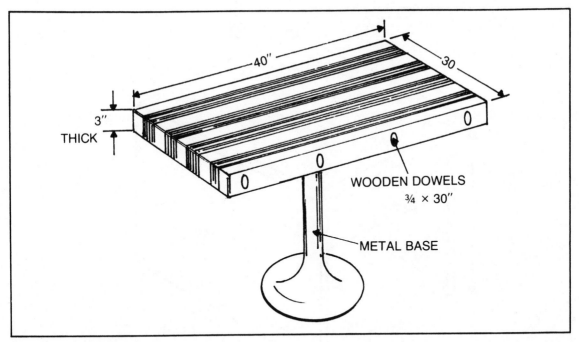

Fig. 8-18. Butcher block table.

available for about $30 at almost any lumber yard or shop that sells "finish-it-yourself" furniture.

Materials

40 pieces ¾-inch plywood, each 3 × 40 inches. Roughly one sheet (4 × 8) any grade.
White glue.
4 hardwood dowels, ¾ inches in diameter, 30 inches long.
Sandpaper.
2 quarts of clear finish.
Metal base.

Directions

With the aid of a table saw, cut 40 strips of plywood; each must be 3 inches wide and 40 inches long. Glue these strips together in groups of six so that all edges are square and exposed. After the glue sets on each batch, drill four ¾-inch diameter holes, evenly spaced. When all five groups have been drilled in this manner, insert the wooden dowels and glue them all together. Bar or pipe clamps will

be necessary for holding the table together until the glue has set up.

To finish, sand the top and sides of the table until they are smooth and no rough texture remains. Next, apply several coats of clear finish, sanding between coats. Finally, attach the tabletop to the metal base.

TV TABLE

Just about every American home could use a project like this. The original plan calls for a finished table that measures 18 × 30 inches. That is about the dimensions of a medium-size color television. You can adjust the measurements to better fit your TV.

Materials

1 sheet (4 × 8 feet) ¾-inch exterior plywood, A-B grade.
White glue.
1 pound of #6d finishing nails.
Sandpaper.
Drawer slider hardware.

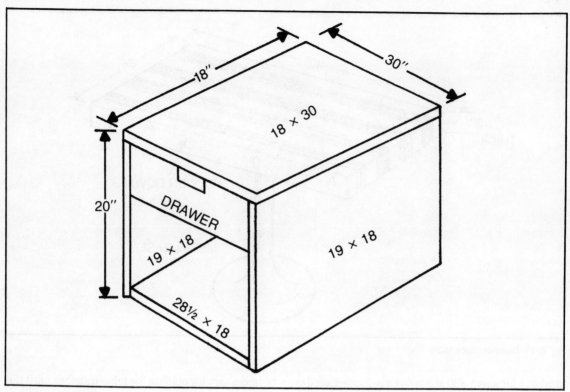

Fig. 8-19. TV table.

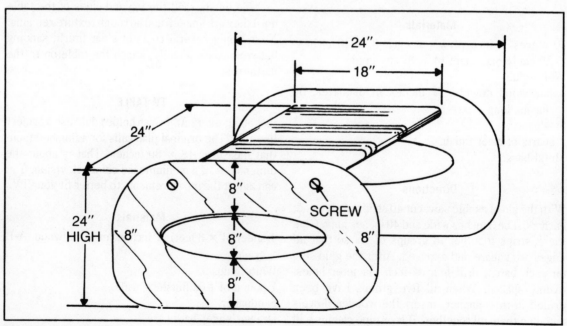

Fig. 8-20. End table #1.

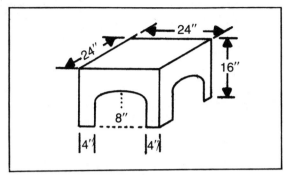

Fig. 8-21. End table #2.

1 quart of primer.
2 quarts of semigloss enamel.

Directions

Begin by cutting all parts from the sheet of plywood as indicated in Fig. 8-19. Next, assemble all parts of the table using white glue and finishing nails. Then build the drawer; see Chapter 5 for information about drawer construction. Finish the table by filling all exposed edges and nail holes. Prime and then apply two coats of semigloss enamel. Remember to sand between coats.

END TABLE #1

This end table (Fig. 8-20) can be used in conjunction with the canvas sling chair described in Chapter 7. Although this is a relatively simple end table to build, you will find a hand-held sabre saw necessary for most of the "freedom" cutting.

Materials

½ sheet (4 × 4 feet) ¾-inch exterior plywood, A-A grade.
Six 2-inch-long #8 wood screws.
Filler paste.
White glue.
Sandpaper.
1 pint of primer.
1 quart of semigloss enamel.

Directions

Begin by cutting two 2-×-2 foot sections from the plywood panel. These will be the legs of the end table and they are best cut as one piece. Clamp the two together and make the rounded edge cuts. Cut

out the centers as shown in Fig. 8-20. Next, cut the tabletop that will measure 18 × 24 inches. Assemble the pieces using white glue and the wood screws. Countersink the screw heads. Next comes the finishing.

To finish, begin by filling all exposed edges and screw holes on the project. After the filler hardens, sand flat and apply primer and two coats of semigloss enamel—sanding between applications.

END TABLE #2

This end table project (Fig. 8-21) is simple to build and it will work well with most types of modernistic furniture. The original plan calls for finishing with primer and semigloss enamel (white), but you can make an even more interesting piece of furniture by covering it with plastic laminate. Keep in mind, however, that this addition will raise the cost and working time considerably.

Materials

½ sheet (4 × 4 feet) ¾-inch-thick exterior plywood, A-D grade.
White glue.
½ pound of #6d finishing nails.
1 pint of primer.
1 quart of semigloss enamel.
Sandpaper.
Wood filler.

Directions

Begin by cutting the top (24 × 24 inches) and four sides (16 × 24 inches) from the half sheet of plywood. Next, make a circular cutout along the bottom of each of the four leg pieces. The plans call for a half-moon type of shape, but you can modify this. Just make all four cutouts the same.

Build a box shape using the four legs, white glue, and finishing nails. Once the base is built, attach the top with more white glue and finishing nails.

To finish the end table, begin by filling all exposed edges and nail holes. After the filler material is dry and hard, sand the entire project until smooth. Apply primer and two coats of semigloss enamel, sanding between coats.

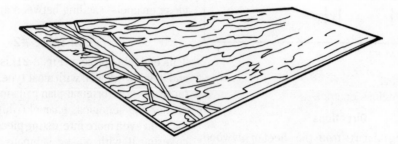

Chapter 9

Children's Furniture

THIS CHAPTER DESCRIBES 12 VERSATILE AND DURable plywood furniture projects. Each piece of furniture is designed to be practical, and some are multipurpose units. Materials lists and directions are provided for each of the projects.

TABLE/ROCKER/CHAIR

Here is a project that your children can lend a hand with, and they will find plenty of uses for the finished project. Depending on which way they stand it, this three-in-one chair can be a rocker, a table, or an everyday chair. This project is fairly simple to construct. You might want to build several of these multipurpose chairs.

Materials

1 sheet (4 × 8 feet) ½ inch exterior, A-B grade.
White glue.
Wood filler.
1 pound of #8d finishing nails.
Sandpaper.
1 pint of primer.
1 quart of semigloss enamel.

Directions

Begin by measuring, marking, and cutting all pieces as shown in Fig. 9-1. You will need two of each. For the curved side panels, you should first cut the pieces square. Then use a cardboard or paper pattern for a guide to cutting the rounded sides. Use a sabre saw for this cutting. If you cut the pieces correctly, the rocker bottom will balance perfectly.

To slot the pieces, drill a hole using a ½-inch drill bit at the end of the proposed slot. Then cut from the edge of the hole. Simply trace the slots of the finished panel onto the uncut piece to ensure a perfect match. After all pieces have been cut and slotted, you are ready for assembly. This is very simple. Use white glue and finishing nails for fastening the pieces together.

To finish, begin by filling all nail holes and exposed edges on the project. This will mean filling all edges. After the filler paste has dried hard, sand everything smooth and apply a coat of primer. Next, apply two coats of semigloss enamel, sanding between coats. After the paint has dried, the project will be ready for action.

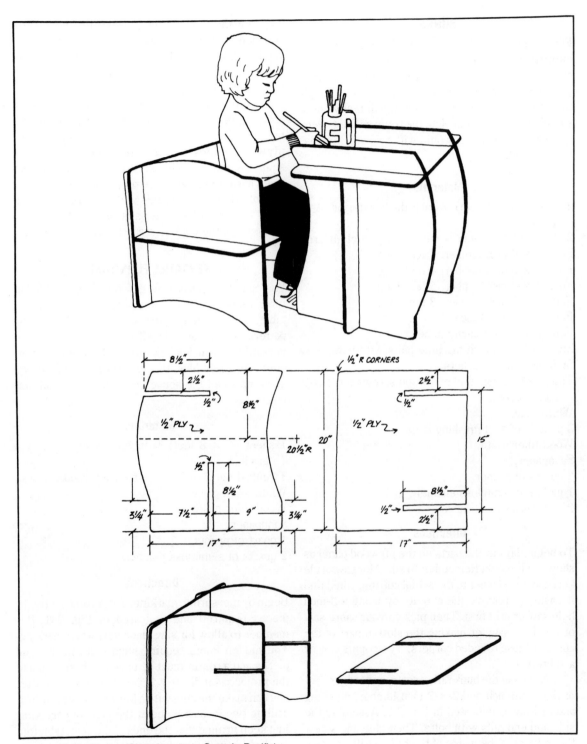

Fig. 9-1. Table/Rocker/Chair (courtesy Georgia-Pacific).

BUNKS

Funny how your children will take a sudden new interest in bedtime. If you want to see that dream come true, take a few hours to construct this good-looking, heavy-duty bunk. It is strong enough to last for years, and your children will really enjoy sleeping in it. As a real plus, the room will not seem quite as crowded as it would with two single beds. See Fig. 9-2.

Materials

2 sheets (4 × 8 feet) ¾-inch-thick exterior, A-A grade.
2 sheets (4 × 8 feet) ⅝-inch-thick particle board.
Four 2-×-6-inch lumber, 7 feet long.
Four 2-×-6-inch lumber, 4 feet long.
Four 2-×-2-inch lumber, 6 feet long.
Four 2-×-2-inch lumber, 3 feet long.
Four 2-×-2-×-18-inch lumber.
Four 1-×-4-×-48-inch lumber.
Sixteen ¼-×-5-inch machine bolts with nuts.
Sixteen ¼-inch washers.
Thirty #12 2-inch flathead wood screws for 2-×-2 inch ledgers.
White glue.
3 pounds of #8d finishing nails.
Wood filler paste.
Sandpaper.
2 quarts of primer.
1 gallon of semigloss enamel.
2 mattresses to fit bunk.

Directions

To begin, lay out the parts on the plywood panel as shown in Fig. 9-2. Remember to allow for saw blade kerfs. When you get to the actual cutting, you'll find it easier to remove the cutouts by using a 3-inch hole saw or drill first. Then pick up your sabre saw or key hole saw for making the slotted part of the cut. For those rounded corners, try a coping saw or a sabre saw.

Next, cut the bunk rails, cleats, and ledgers out of the 2-×6-inch and 2-×-2-inch lumber, notching and drilling as indicated in Fig. 9-2. Assemble the side and end rails with bolts. Then glue and screw the ledgers to the inside of the rails. Drill accurate

holes for the machine bolts. Next, the ledgers are attached to the end panel and the cleats to the vertical side panels. Bolt the bunks together and fit in both top and bottom braces. Now that the project is assembled, it is ready for finishing.

To finish, begin by making sure there are no sharp corners. Use a wood rasp or plane for rounding. Fill all bolt and nail holes and all exposed plywood edges. Your intention is to create smooth—and safe—lines. After the filler paste has dried hard, sand the entire project smooth. Apply a coat of primer. Follow this with two coats of semigloss enamel. When the paint dries, add the mattresses and the bunk is ready for years of service.

VERSATILE FURNITURE

You can choose from six different pieces of furniture: a desk, a set of shelves for toys or books, a table, a doll's bed, and a love seat. The cutting pattern is the same in all cases. How's that for versatility? You just assemble the pieces differently. As a real plus, this furniture is tough. It will stand up to all the abuse your little ones can dish out.

Materials

1 sheet (4 × 8 feet) ¾-inch-thick exterior, A-A grade.
Twenty-Four 2-inch #8 roundhead wood screws.
White glue.
Wood filler paste.
Sandpaper.
1 quart of primer.
2 quarts of semigloss enamel.

Directions

Begin by measuring, marking, and cutting out the 10 pieces required and indicated in Fig. 9-3. Remember to allow for saw blade kerf when marking. The hidden joints require blind slots in the end pieces and a router must be used for these to make the project as indicated. If you don't own a router, you can make the cuts with a key hole saw after first drilling two ¾-inch holes at the ends of each slot. Just keep in mind that the ends of the seat, tabletop, or shelves will then be visible. In this case, you

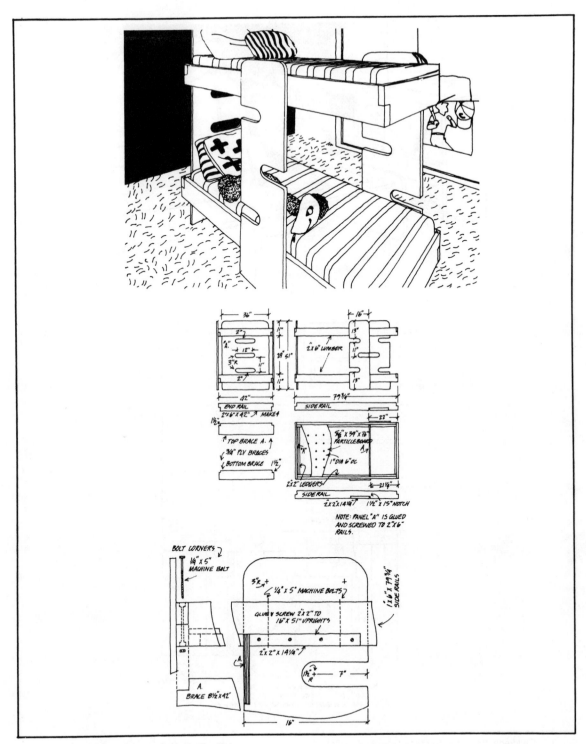

Fig. 9-2. Bunk Beds (courtesy Georgia-Pacific).

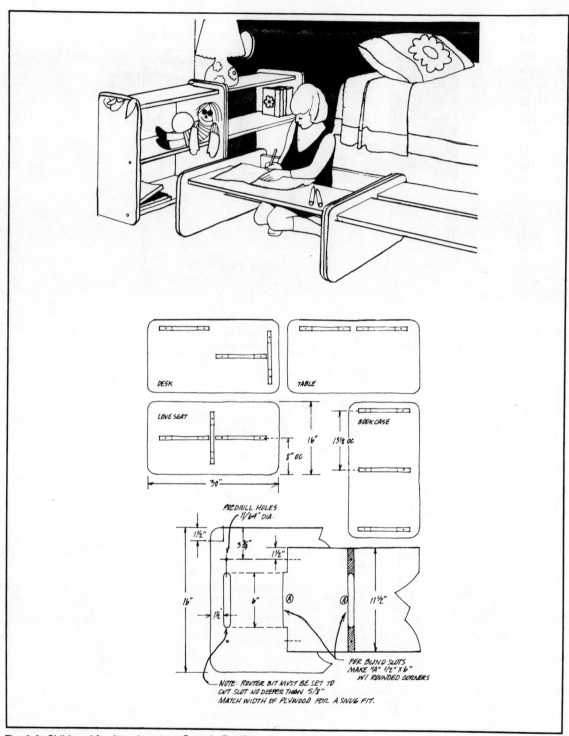

Fig. 9-3. Childrens' furniture (courtesy Georgia-Pacific).

must also make the tongues ¾ of an inch longer (on both sides) to fit flush with the outside.

After all of the pieces have been cut and slotted, assemble the project using the screws and white glue. Round off all of the corners and fill all screw holes and exposed panel edges. After the filler paste has dried hard, sand the entire project smooth and apply a coat of primer. Next, apply two coats of semigloss enamel, sanding between coats. After the paint dries, the project is ready for use.

TOY STORAGE BOX

Kids seem to accumulate toys faster than parents can keep up with them. One sure solution is to build a toy box for storage (Fig. 9-4). Put wheels on the bottom and the box can be wheeled from one room to the next. The next thing to do is convince your children that their toys go into the box when not in use. For that part, you are really on your own.

Materials

1 sheet (4 × 8 feet) ½-inch exterior, A-B grade.
White glue.
1 pound of #8d finishing nails.
Wood filler paste.
Sandpaper.
Rope; about 24 inches, for handles.
4 caster-type wheels.

1 quart of primer.
2 quarts of semigloss enamel.
Decals of animals for sides.

Directions

Begin by cutting the plywood into the following size pieces:

   Two 36 × 16 inch; sides.
   Two 16 × 16 inch; ends.
   One 16 × 36 inch; bottom.

Assemble the pieces with white glue and nails according to the diagram. Then drill two ½-inch holes in the ends for the rope handles. The last part of the construction is to add the caster wheels to the bottom.

To finish, begin by filling all nail holes and exposed edges. After the filler paste has dried hard, sand the entire project smooth and apply a coat of primer. Follow this with two coats of semigloss enamel, sanding between coats. Apply decals of favorite animals or TV characters to the sides, and fill up with toys.

HANDY STOOL

Sooner or later your child will want to start washing his hands and face and brushing his teeth just like the rest of the folks. The only problem is that junior is not tall enough to reach the bathroom sink with-

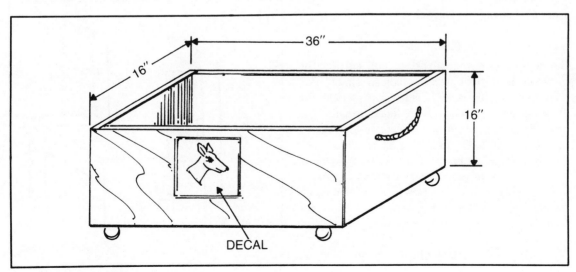

Fig. 9-4. Toy storage box.

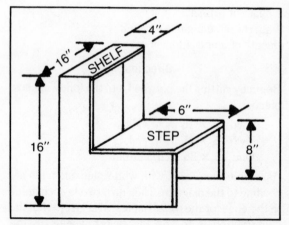

Fig. 9-5. Handy stool.

out assistance. One good solution to this problem is to build a small stool that will enable your child to wash at the sink. The project is simple and a real aid in getting your child up safely to sink height.

Materials

½ sheet (4 × 4 feet) ¾-inch-thick exterior, A-B grade.
White glue.
1 pound of #8d finishing nails.
Wood filler paste.
Sandpaper.
1 pint of primer.
1 quart of semigloss enamel.

Directions

Begin by measuring, marking, and cutting the plywood into the four pieces as indicated in Fig. 9-5. Note that the sides are "L" shaped. Assemble the pieces using white glue and the finishing nails. The last step is to finish off the project as follows.

To finish, begin by filling all nail holes and exposed edges. After the filler paste dries hard, sand the entire project smooth and apply a coat of primer. Follow this with two coats of semigloss enamel, sanding lightly between coats. Now the stool is ready for bathroom service.

SMALL CHAIR

Every child should have his or her own chair, but

have you checked the prices for childrens' furniture lately. For just a few dollars and a few hours of your time, you can build chairs like the one shown in Fig. 9-6. They will serve your children well.

Materials

½ sheet (4 × 4 feet) ½-inch-thick exterior, A-B grade.
White glue.
½ pound of #8d finishing nails.
Wood filler paste.
Sandpaper.
1 pint of primer.
1 quart of semigloss enamel.

Directions

Begin by measuring, marking, and cutting out the seven pieces necessary for this project (Fig. 9-6). Note that the two side legs have a semicircular cutout along the bottom edge. A sabre saw is the best tool for this type of cutting. When all of the pieces have been cut, assemble the project using white glue and finishing nails. After the glue has dried—overnight is best—the project is ready for finishing.

To finish, begin by filling all nail holes and exposed edges. After the filler has dried hard, sand

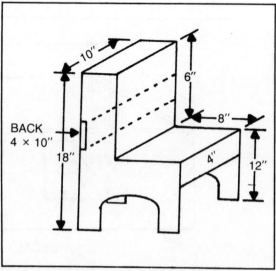

Fig. 9-6. Small chair.

the entire project smooth and apply a coat of primer. Follow this with two coats of semigloss enamel, sanding lightly between coats. After the paint dries, the chair is ready for use.

STORAGE BED

Here is a good project for when your child is ready to move from the crib to a real bed. In addition, to providing a safe place to sleep, this bed also offers underneath storage space.

Materials

2 sheets (4 × 8 feet) ½-inch exterior, A-D grade.
White glue.
5 pounds of #8d finishing nails.
Wood filler paste.
Sandpaper.
2 sets drawer slider hardware.
2 drawer pulls or knobs.
Foam mattress with cover to fit.

Directions

Begin by measuring, marking, and cutting the plywood as follows:

    One 36 × 60 inch; top.
    Two 12 × 60 inch; sides.
    Two 12 × 34½-inch; ends.
    Two 7 × 24 inch; drawer fronts.
    Two 6 × 22 inch; drawer backs.
    Four 6 × 24 inch; drawer sides.
    Two 22 × 24 inch; drawer bottoms.

Assemble the pieces with white glue and finishing nails as shown in Fig. 9-7. After the basic bed has been constructed, make the cutout holes for the drawers (these will be 6 × 23 inches each). Then you can turn your attention to building the drawers themselves. Consult Chapter 5 for information about how to do this. Install the drawer sliders and the drawers.

To finish, begin by filling all nail holes and exposed edges. After the filler paste has dried hard, sand the entire project smooth and give one coat of primer. Follow this with two coats of semigloss enamel, sanding lightly between coats. Add the covered mattress and store the crib.

ANIMAL CHAIR

Here is a project that is fun to build and one that your child will enjoy using for a long time. The original plans call for an animal design, but you can change this if your child prefers another type of animal—an elephant for example. Just draw carefully before cutting.

Materials

1½ sheets (4 × 8 feet) ½-inch-thick exterior, A-B grade.
Wood filler paste.
One 24-inch-long wooden dowel, ¾ inch in diameter.
Sandpaper.
White glue.

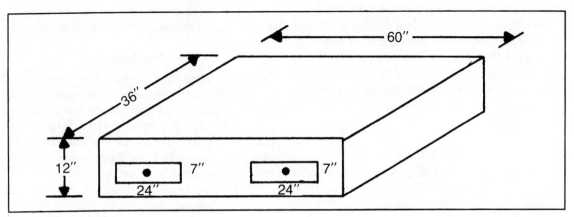

Fig. 9-7. Storage bed.

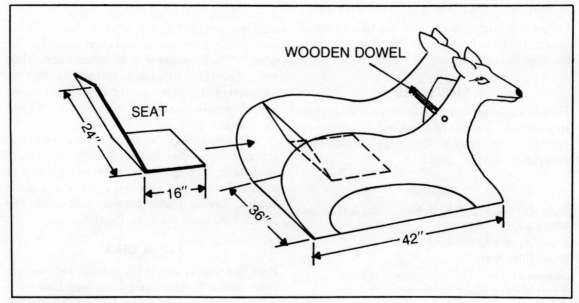

Fig. 9-8. Animal chair.

1 pound of #8d finishing nails.
1 quart of primer.
2 quarts of semigloss enamel in colors, as required.

Directions

Begin by drawing an animal design on one 4-×-4-foot piece of plywood. Place another 4-×-4 foot sheet under this and cut out two patterns. Cut the seat (two pieces 24 × 24 and 24 × 16 inches). Assemble the pieces as shown in Fig. 9-8 using white glue and finishing nails. Install the wooden dowel. Now the project is ready for finishing.

To finish, begin by filling all nail holes and exposed plywood edges. After the filler has dried hard, sand the entire project smooth—removing any sharp edges. Apply a coat of primer. When this dries, apply two coats of semigloss enamel, adding eyes, mouth, etc. After the paint dries, the project is ready for use.

DOLL CRADLE

Here is a nice plan for a doll cradle that you can turn out in a matter of hours. The basic design can be modified by cutting more intricate scroll work around the headboard. This is a very inexpensive project because you use ¼-inch-thick plywood as the building material.

Materials

½ sheet (4 × 4 feet) ¼-inch thick interior, A-B grade.
White glue.
Wood filler paste.
1 pound of #4d finishing nails.
Sandpaper.
1 pint of primer.
1 quart of semigloss enamel.
1 small foam cushion, covered for mattress.

Directions

Begin by cutting the two end pieces (foot 16 × 15 and head 16 × 24 inches). Cut these square and then use a sabre saw to cut a suitable design as shown in Fig. 9-9. Next cut the two sides (10 × 36 inches) and bottom (12 × 26 inches). Now assemble the components using white glue and the finishing nails. The next step is to finish off the project.

To finish, begin by filling all nail holes and exposed edges on the project. After the filler has dried hard, sand the entire project smooth and apply

248

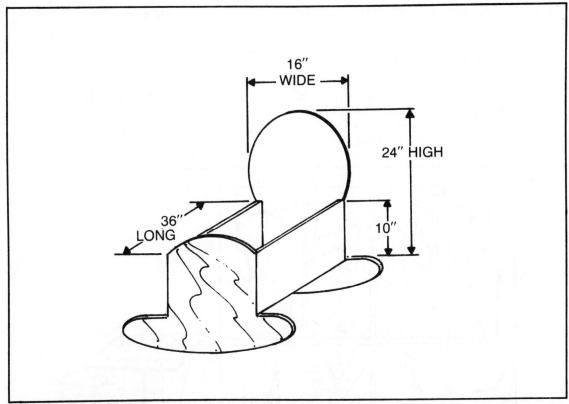

Fig. 9-9. Doll cradle.

a coat of primer. Apply two coats of semigloss enamel, sanding lightly between coats. The project is complete when the paint has dried.

SADDLE-SEAT DESK

Here is a weekend workshop project that will bring years of pleasure to any child: a saddle-seat desk that won't wobble. Its three legs assure even support. It is a safe place for your child to draw or work on small projects.

Materials

1 sheet (4 × 8 feet) ¾-inch-thick hardwood plywood, A-B grade.
White glue.
Wood filler paste.
Sandpaper.
Eight 2-inch-long countersink woodscrews (#8).
1 pint of primer.

1 quart of semigloss enamel.
One 24-inch long ¼ round molding-pencil rail.
6 wire brads, 1 inch long.

Directions

Begin by measuring, marking and cutting the plywood according to the diagram shown in Fig. 9-10. You will need four pieces. Use a hand-held circular-saw for all straight cuts and a sabre saw for the rounded and slotted cuts. After all the parts have been cut, assemble the project by fitting the pieces together and fastening with white glue and screws. Attach the pencil rail with wire brads and glue.

To finish, begin by filling the screw holes and all exposed edges on the project. After the filler paste has dried hard, sand the entire project smooth and apply a coat of primer. Apply two coats of semigloss enamel, sanding lightly between coats.

After the last coat dries, the saddle desk is ready for use.

BUNK BED WITH SHELVES

With this bunk-bed design your childrens' room will have more space because the beds are vertical. In addition, the end of these bunk beds is also a bookcase. If you would like, you can change the basic plan and include a desk in the bookcase.

Materials

3 sheets (4 × 8 feet) ¾-inch-thick exterior, A-B grade.

2 sheets (4 × 8 feet) ⅝-inch particle board.

Two 2-×-6 lumber, 72 inches long.

Two 2-×-6 lumber, 34½ inches long.

Four 2-×2-×-72-inch lumber.

Four 2-×-2-×-34½-inch lumber.

5 pounds of #8d finishing nails.

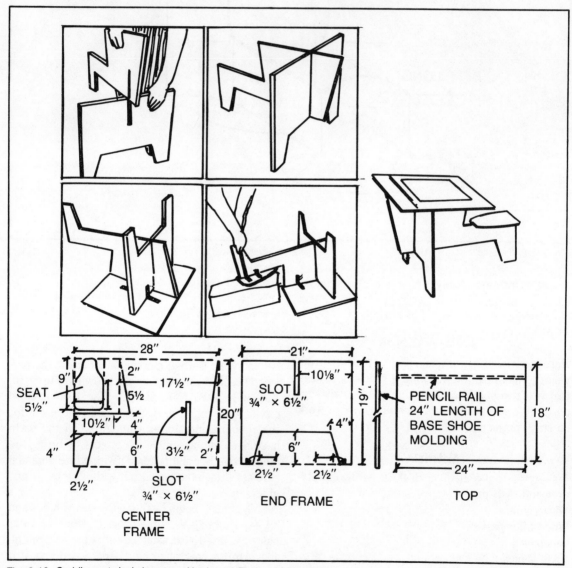

Fig. 9-10. Saddle-seat desk (courtesy Hardwood Plywood Mfg. Assoc.).

250

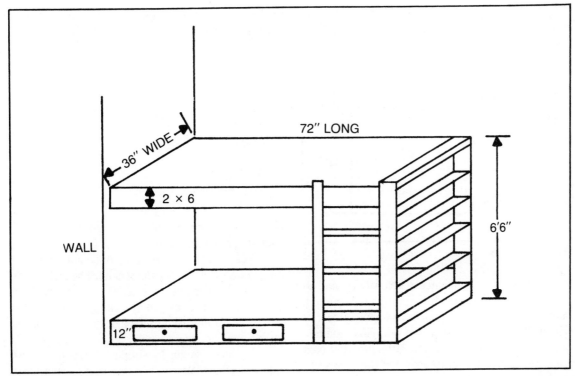

Fig. 9-11. Bunk beds.

White glue.

Sixteen 4-inch long carriage bolts, with nuts and washers.

2 sets drawer hardware; slider mechanisms and pulls.

8 toggle bolts, for attaching top bunk to wall.

Sandpaper.

2 quarts of primer.

1 gallon of semigloss enamel.

2 mattresses to fit the bunks.

Wood filler paste.

Directions

Begin by building the top bunk frame using 2-×-6-inch lumber. When complete, it will measure 36 × 72 inches. Attach the 2-×-2-inch lumber inside this frame, ⅝ of an inch below the top edge (Fig. 9-11). Use the carriage bolts and white glue for this. Later, the ⅝-inch particle board will fit inside on top of these ledgers.

Now build the bottom bunk using plywood for the frame (12 inches high and also 36 × 72 inches). Cut the holes for the drawers (12 × 24 inches) and make the drawers. Consult Chapter 5 for information on how to do this. Install the 2-×-2-inch ledger inside this frame and cut the ⅝-inch particle board to fit.

Now build the bookcase for the end of the bunk. Keep in mind that this bookcase holds up the top bunk and is also attached to the bottom bunk. It will measure 78 inches high and be 36 inches wide. With the bottom bunk in place, attach the bookcase to the end. See Fig. 9-11.

With the help of some friends, position the top bunk on the wall and fasten it in place with toggle bolts (to the wall). The end of the top bunk is also attached to the bookcase. Once the top bunk frame has been secured, cut and insert the ⅝-inch particle board onto the 2-×-2-inch ledger inside the frame. The last thing you need to do is build a ladder up to the top bunk. This can be easily done with the remaining ¼-inch-thick plywood.

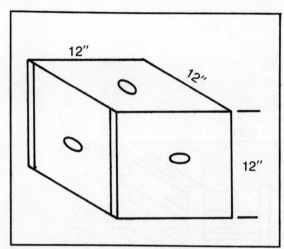

Fig. 9-12. Box stool.

Finish by filling all nail and screw holes and all exposed edges. After the filler paste has hardened, sand the entire project smooth and apply a coat of primer. Then apply two coats of semigloss enamel, sanding lightly between coats. After the last coat dries, lay down the mattresses and the bunks are ready for sleeping.

BOX STOOL

Each side of this cube (Fig. 9-12) has a hand slot so this stool can be carried easily. It is strong and safe. Paint it a bright color.

Materials

½ sheet (4 × 4 feet) ½-inch thick exterior, A-D grade.
White glue.
Wood filler paste.
¼ pound of #6d finishing nails.
Sandpaper.
1 pint of primer.
1 quart of semigloss enamel.

Directions

Begin by cutting the plywood into 12-×-48-inch long strips. Next, cut six pieces, from the strips, each measuring 12 inches long. Assemble the cube using white glue and finishing nails. The last step is to cut hand holes in each side. This can be done by drilling a hole first and then making the cut with a sabre saw. After the holes have been cut, the cube is ready for finishing.

To finish, begin by filling all nail holes and exposed edges. After the filler paste dries hard, sand the entire cube smooth. Apply a coat of primer. Next, apply two coats of semigloss enamel, sanding lightly between coats. The project will be ready for use when the final coat dries.

Chapter 10

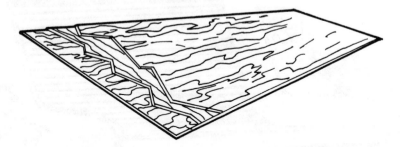

Outdoor Furniture

THIS CHAPTER CONTAINS MATERIALS LISTS and step-by-step instructions for 11 outdoor plywood furniture projects. Some of the projects are for beginning woodworkers and others are for advanced woodworking enthusiasts. These sturdy projects will provide years of service.

CHAISE LOUNGE

Turn that seldom-noticed backyard corner into a seating area over the weekend with this distinctive chaise lounge. It looks expensive, but it isn't. This project is actually quite simple to build, and it is sure to give you years of outdoor seating pleasure.

Materials

2 sheets (4 × 8 feet) ¾-inch-thick exterior, A-B grade.
21 pieces 2-×-2-×-60-inch lumber; redwood.
4 pieces 1-×-2-×-60-inch lumber; redwood.
4 pieces 2-×-4-×-61½-inch lumber; redwood.
4 pieces 2-×-4-×-61½-inch lumber; redwood.

2 pieces 2-×-4-×-60-inch lumber; redwood.
8 1-×-4-inch metal corner braces, 58½ inches long.
5 pounds of #8d galvanized finishing nails.
Waterproof glue.
1 quart of transparent stain for plywood sides.
1 gallon of boiled linseed oil for redwood.
Sandpaper.
Exterior wood filler paste.

Directions

Begin by measuring, marking, and cutting the two end panels from the plywood. Next, make the notch cuts for the 2-×-4-inch lumber crossbraces. See Fig. 10-1. Use a sabre saw for this cutting. Following the diagram shown in Fig. 10-1, frame in the seating area and cut the plywood for the top and back.

Using glue and galvanized finishing nails, apply the 2-×-2-inch lumber as seating slats and the 1-×-2-inch lumber for back and top boards. Be sure to consult the diagram often so you will know where

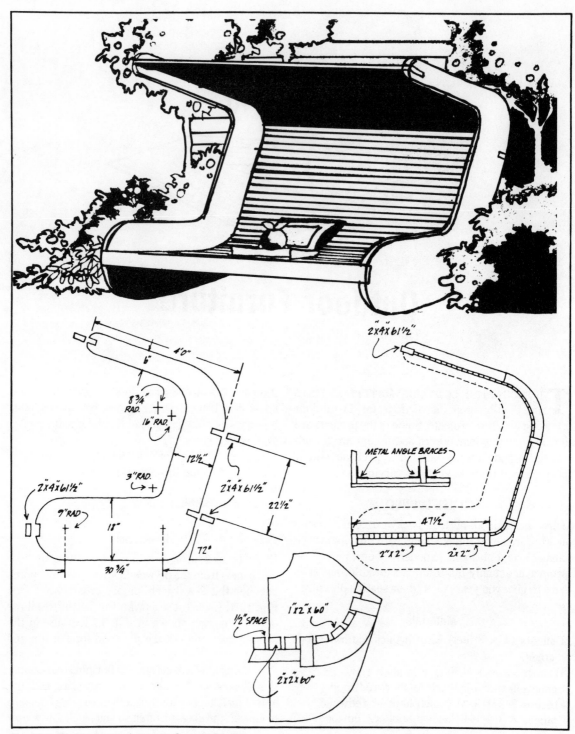

Fig. 10-1. Chaise lounge (courtesy Georgia-Pacific).

all the parts go. After all of the seating, back and top slats have been installed, the project is ready for finishing.

To finish, begin by filling the exposed edges and all nail holes in the plywood. Use exterior-grade filler paste for this. After the filler has dried hard, sand the entire project smooth. Then apply a coat of transparent stain to all plywood. Next, you can turn your attention to finishing the redwood seating slats. Redwood ages beautifully without any help, but you will want to coat all of the redwood slats with linseed oil to prevent the redwood from drying out and checking. Apply a generous coat of linseed oil. Use a linseed-oil-soaked rag for this. Let the linseed oil soak in for several hours and then wipe off the excess. In about one day, the redwood will be ready for use.

LOUNGING CHAIR

Here is a durable, sturdy outdoor chair that is great for lounging on a summer afternoon. The main differences between this design and the garden-variety aluminum lawn chair is that this one will last a long time. It is pleasing to look at and comfortable. Chances are very good that you will want to build several of these outdoor chairs once you see how easy it is. The original design calls for redwood, but if economy seating is your intention, you can substitute Western red cedar.

Materials

To make one outdoor chair, buy the following:
½ sheet (4 × 4 feet) ¾-inch-thick exterior, A-C grade.
Two 1-×-3-inch-by-8-foot-long lumber; redwood or cedar.
Two 2-×-3-inch-by-8-foot-long lumber; redwood or cedar.
One 2-×-3-inch-by-6-foot-long lumber; redwood or cedar.
Waterproof glue.
Sandpaper.
Exterior wood filler paste.
1 pound of #8d galvanized finishing nails.
1 quart of exterior wood stain finish.

1 quart of boiled linseed oil for redwood or cedar.
1 canvas-covered cushion for seat.

Directions

Begin by cutting up the plywood and lumber into the following size pieces:

One 19½-×-17-inch plywood.
One 2-×-3-×-16½-inch lumber.
Five 2-×-3-×-22½-inch lumber.
Four 2-×-3-×-25-inch lumber.
Five 1-×-3-×-26-inch lumber.

Assemble the parts of the chair using waterproof glue and the galvanized finishing nails. With a nail set or punch, drive all the nailheads just below the surface. Consult Fig. 10-2A and 10-2B to see how the parts go together; it is really quite straightforward. After all of the parts have been fastened, you can begin finishing off the chair.

To finish, start by filling the exposed edges and nailholes in the plywood. After the exterior wood filler paste has dried hard, sand the entire chair smooth. Then give two coats of stain finish to the plywood seat. Give a liberal coating of linseed oil to the redwood or cedar lumber parts of the chair. Allow the linseed oil to soak in for a few hours and then wipe off the excess. Add one cushion and the seat is ready for use. You should apply a light coating of linseed oil to the chair once a year (in the spring) or more often if you discover cracking.

PICNIC TABLE

Substantial, good looking and built in just a few hours, this one-piece picnic table will be a fine addition to your patio, deck, or family recreation area. Built from ¾-inch-thick exterior plywood, 2-×-6-inch and 2-×-8-inch redwood lumber, you should be able to put this table together in just a few hours. It is large enough to seat six comfortably and eight in a pinch. See Fig. 10-3.

Materials

2 sheets (4 × 8 feet) ¾-inch-thick exterior, A-B grade.

Fig. 10-2A. Lounge chair (courtesy Georgia-Pacific).

Four 2-×-8-inch redwood lumber, 6 feet long.
Ten 2 × 6 inch redwood lumber, 6 feet long.
Sixteen ¾-×-3½-inch hardwood dowels.
Twenty 1-inch-long wood screws.
3 pounds of #8d galvanized finishing nails.
Waterproof glue.
Exterior wood filler paste.
Sandpaper.
1 quart of exterior stain finish.
1 gallon of boiled linseed oil; for redwood.

Directions

Begin by measuring, marking, and cutting the plywood for the end panels. Note that each end is composed of two pieces that have been laminated together with waterproof glue. It is usually best to cut two panels at a time with a sabre saw. This way you can be certain that the pieces will be exactly the same dimensions. After you have cut out four end pieces, laminate two together for each end. This is best done with waterproof glue and 1-inch long wood screws. Countersink the heads.

Cut and sand smooth the notches for the 2-×-8-inch lumber crossmembers, filling any cavities with exterior wood filler paste. Drill ¾-inch holes in the 2-×-8-inch lumber as indicated in Fig. 10-3. Once the crossmembers have been secured in the end panels, drive ¾-×-3½-inch-long wood dowels into the drilled holes. Next, attach the 2-×-6-×-72-inch long lumber for the tabletop and seating. Space these about ¼-inch apart and use waterproof glue and galvanized finishing nails for the fastening.

To finish, begin by filling all nail holes and

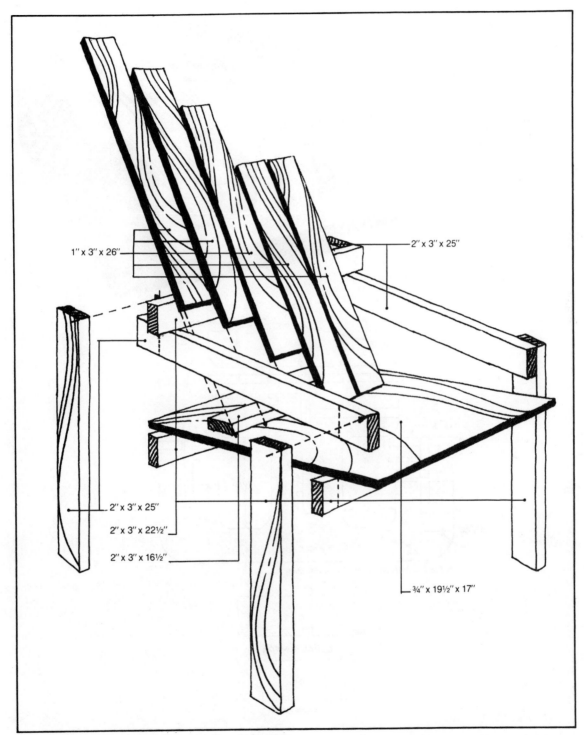

1″ x 3″ x 26″

2″ x 3″ x 25″

2″ x 3″ x 25″

2″ x 3″ x 22½″

2″ x 3″ x 16½″

¾″ x 19½″ x 17″

Fig. 10-2B. Lounge chair details (courtesy Georgia-Pacific).

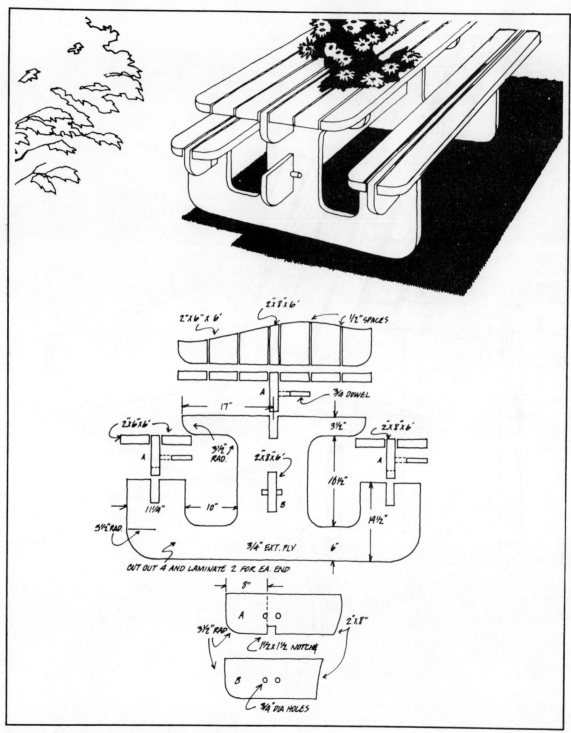

Fig. 10-3. Picnic table (courtesy Georgia-Pacific).

exposed edges on the plywood ends of the project. After the filler paste dries hard, sand the plywood smooth and apply two coats of stain finish. Next, finish off the redwood top and seating. This is done by sanding all redwood surfaces smooth (and by rounding corners if this has not been done already). Apply a liberal coat of boiled linseed oil. Allow this to soak in for several hours and wipe off the excess. Apply additional coats of linseed oil throughout the season to prevent cracking of the redwood.

BENCH

Lawn and garden furniture—traditionally made from aluminum tubing and plastic webbing—is common around many homes. It usually gets dirty easily and does not last more than about two seasons. This sturdy outdoor bench will last and it will stay good looking almost indefinitely. It is also easy to build. See Fig. 10-4.

Materials

½ sheet (2 × 8 feet) ¾-inch exterior plywood, A-D grade.
Two 2-×-4-×-19½-inch redwood; bench ends.
Two 2-×-4-inch-×-8-foot redwood; bench sides.
Two 2-×-6-×-15½-inch redwood; under bench supports.
Two 4-×-4-inch-×-4-foot redwood; legs.
½ bag fast-mixing cement; for setting posts.
4 carriage bolts, 7 inches long, with washers and nuts.
1 pound of #6d galvanized finishing nails.
2 pounds of #16d hot-dipped galvanized nails.
Sandpaper.
1 quart of clear finish.

Directions

Begin by ripping down the plywood into strips that measure 2 inches wide by 8 feet long. Build the frame for the bench. This involves nailing the short 2-×-4-inch lumber to the ends of the 8-foot lengths. Install the 2-×-6-inch lumber so that the tops are ¾ of an inch below the top of the bench. Nail the 2-inch strips of plywood into the bench with the galvanized

finishing nails. When done properly, the top of the plywood strips will be flush with the top of the bench and the 2-×6-inch lumber will extend below.

Now you must dig two holes and set the 4-×-4-inch-×-4-foot-long lumber into cement in the holes. After the cement hardens, attach the bench (through the 2-×-6 lumber) to the secure 4 × 4's. Use the carriage bolts for this. The last step is to sand the entire project smooth and apply two coats of clear finish.

POTTING TABLE

If someone in your family has a green thumb, this-easy-to-build potting table is a sure-fire winner. The unit is compact, versatile, and it looks good. Put it in the family room, on the back porch, in the garage, or even out on the patio. Wherever you locate this potting table, it is sure to attract comments and, more importantly, get used.

Materials

3 sheets (4 × 8 feet) ¾-inch-thick exterior, A-B grade.
1 sheet (4 × 8 feet) ¼-inch-thick pegboard.
Three 2-×-4-×-72-inch lumber.
Six 2-×-4-×-24-inch lumber.
Fourteen 2-×-4-×-22½-inch lumber.
Two 2-×-4-×-4-inch lumber.
One 2-×-6-foot piece plastic laminate (optional).
One 4-foot-long fluorescent light fixture (optional).
Two 2-inch butt hinges.
Waterproof glue.
1 quart of creosote.
5 pounds of #8d galvanized finishing nails.
Eighteen #10 roundhead wood screws with grommets.
1 quart of exterior primer.
2 quarts of exterior semigloss enamel.
Sandpaper.
Exterior wood filler paste.

Directions

Starting with the 2-×-4-inch lumber, precut all of your lumber to length (as indicated in the materials list). Build three frames with them (each measuring

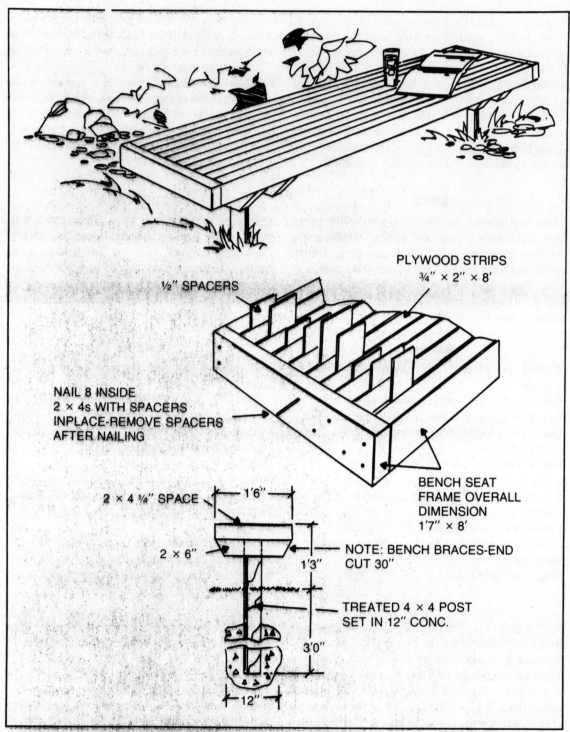

½" SPACERS

PLYWOOD STRIPS
¾" × 2" × 8'

NAIL 8 INSIDE
2 × 4s WITH SPACERS
INPLACE-REMOVE SPACERS
AFTER NAILING

BENCH SEAT
FRAME OVERALL
DIMENSION
1'7" × 8'

2 × 4 ¼" SPACE

1'6"

2 × 6"

NOTE: BENCH BRACES-END
CUT 30"

1'3"

TREATED 4 × 4 POST
SET IN 12" CONC.

3'0"

12"

Fig. 10-4. Outdoor bench (courtesy Georgia-Pacific).

2 × 6 feet). Next, cut three ¾-inch plywood shelves (2 × 6 feet). Attach the plywood to the frames. To make the planter box, cut six pieces of 2-×-4-inch lumber to a length of 24 inches. With an eye on the diagram shown in Fig. 10-5, glue and nail these together and the planting box is complete.

Next you can turn your attention to the side panels. Cut these from the remaining plywood according to Fig. 10-5. Drill holes for the wood screws and attach the sides of the table to the shelves. Begin by attaching the bottom frame and shelf, then the middle, and finally the top. Use waterproof glue and wood screws for this. Attach the pegboard back. If you are planning to include a plastic laminate top, do so at this time. Then you can turn your attention to finishing off the potting table.

To finish, begin by filling all nail holes and exposed plywood edges. After the filler has dried hard, sand the entire project smooth. Apply a coat of primer to all surfaces (omit the plastic laminate top, if one exists). Then apply two coats of semigloss enamel. When the paint dries, all that will remain is to coat the inside of the planter box with creosote. Allow this to dry for about one day. Then fill the box with soil and get potting.

SANDBOX

Make yourself a hero, Dad! Probably the simplest project to build, this sandbox will provide hours of fun for your little ones. First, buy only clean "pool sand" for the fill in the box. This is a very clean type of sand that you can be fairly sure is safe for your kids to play in. Secondly, it is a good idea to cover the sandbox when not in use—certainly at night. This will keep night visitors out of the box. A large sheet of plastic sheeting will work for this.

Materials

1⅛ sheets (4 × 8 and 1 × 4 feet) ¾-inch exterior, A-B grade.
One 2-×-2-inch-pressure-treated lumber, 8 feet long.
Fifty 1½-inch-long-flathead-galvanized wood screws.
Wood filler paste.
Sandpaper.

1 quart of exterior primer.
2 quarts of exterior semigloss enamel.
50 pounds of clean pool sand.

Directions

Follow the cutting diagram in Fig. 10-6. Make allowances for saw blade kerfs between adjacent parts. Secure the bottom panel to the 2-×-2-inch lumber with the galvanized wood screws. Attach the end panels to the bottom panel with the screws as well. Drive the screws about 4 inches apart and make sure the tops are countersunk just below the surface.

Place the side panels in position and secure them with wood screws, also placed about 4 inches apart. Screw the seats in place. Next, with a wood rasp or Surform tool, round off all sharp corners. Now the project is ready for finishing.

To finish, begin by filling all nail holes and exposed edges. After the filler paste dries hard, sand the entire project smooth and apply two coats of exterior primer. Next, apply two coats of exterior semigloss enamel, sanding lightly between coats. After the last coat dries, fill the box with sand and add a few kids.

BARBECUE STORAGE

From all outward appearances, it looks just like another planter. But look inside and it is a complete storage area for all of your barbecue utensils and charcoal briquettes. This is an easy project to build and you can put the entire unit together in just a few hours. This project is made to last because it is made from exterior plywood siding. See Fig. 10-7.

Materials

3 sheets (4 × 8 feet) ⅝-inch, texture 1-11 exterior siding.
Six 2-×-8-×-27-inch lumber.
Six 2-×-8-×-18-inch lumber.
Three 18-×-24-×-¾-inch exterior plywood.
One 9-×-22-×-¾-×⅝-inch exterior plywood.
Four 1-×-4-×-60-inch lumber.
One 1-×-4-×-22¼-inch lumber.
Four ¾-×-¾-×-18-inch lumber.
Four ¾-×-¾-×-22½-inch lumber.

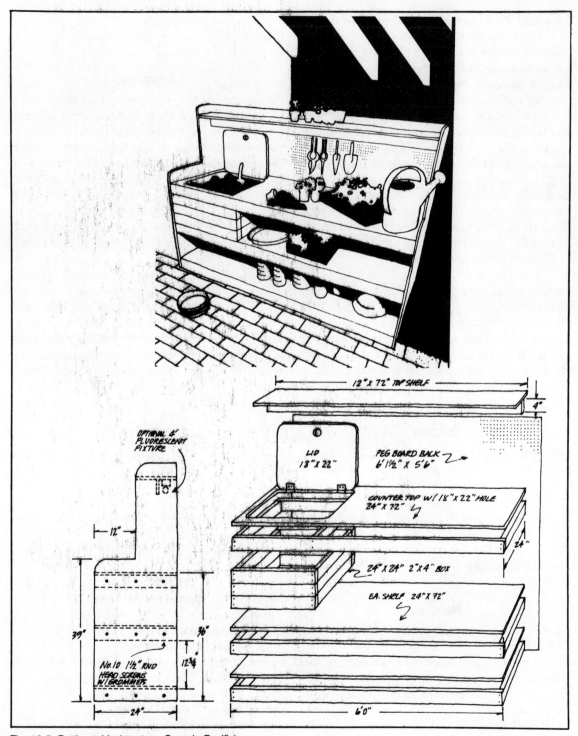

Fig. 10-5. Potting table (courtesy Georgia-Pacific).

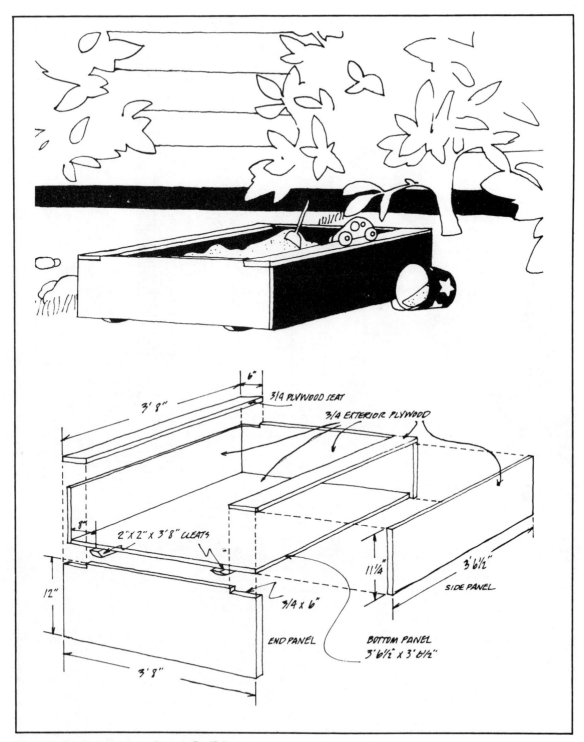

Fig. 10-6. Sandbox (courtesy Georgia-Pacific).

Labels within figure:
6"
3' 8"
3/4 PLYWOOD SEAT
3/4 EXTERIOR PLYWOOD
8"
2" X 2" X 3' 8" CLEATS
11¼"
3' 6½"
SIDE PANEL
12"
3/4 x 6"
END PANEL
BOTTOM PANEL
3' 6½" x 3' 6½"
3' 8"

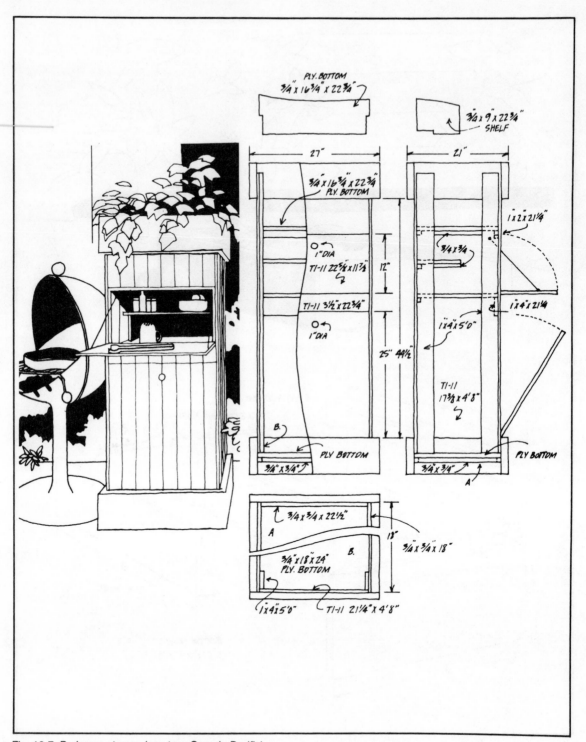

Fig. 10-7. Barbecue storage (courtesy Georgia-Pacific).

Five ¾-×-¾-×-21¼-inch lumber.
Two ¾-×-¾-×-5½-inch lumber.
Four ¾-×-¾-×9¾-inch lumber.
One 1-×-2-×-21¼-inch lumber.
Four 1-×-4-×-28¼-inch lumber.
Two 14-inch pieces of light chain.
2 cabinet butt hinges.
1 pound of #2d galvanized finishing nails.
3 pounds of #8d galvanized finishing nails.
½ gallon of exterior stain finish.
Sandpaper.
Exterior wood filler paste.
2 cabinet knobs.

Directions

Begin by framing the bottom of the barbecue storage unit using the 2-×-8-inch lumber. Then build the same type of frame for the top. Next, following the diagram shown in Fig. 10-7, cut the texture 1-11 exterior siding, front and back panels. Attach 1-×-4-inch corner brackets. Attach the precut bottom panel into place. Now you are ready to attach the top planter box. Nail the planter bottom panel to the top of the 1-×-4 inch lumber corner braces as shown in Fig. 10-7. Nail the 2-×-8-inch planter frame together and line with plastic sheeting to make it waterproof.

The finishing touches are easy. Begin by cutting openings for the doors (allow room to attach the hinges). Next attach chain on both sides of the door to prevent it from falling below horizontal. Attach a knob to the front. The last step is to add the top shelf inside the unit.

To finish off the project, fill all nail holes and exposed edges with exterior wood filler paste. After this dries, sand everything smooth and apply a coat of stain sealer over the entire unit. When this dries, the barbecue storage unit is ready for use.

CHAIR SIDE TABLE

Here is a good project for all of that scrap plywood you have been saving. While the original design calls for plywood that is ¾ of an inch thick, you can substitute ⅝-inch-thick or ½-inch-thick pieces as long as you use exterior plywood (any grade). You will probably want to make several of these small tables for around the patio or deck.

Materials

15 pieces ¾-inch-thick exterior plywood, any grade, each cut 2 inches wide and 24 inches long.
2 hardwood dowels, ¾ × 24 inches.
Four 2-×-2-×-19-inch lumber.
1 pint of clear coating; exterior.
Sandpaper.
1 pound of #4d finishing nails, galvanized.

Directions

Begin by cutting 15 strips of plywood, each 2 × 24 inches. Drill ¾-inch holes (one at each end and located 1½ inches in from the end). Then slide one dowel through all of the holes on one end of the strips and do the same for the other dowel. Now position the strips along the dowel so that there is about ½ inch of space between each. Tack each strip at this location with a finishing nail at each end. The next step is to attach the legs. Place one at each corner and tack it in place with three finishing nails. Now the project is ready for finishing.

To finish, sand the top and legs of the table. Apply two coats of clear finish. When the final coat dries, the small table is ready for service.

HANGING FLOWER-POT HOLDER

Here is another project for some of those scrap pieces of plywood you have laying around the workshop. This project will help to add flowers to your patio or deck. See Fig. 10-9.

Materials

For each planter:
1 scrap piece ¾-inch-thick exterior plywood, any grade 6 × 18 inches.
Rope or chain for hanging.

Directions

Cut the plywood to 6 × 18 inches. Next, cut three holes, evenly spaced, in the face. The holes should be large enough to fit a 4-inch flower pot snugly. Cut

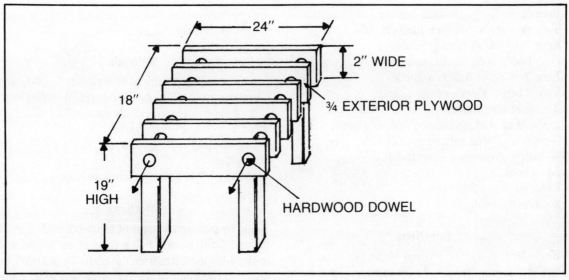

Fig. 10-8. Chair side table.

these holes with a sabre saw fitted with a special plywood cutting blade. Then drill a ½-inch diameter hole at each end. Insert a length of rope into these holes and hang the unit from a tree limb or other suitable support.

SMALL TABLE

This small, easy-to-build outdoor table will come in very handy around the patio, especially when you are entertaining. It is designed to be sturdy and to last for a long time. See Fig. 10-10.

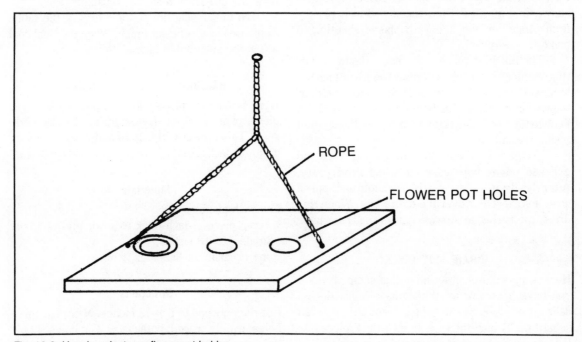

Fig. 10-9. Hanging planter or flower-pot holder.

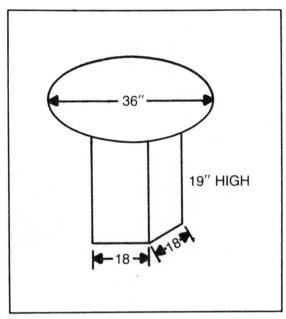

Fig. 10-10. Small outdoor table.

Materials

½ sheet (4 × 4 feet) ½-inch-thick exterior, A-D grade, base.

½ sheet (4 × 4 feet) ¾-inch-thick exterior, A-D grade, top.

Wood filler paste.

1 pound #8d galvanized finishing nails.

Sandpaper.

1 pint of exterior primer.

1 quart of exterior semigloss enamel.

Waterproof glue.

Directions

Begin by cutting the ½-inch thick plywood for the base. You will need 4 strips, each 18 × 19 inches. Fasten these together using waterproof glue and finishing nails. Next, cut the top from the ¾-inch-thick plywood. It is circular so you must use a sabre saw for the cutting. Attach the top to the base from above. Use glue and finishing nails for this. Now you are ready for finishing.

Begin the finishing stage by filling all nail holes and exposed edges. After the filler has dried hard, sand the entire project smooth and apply a coat of exterior primer. Apply two coats of exterior semi-gloss enamel, sanding lightly between coats. The project is ready for use after the paint dries.

PLANTER BOX

Here is a good basic project that will take only a few hours to complete. While the original design calls for a planter box that is 6 feet long you can make one shorter if space requires. Before using the planter, it is a good idea to line the insides with plastic sheeting material.

Materials

1 sheet (4 × 8 feet) ¾-inch-thick exterior plywood, A-D grade.

½ sheet (2 × 8 feet) ¾-inch thick, CDX plywood (bottom).

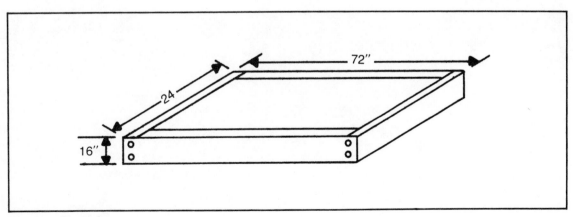

Fig. 10-11. Planter box.

Waterproof glue.
2 pounds of #10d hot-dipped galvanized box nails.
Wood filler paste.
Sandpaper.
1 quart of exterior primer.
2 quarts of exterior semigloss enamel.

Directions

Begin by cutting the full sheet of plywood into strips 16 inches wide and 8 feet long. Now you will need to laminate these strips in groups of twos, each 16 inches high, 1½ inches thick and 8 feet long. Use waterproof glue and nails for this. After the glue sets, about 8 hours, cut the strips into the following pieces:

two 24 inch strips.
two 72 inch strips.

These are the sides and ends of the planter. Nail them together to make a rectangular-shaped box. Attach the bottom using the CDX plywood cut to 24 × 72 inches. Use waterproof glue and nails for this attachment. Now turn the planter over and you can begin finishing.

To finish, begin by filling all nail holes and exposed edges. After the filler has dried hard, sand the entire project—outside only—smooth and apply a coat of primer. Follow this with two coats of semigloss enamel, sanding lightly between coats. After the last coat dries, line the inside of the planter with plastic sheeting and you are ready to fill the unit with clean top soil.

Chapter 11

Miscellaneous Furniture

THERE ARE 18 VARIED PLYWOOD FURNITURE projects described in the chapter. Each of these units is designed to be durable and practical. There are easy-to-build projects and some designed for the advanced woodworker. All of the projects have materials lists and directions.

FOLD-DOWN TABLE

There are few of us who couldn't use an extra work area around the house. Whether it's for sewing, repairing appliances, or just hobby work, this fold-down table takes up very little room. This table is very simple to make and quite handy around the home.

Materials

½ sheet (4 × 4 feet) ¾-inch exterior, A-C grade.
One 21-inch-long piano hinge.
White glue.
1 pound of #6d finishing nails.
Filler paste.
Sandpaper.
6 molly bolts.

1 quart of primer.
2 quarts of semigloss enamel.

Directions

Begin by measuring, marking, and cutting all parts of this project from the half sheet of plywood. See Fig. 11-1. Assemble the cabinet using white glue and finishing nails. Then you can start building the table. Begin by notching section "B" (tabletop) so that the upright base ("A") fits snuggly into place. Then glue and nail the braces ("C") into place. Now attach the tabletop to the support brace and the wall brace ("D") using the piano hinges. To finish, attach the remaining wall brace ("D") directly to the wall using the molly bolts or by screwing directly into the wall studs. Attach the wall brace ("D") to the tabletop to the now secure wall piece ("D").

To finish the table and shelf, begin by filling all nail holes and exposed edges. When the filler material has dried hard, sand everything smooth and apply a coat of primer to all surfaces. Next apply two coats of semigloss enamel, sanding between coats.

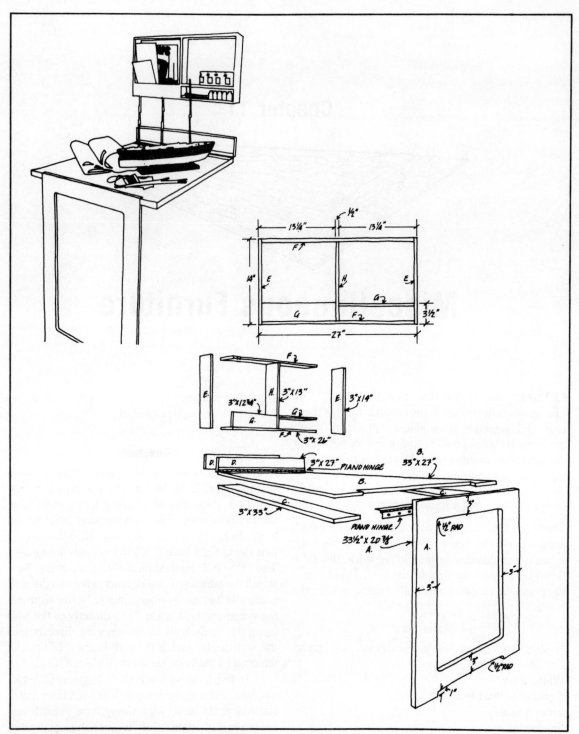

Fig. 11-1. Fold-down table (courtesy Georgia-Pacific).

After the last coat is dry, the table is ready to be pressed into service.

TV TRAYS

The American addiction to television has spawned a number of projects for the do-it-yourselfer, assuming of course that he or she can tear himself away from the boob tube long enough to put the pieces of a project together. The three TV trays in this project can be built in a few hours and at a nominal cost. Even if you don't watch a lot of television, you will probably find a number of uses for these handy trays. The original design comes from the Hardwood Plywood Manufacturers Association.

Materials

½ sheet (4 × 4 feet) ¼-inch-thick, exterior plywood, A-B grade.

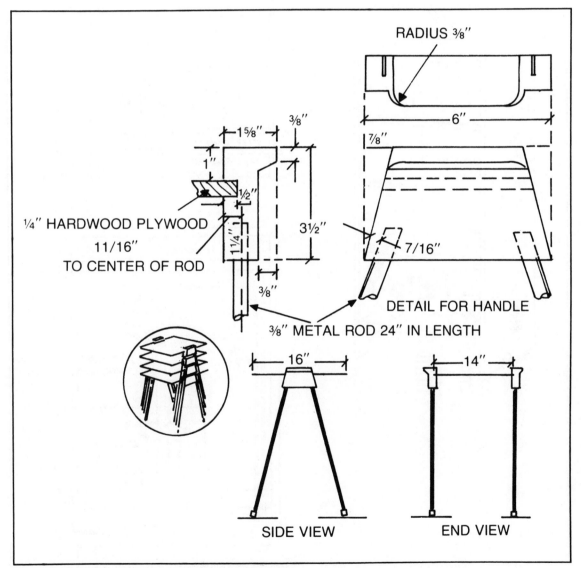

Fig. 11-2. TV trays (courtesy Hardwood Plywood Mfg. Assoc.).

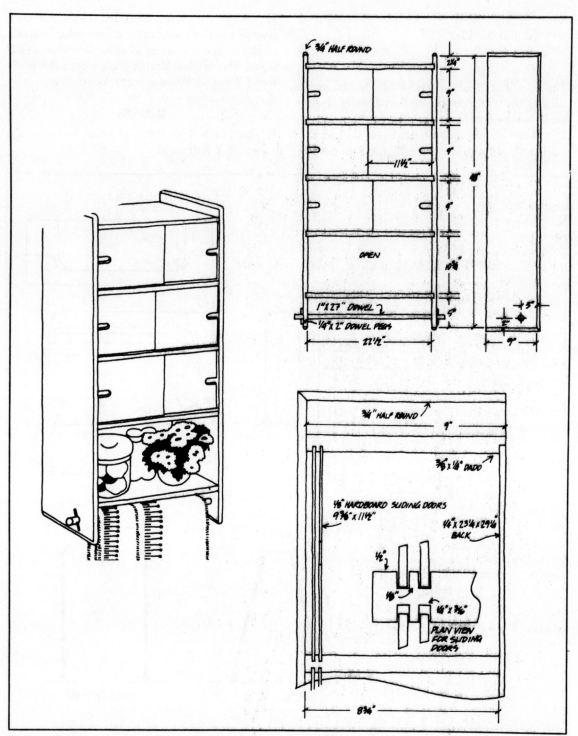

Fig. 11-3. Odds-and-ends shelf (courtesy Georgia-Pacific).

Six 6-inch-long pieces of 2 × 4, in a species similar to that of the plywood.

6 metal rods, 7/16 of an inch in diameter, 24 inches long.

6 rubber caps for the ends of the rods.

1 pint of stain.

1 quart of clear finish.

Edge filler paste.

White glue.

Sandpaper.

Directions

Begin by cutting three pieces (each 16 × 14 inches) from the sheet of plywood; these will become the trays. Next you must work on the handles (6-inch sections of 2-×-4-inch lumber). Each must have two holes (for the metal rod), be shaped as shown, and have a ½-inch notch into which one side of the tray will slide. The detail for each handle is shown in Fig. 11-2.

After all of the handles have been constructed, fit two handles to each tray (use white glue to fasten each). Then insert the metal legs with the rubber caps on the feet.

To finish, begin by filling all exposed edges. After the filler has dried hard, sand everything smooth and apply a coat of stain. Apply two coats of clear finish, sanding between coats.

ODDS-AND-ENDS SHELF

Is there anybody who couldn't use a little extra storage room for odds and ends that collect in almost every room in the home—especially the bathroom? Using nothing more than plywood, hardboard, and wood trim, you should have little problem building this handy shelf in a few hours.

Materials

½ sheet (4 × 4 feet) ¾-inch exterior plywood, A-A grade.

¼ sheet (2 × 4 feet) ¼-inch exterior plywood, A-D grade.

¼ sheet (2 × 4 feet) ⅛-inch hardwood paneling; door material.

1 hardwood dowel, 1 inch in diameter, 26½ inches long.

8 feet of ¾-inch, half-round trim.

2 hardwood dowels, ¼ inch in diameter, 2 inches long.

1 pound of #4d finishing nails.

Wood filler paste.

White glue.

Sandpaper.

1 pint of primer.

1 quart of semigloss enamel.

Directions

Begin by measuring, marking, and cutting all pieces from the plywood. Next, mark the spacing for the shelves on each of the side panels. Then dado each of the side panels to accommodate the shelves. Dado the door grooves ½ inch back from the forward edge of each shelf. Assemble the shelves and side pieces, leaving one side off until the doors are placed into the dado runner slots. Now attach the remaining side piece and glue nail into place.

Attach the optional dowel pegs and the towel by drilling each of the holes as shown in Fig. 11-3. Then turn the project over and glue/nail the back panel in place. Drive nails through the back panel into the sides and shelves of the project.

To finish, begin by filling all exposed edges and nail holes. After the filler material has dried hard, sand everything smooth. Apply one coat of primer and two coats of semigloss enamel, sanding lightly between coats.

ROOM DIVIDER WITH PLENTY OF STORAGE

This project (Fig. 11-4A) provides a great deal of storage space. At the same time, you will be partially dividing a room into more functional units.

Materials

4 panels ¾″ × 4′ × 8′ G-P interior grade plywood.

1 panel ¼″ × 4′ × 8′ G-P interior grade plywood.

1 piece ⅜″ × 1½″ × 6′ lumber.

8 cabinet pulls.

4 pairs cabinet hinges.

Directions

As you can tell from Fig. 11-4B, there are quite a few cuts required for this project. Therefore it is

Fig. 11-4A. Room divider with storage space (courtesy Georgia-Pacific).

important that you make certain of your measurements and that you cut with precision. If you do not have a table saw at your disposal, I would recommend that you have all of the pieces cut at your local lumber yard. This will add a few additional dollars to the total cost of the project, but at least you can be reasonably certain that the pieces will be cut according to plan.

Just as much care, and then some, is required during the assembly of this room divider. Work very carefully and with the diagram close at hand. White glue (water base) and 6d finishing nails are the materials you will require for assembly.

After the room divider is all put together and the glue joints have dried—at least overnight—you can begin the finishing. The bulk of this work will be filling the exposed edges of the plywood. It is very important to work carefully. Keep in mind that your intention is to simply fill the end grain of the plywood and not build it up.

Sand all parts of the divider and either stain and cover with a clear coating or prime and paint a suitable color. White is a good basic color that will blend in well with most types of decor. On the other hand, if you prefer a stain, go with a lighter tone so that the natural beauty of the veneer can show through well.

If you decide to build this room divider with storage space, allow yourself plenty of time for the project. Accomplish all cutting and assembly tasks in an unhurried manner. Then finish off the project with several coats of finish material. If you take the care necessary to build this room divider according to the diagram, you will end up with a functional piece of furniture that will easily give a lifetime of silent service.

THREE-TIER WINDOW BOX

This window planter box attaches to an exterior wall of your home with only one bracket and the law of gravity takes care of the rest. Suspended from one another, the three tiers can easily be removed

274

for spring planting and cleaning. The entire project can be built in one weekend at a fairly low cost.

Materials

2 sheets (4 × 8 feet) ¾-inch exterior plywood, A-D grade.
Two 1-×-4-×-52-inch lumber; cedar looks nice.
Three 1-×-4-×-54-inch lumber; cedar.
Four 1-×-4-×-56-inch lumber; cedar.
Four hardwood dowels, ¾ × 3¼ inch.
Nine 3-inch-long wood screws; brass.
Twelve ½-inch-long wood screws; brass.
1 quart of creosote.
1 pound of #4d galvanized finishing nails.
Sandpaper.

Directions

Begin by measuring, marking, and cutting patterns for each of the end, back, and bottom panels. After each has been cut from the plywood, round off the corners as indicated in Fig. 11-5. Slot the end pieces ¾ × 3½ inches and drill ⅞-inch holes as indicated. Assemble the units and attach "A" to the framing members of your exterior wall using the 3-inch long wood screws. Attach the other units to "A" using the wooden dowels.

The last steps involve applying a coat of creosote to all interior surfaces and sanding the outside of each planter. The creosote will prevent deterioration of the boxes, but you should wait at least 24 hours before filling the planters with dirt. This will give the plywood a chance to absorb the creosote.

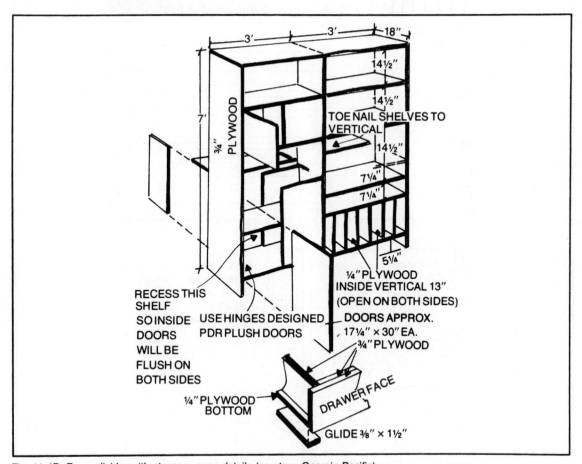

Fig. 11-4B. Room divider with storage space details (courtesy Georgia-Pacific).

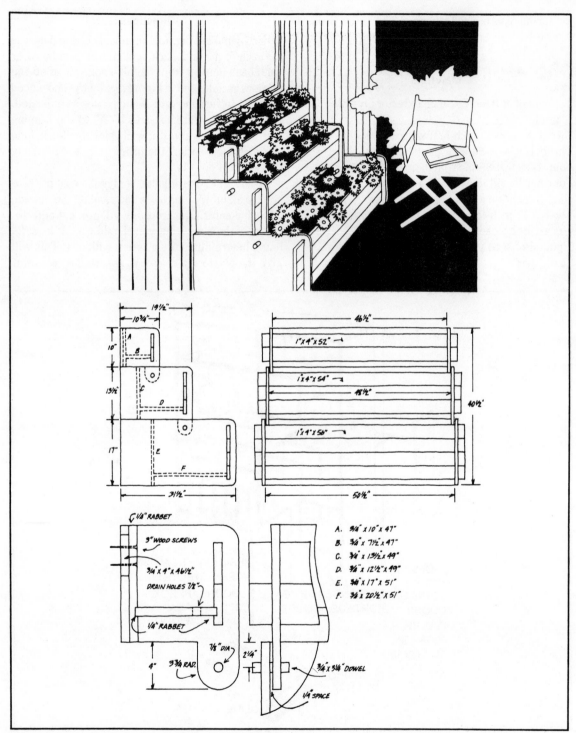

Fig. 11-5. Three-tier window box (courtesy Georgia-Pacific).

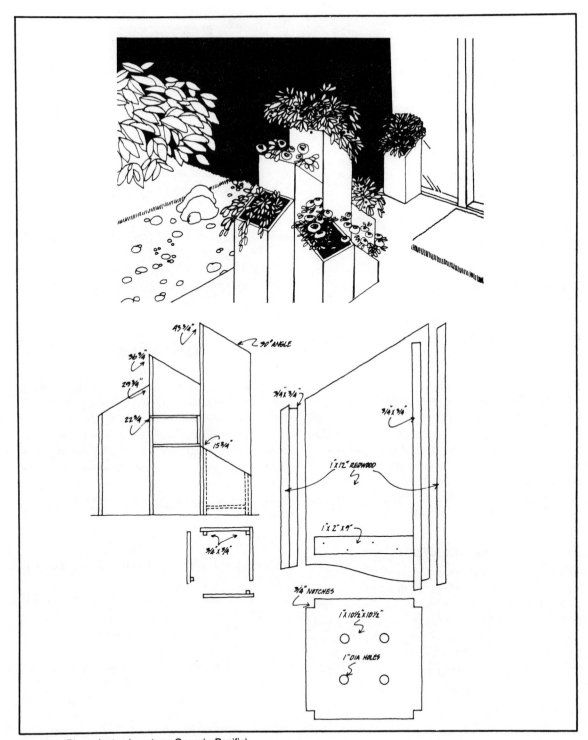

Fig. 11-6. Plant cluster (courtesy Georgia-Pacific).

PLANT CLUSTER

Contemporary and easily built in an afternoon, this organ pipe planter cluster works both indoors and out. Take a look around that favorite porch, deck, or family room. It looks good and fits anywhere so you might want to build several for special plants around the home. See Fig. 11-6.

Materials

2 sheets (4 × 8 feet) ¾-inch exterior plywood, A-D grade.
Waterproof glue.
2 pounds of #6d galvanized finishing nails.
Sandpaper.
1 quart of creosote.
1 quart of stain.
2 quarts of clear finish.

Directions

Begin by cutting all parts as indicated in the diagram. Assemble each of the three planter columns. It is strongly recommended that you apply a finish to all units before attaching a cluster.

To finish, coat the interior of each column with creosote; allow this to dry for 24 hours. Sand all exterior surfaces. Apply a coat of stain. After this dries, apply two coats of clear finish, sanding between coats. The last step is to attach the planter columns in groups of three. This can be done with nails or by careful positioning. Then fill each with good topsoil and add your favorite plants.

PLANTER DIVIDER

Take one plain living room and add this planter/room divider and the whole room takes on a new look. This project not only provides a place for your favorite plants, but also effectively helps to divide up a room into sections. The entire project is easy to build and it will enhance the interior of any room in your home.

Materials

2 sheets (4 × 8 feet) ¾-inch exterior plywood, A-D grade.
1 pound of #6d galvanized finishing nails.

Waterproof glue.
Wood filler paste.
Sandpaper.
Plastic liner or plastic trays to fit inside.
2 quarts of primer.
3 quarts of semigloss enamel.

Directions

Begin by measuring, marking, and cutting all parts for the project. Assemble the pieces as shown in Fig. 11-7. Use waterproof glue and galvanized finishing nails for the fastening. To make the interior waterproof, you can simply line it with plastic sheeting or place plastic trays under plants.

To finish, first fill all nail holes and exposed edges with wood filler paste. After this material has dried hard, sand everything smooth and apply a coat of primer. Apply two coats of semigloss enamel, sanding between coats.

PLATFORM BED

Ever notice how many things accumulate under a bed? Here is a way to put an end to that and get organized a bit more as well. This project is a platform bed complete with ample storage. If you have ever wondered how to get more use from some of the wasted space around your home, this could be one solution. This project is easy to construct and nice to look at as well. As an added benefit, this bed makes a good project for the guest room.

Materials

2 sheets (4 × 8 feet) ¾-inch exterior plywood, A-D grade.
½ sheet (4 × 4 feet) ¼-inch exterior plywood, A-D grade.
Three 2-×-4-inch-×-6-foot lumber.
Five 2-×-2-inch-×-6-foot lumber.
1 sheet (4 × 8 feet) ⅝-inch particle board.
Two 2-×-2-inch-×-10-foot lumber.
Two ¾-inch-×-37½-inch piano hinges, with screws.
Eight ¼-×-3½-inch carriage bolts, with nuts.
Thirty-six #12 flathead wood screws.

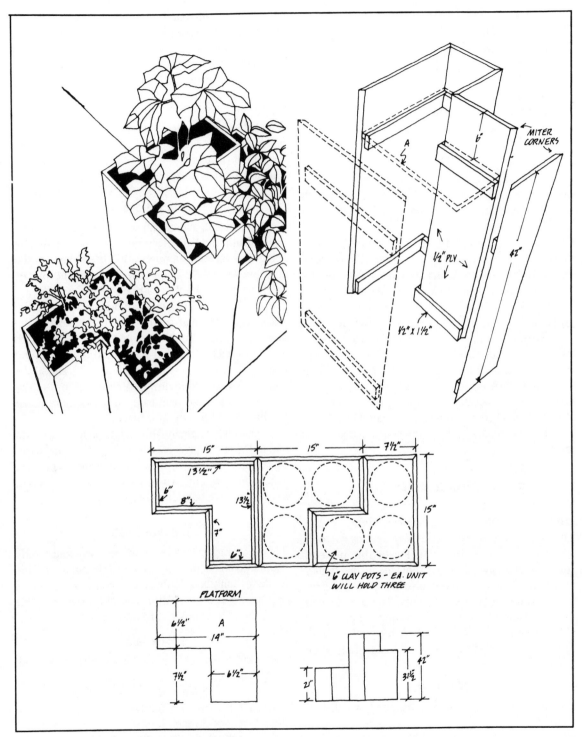

Fig. 11-7. Plant divider (courtesy Georgia-Pacific).

White glue.
Wood filler paste.
2 pounds of #8d finishing nails.
Sandpaper.
2 quarts of primer.
3 quarts of semigloss enamel.
1 foam pad, 75 × 39 inches.
Fabric to cover the foam pad.

Directions

Begin by building the base of this bed using the precut 2-×-4-inch and 2-×-2-inch lumber. Notch the 2-×-4-inch lumber to assure a tight fit with the 2-×-2-inch supports. Construct the end panels, drilling where necessary, as shown in Fig. 11-8. Once the end panels are in place, attach the remainder of the framework as shown. Glue and screw the ledgers in place. Cut and attach the storage doors. Note that these doors have holes rather than handles. Now the project is ready to be finished.

To finish, begin by filling all exposed edges and nail holes. After the filler paste dries hard, sand everything smooth and apply a coat of primer. When the primer has dried, paint the project with two coats of semigloss enamel, sanding between coats. When the final coat of semigloss enamel has dried, lay the mattress in place and you are ready for guests.

FIREPLACE BENCH

This fireplace bench lets you store kindling, firewood, and newspapers in plain sight. At the same time it gives you a little extra seating room. If you are wondering where to locate this project, consider one side of your fireplace, in the family room, or almost anywhere else close to the fireplace. While this project is designed for use close to the fireplace, you can probably find a number of alternative uses even if you don't have a fireplace. This is a fun project to build and it looks great when finished.

Materials

1 sheet (4 × 8 feet) ¾-inch exterior plywood, A-B grade.
Two 1½-inch half-round moldings, 8 feet long.

One ¾-inch half-round molding, 4 feet long.
One ¾-inch quarter-round molding, 4 feet long.
1 cushion for the top, 45 × 22¼ inches.
1 pound of #8d finishing nails.
¼ pound of wire brads 1½ inches long for attaching moldings.
White glue.
Edge filler paste.
Sandpaper.
1 quart of primer.
2 quarts of semigloss enamel.

Directions

Measure, mark, and cut all parts from the plywood panel. Build the side pieces of the bench by nailing and gluing the end supports ("F") to each end of the side pieces ("A"). Then glue and nail the pieces marked "B" to the pieces marked "E".

With a careful eye on the diagram shown in Fig. 11-9, attach the half-round trim to the base of the bench as shown. Attach the remainder of the bench pieces to each other and install the quarter-round trim in the joints between sections "A" and "D/A and C." For the top trim, miter the corners of the 1½-inch half-round trim to form the corners. Glue the half-round pieces into place.

To finish, begin by filling all exposed edges and nail holes in the project. After the filler dries hard, sand everything smooth and apply a coat of primer. This is followed by two coats of semigloss enamel, sanding lightly between coats.

STACKABLE BEDS

This is a practical project that can turn your family room into a guest room in a matter of minutes. This modular bunk bed doubles as a couch when not in use as a spare bed. After you build one of these handy beds, you might be tempted to build another.

Materials

1 sheet (4 × 8 feet) ¾-inch-thick exterior plywood, A-B grade.
2 sheets (4 × 8 feet) ⅝-inch particle board.
Four 2-×-2-×-81-inch lumber.
Four 2-×-2-×-36-inch lumber.
2 foam mattresses 75 × 38 inches.

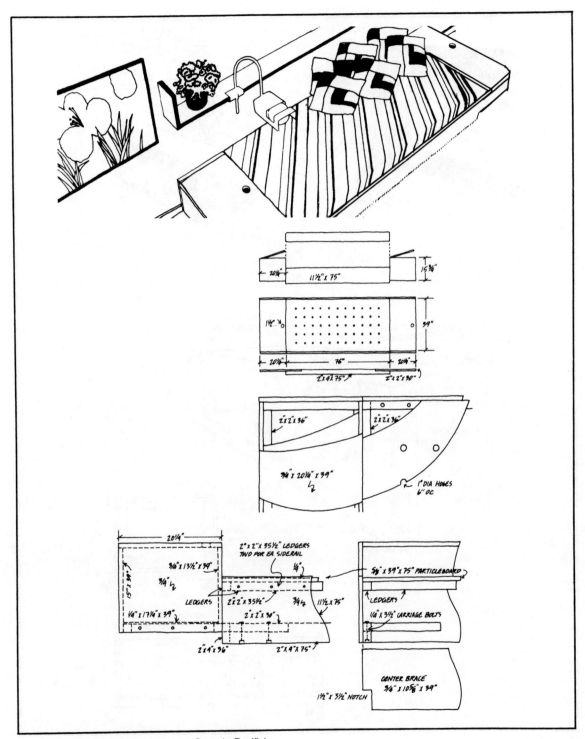

Fig. 11-8. Bed with storage (courtesy Georgia-Pacific).

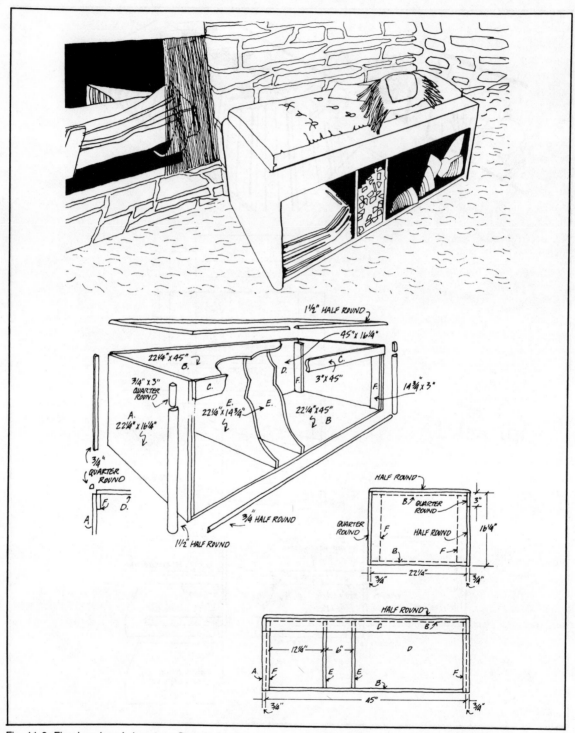

Fig. 11-9. Fireplace bench (courtesy Georgia-Pacific).

1 pound of #6d finishing nails.
White glue.
Edge filler paste.
Sandpaper.
2 quarts of primer.
3 quarts of semigloss enamel.

Directions

Measure, mark, and cut out all parts from the plywood sheet, making sure to allow for saw blade width. Then cut the two hand holes in each of the bed ends—a sabre saw is useful here—and round off the top edges as well. Cut the 2-×-2-inch ledgers and attach them to the inside of the side panels, measuring down 3 inches from the top edge. Use glue and nails for this. Assemble the two plywood frames, once again using glue and nails. Now attach the reinforcing blocks in each corner below the already in place ledgers.

The next step is to cut a 36-×-84-inch rectangle from each of the sheets of particle board. Drill ventilation holes in these—as shown in Fig. 11-10—and lay each panel into place in the frames. The last step is to attach the corner hinges.

To finish, begin by filling all nail holes and exposed panel edges. After the filler paste hardens, sand everything smooth and apply one coat of primer. This is followed by two coats of semigloss enamel, sanding lightly between coats. The last step in the project is to cover the foam pads with an attractive fabric and lay it in place. You might also want to add a few decorative pillows as well.

WINE RACK

This project looks great on the kitchen counter or buffet and it goes together very quickly once you have the parts made. This wine rack, in addition to being a good place to store wine, also adds a touch of class to almost any room. The plans result in one wine rack that will hold 12 bottles of wine and eight wine glasses (with long stems). You might want to build several of these for your home or possibly to give as gifts.

Materials

2/3 sheet (4 × 6 feet) ½-inch-thick interior ply-

wood, A-B grade.
Four ½-×-12-inch half-round molding.
¼ pound of #4d finishing nails.
White glue.
Wood filler paste.
Sandpaper.
1 pint of primer.
1 quart of semigloss enamel.
Masking tape and enamel paint for graphics (optional).

Directions

Begin by cutting the plywood into two pieces measuring 12 inches wide by 6 feet long. From these two pieces, cut two boards 16½ inches long and three boards 16¼ inches long. Following the diagram shown in Fig. 11-11, rabbet each of the 16¼-inch pieces with a ½-×-⅛-inch rabbet, and make the same cut along the 12-inch edge of each of the 16½-inch pieces. Pick one of the 12-×-16¼-inch pieces and trim the back edges ¾ of an inch to allow room for insetting the back panel. This panel should be square and measure 15¼ inches on a side.

Assemble all of the pieces, including the back, with glue and nails. Then construct the inside of the rack. From the remaining plywood, cut two pieces measuring 8¾ × 11¼ inches and rabbet the boards following the details in the diagram. Cut eight pieces 33¾ × 11¼ inches. Glue the pieces following the drawing shown in Fig. 11-11. Cut four pieces measuring 1⅜ × 11¾ inches and four ½-inch dowels, each 11¼ inches long. Assemble the pieces according to the diagram and you are then ready to finish off the project.

To finish, begin by filling all nail holes and exposed edges. After the filler has dried hard, sand everything smooth and apply one coat of primer. After the primer is dry, apply two coats of semigloss enamel, sanding between coats. When the final coat dries, the wine rack is ready to be pressed into service.

PLANT STAND

This is an attractive plant stand that is easy to build. The design is unusual and functional as well. Consider building several of these plant stands for a few rooms in your home or outside on the patio or deck.

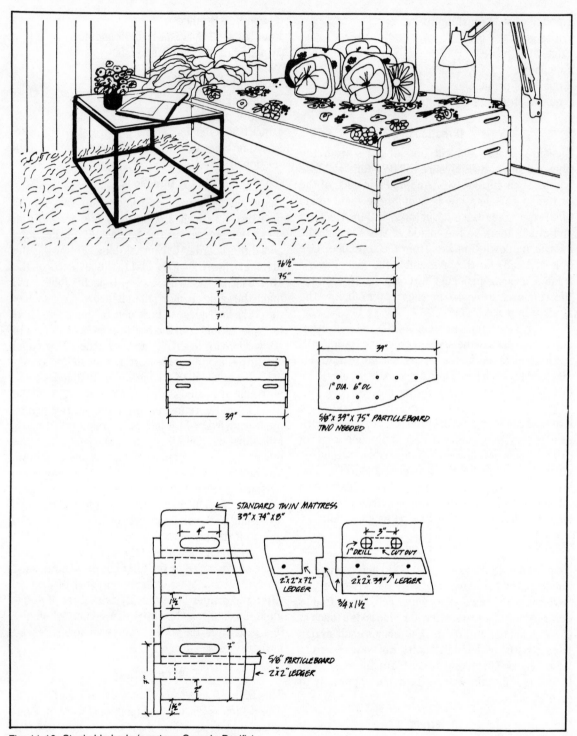

76½"
75"
7"
7"

39"

39"

1" DIA. 6" OC

5/8" X 39" X 75" PARTICLEBOARD
TWO NEEDED

STANDARD TWIN MATTRESS
39" X 74" X 8"

4"

1½"

2"X 2"X 72"
LEDGER

3"

1" DRILL   CUT OUT

2"X 2"X 39" LEDGER

3/4 X 1½"

7"

7"

2"

5/8" PARTICLE BOARD

2"X 2" LEDGER

1½"

Fig. 11-10. Stackable beds (courtesy Georgia-Pacific).

284

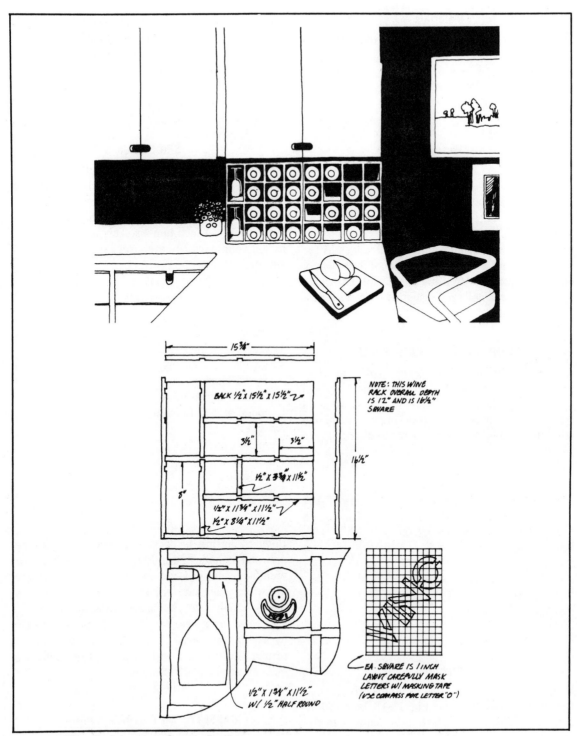

Fig. 11-11. Wine Rack (courtesy Georgia-Pacific).

Materials

¼ sheet (2 × 4 feet) ¾-inch exterior plywood, A-A grade.
White glue.
¼ pound of #6d finishing nails.
Wood filler paste.
Sandpaper.
1 pint of primer.
1 quart of semigloss enamel.

Directions

Begin by cutting out the three pieces of this project as indicated in Fig. 11-12. Assemble the pieces; "A" slips into "B," and "C" slips into "D." Next finish off the project by filling all nail holes and edges. After filler dries hard, sand everything smooth and apply one coat of primer. After this dries, apply two coats of semigloss enamel, sanding lightly between coats. Add one plant.

PLANT OR KNICKKNACK SHELF

This is a good project for scrap pieces of ¾-inch A-A plywood. The basic design will easily hold a medium-size plant or two small plants. It is a good project for developing woodworking skills and one that offers a good solution for what to do with spare plants.

Materials

2 pieces of plywood (¾-inch-thick, exterior, A-A grade): one 12 × 8 inches for the shelf and one 8 × 6 inches for leg support.
White glue.
3 #6d finishing nails.
2 pieces of scrap tin 1 × ½ inch.
Filler paste.
Sandpaper.
½ pint of primer.
½ pint of semigloss enamel.

Directions

Begin by cutting the two pieces of this project from the plywood as indicated in Fig. 11-13. Using white glue and finishing nails, fasten the support to the shelf from above. Finish by filling the edges and sanding the work smooth. Give the project one coat of primer and two coats of semigloss enamel, sanding between coats. To hang the project, make metal tabs (with holes toward the top) and attach these to the plant shelf. Almost any scrap tin can be used for these tabs. Fasten the project to the wall with long wood screws for molly bolts.

SPICE RACK

Here is a project that can be the solution to having all of those spice jars around the kitchen stove. The original plan calls for using 1-×-2-inch lumber for the shelves, but you can easily modify this by substituting 1-×-4-inch lumber. This might be necessary if your spice jars are larger than a typical salt shaker.

Materials

1 piece of exterior plywood, ¾ of an inch thick, A-D grade.
12 feet 1-×-2 inch lumber cut as follows:
    Two 24-inch pieces; sides.
    Two 20-inch pieces; top and bottom.
    Two 18½-inch pieces; shelves.
¼ pound of #4d finishing nails.
Sandpaper.
1 pint of primer.
1 quart of semigloss enamel.
White glue.
2 molly bolts.

Directions

Begin by cutting the back of the spice rack from the plywood as indicated in Fig. 11-14. Build the rack with the pieces of 1-×-2-inch lumber. Be certain to use white glue along with the finishing nails. Attach the rack to the back, being sure to center the rack.

Now you are ready to finish the project. Begin by sanding all surfaces, and then apply a coat of primer. Follow this with two coats of semigloss enamel, sanding between coats. You can hang the spice rack close to the stove using molly bolts.

CASSETTE TAPE STORAGE RACK

This little project is the solution to two problems:

Fig. 11-12. Plant stand (courtesy Georgia-Pacific).

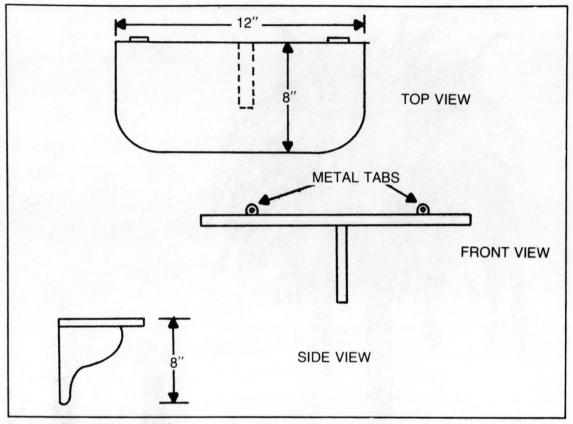

Fig. 11-13. Plant or knicknack shelf.

what to do with scrap plywood and what to do with your loose cassette tapes. The easiest way to construct this project is on a table saw or with the aid of a router. Without either of these tools, the project becomes very difficult to make. The original design results in a free-standing cassette rack that will hold 10 tapes in their plastic boxes.

Materials

Plywood as follows:

Two 5¼-×-2-inch pieces; top and bottom.
Two 5¼-×-2-inch pieces; sides.
White glue.
8 #6d finishing nails.
Primer.
Semigloss enamel.
Filler paste.
Sandpaper.

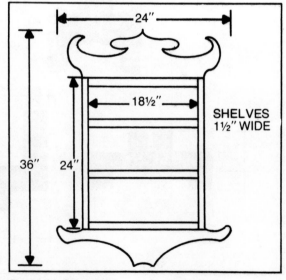

Fig. 11-14. Spice rack.

Directions

Make rabbet cuts, ¼ inch deep and spaced approximately ½ inch apart, on both of the side pieces of this rack. Assemble the rack, as shown in Fig. 11-15, with white glue and finishing nails. Fill all nail holes and exposed edges. Sand flush and coat with primer. When dry, apply two coats of semi-gloss enamel. The project is ready for service.

RIFLE AND SHOTGUN WALL RACK

The best place for rifles and shotguns is displayed on a wall rack. They will be out of harms way here and this unit makes a nice wall decoration for your den. This wall rack is simple to build and it will easily hold four rifles or shotguns.

Materials

¾-inch exterior plywood, A-A grade cut as follows:

Two 8-×-48-inch pieces for the rack.
Two 36-×-3-inch pieces for the ladder back.

White glue.
Eight 1½-inch-long wood screws.
2 molly bolts (for wall fastening).
Filler paste.
½ pint of stain.
1 pint of clear finish.
Sandpaper.

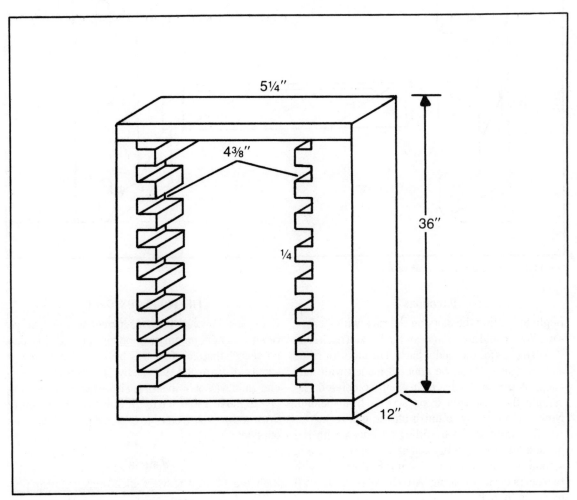

Fig. 11-15. Cassette tape storage rack.

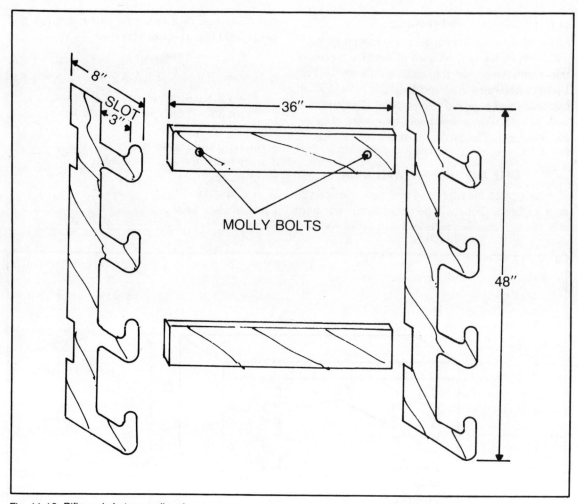

Fig. 11-16. Rifle and shotgun wall rack.

Directions

Begin by cutting the slots on the rack with a sabre saw. You should also notch cut the back of each rack ¾ × 3 inches for the ladder back. The slots for rifles and shotguns should be about 3 inches wide and deep. When both sides have been completed, assemble the rack wtih wood screws from behind. Now you are ready to finish off the gun rack.

To finish, begin by filling all edges with the paste filler. After it is dry and hard, sand everything smooth and apply a coat of stain. Follow this with two coats of clear coating. Attach the rack to a wall using molly bolts.

FIREWOOD BOX/CART

Everyone knows that a fireplace or wood stove requires a fair amount of wood for burning. It is also no secret that the fire will be easier to tend if a supply of firewood is closeby. This project offers one good way of both storing firewood and allowing you to move a load easily. It holds a fair amount of firewood so you won't have to make frequent trips outside.

Materials

2 sheets (4 × 8 feet) ¾-inch-thick exterior plywood, A-B grade.

14 feet 2-×-4 inch lumber cut as follows:
    Two 24 inch.
    Two 60 inch.
White glue.
1 pound of #8d finishing nails.
Four caster-type wheels with screws for attaching them.
Sandpaper.
Eight 16d common box nails for constructing the frame.
Filler paste.
1 quart of stain.
2 quarts of clear finish.

Directions

Cut the plywood as follows:

    Two 24-×-36-inch pieces with rounded front corners for the sides.
    One 60-×-36-inch piece for the back.
    One 24-×-60-inch piece for the bottom.

Assemble the pieces as shown in Fig. 11-17. Then build the 2-×-4-inch frame using the 16-penny nails and white glue. Attach the 2-×-4 frame to the bottom of the wood box. Add the caster-type wheels (one to each corner).

To finish, begin by filling all nail holes and exposed edges. When the filler has dried hard, sand everything smooth and apply a coat of stain. Apply two coats of clear finish, sanding between coats.

WATER BED PLATFORM FRAME

Easily the most expensive part of any water bed is the frame in which the mattress lies. You can build a suitable water-bed frame for a queen-size water bed for a fraction of the cost, even if you only have moderate woodworking skills. Simply follow the diagram shown in Fig. 11-18 and you can't go wrong.

Materials

3 sheets (4 × 8 feet) ¾-inch thick exterior plywood, A-D grade.
23 feet 2 × 6-inch lumber cut as follows for platform:
    Two 5-foot pieces.
    Two 6-foot-6-inch pieces.
White glue.
½ pound of 16d nails.
2 pounds of #8d finishing nails.
Filler paste.

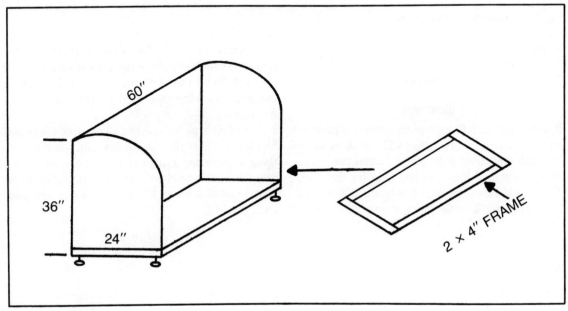

Fig. 11-17. Firewood box/cart.

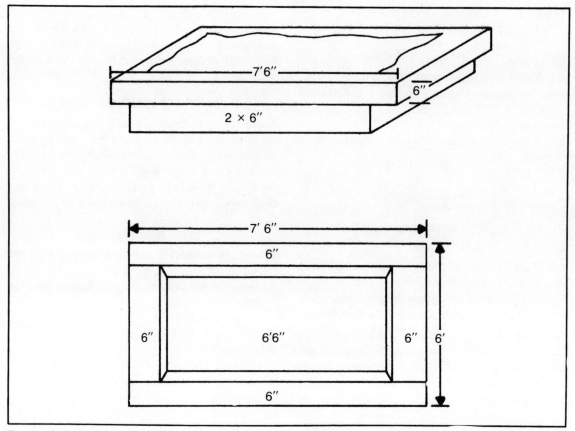

Fig. 11-18. Water bed platform frame.

Sandpaper.
2 quarts of primer.
3 quarts of semigloss enamel.

Directions

Begin by cutting one and one-half sheets of plywood into strips measuring 6 inches wide and 8 feet long. You will end up with 12 pieces. Build two three-sided columns 7 feet 6 inches long for the sides. Then build two three-sided columns 5 feet long. Now attach these to the one and one-half sheets of plywood that are left. The plywood sheets are the bottom of the bed and the columns are the sides of the bed. Build the platform using the 2-×-6-inch lumber. Attach the water-bed frame to the platform from above.

To finish, begin by filling all exposed edges and nail holes. After the filler dries hard, sand everything smooth and apply one coat of primer. Apply two coats of semigloss enamel, sanding between coats. Install a water bed liner, a water bed mattress, and fill.

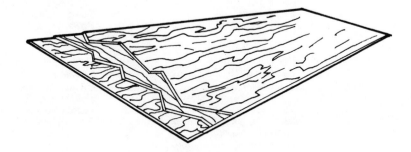

Index